A
Writer's
Companion

❖❖❖

A
Writer's
Companion

❖❖❖

SECOND EDITION

Richard Marius

Harvard University

❖❖❖

McGraw-Hill, Inc.

New York   St. Louis   San Francisco   Auckland   Bogotá
Caracas   Hamburg   Lisbon   London   Madrid   Mexico   Milan
Montreal   New Delhi   Paris   San Juan   São Paulo   Singapore
Sydney   Tokyo   Toronto

This book was developed by
STEVEN PENSINGER, INC.

A Writer's Companion

1 2 3 4 5 6 7 8 9 0 DOC DOC 9 5 4 3 2 1 0

ISBN 0-07-557252-4

This book was set in New Baskerville by the College Composition
Unit in cooperation with Black Dot, Inc.

*The editors were Steven Pensinger and David Dunham;
the designer was Jo Jones;
the production supervisor was Janelle S. Travers.
New drawing was done by Troy Todman.
R. R. Donnelley & Sons Company was printer and binder.*

Library of Congress Cataloging-in-Publication Data

Marius, Richard.
A writer's companion / Richard Marius.—2nd ed.   p.   cm.
Includes bibliographical references.
ISBN 0-07-557252-4
1. English language—Rhetoric.   2. Exposition (Rhetoric)
I. Title.
PE1429.M27   1991
808'.042—dc20   90-5774

About
the Author

❖❖❖

*R*ichard Marius has directed the Expository Writing Program at Harvard since 1978. He is a graduate in journalism of the University of Tennessee and holds the M.A. and the Ph.D. from Yale University. He taught European history at Gettysburg College and at the University of Tennessee before he went to Harvard. He is the author of biographies of Martin Luther and Thomas More and three novels as well as several books on writing. With Harvey Wiener, he is co-author of *The McGraw-Hill College Handbook*.

For
Willis C. Tucker
and
John Lain
Beloved Professors
The School of Journalism
of
The University of Tennessee

Contents

❖

Preface

❖ ❖ ❖

*T*he first edition of this book, published in 1985, met with success beyond my imagining. I have received more correspondence from readers about it than I have had from anything else I have ever written. It has turned up in unexpected places, and unexpectedly people in Europe, Asia, Africa, and Australia have written me about it—not to mention a host of people here in the United States. For this response I am deeply grateful. I hope readers continue to let me know what they think about the book, what they like and what they would change or add.

It is in the nature of writers to become dissatisfied with their creations. I have taught regularly out of the first edition, seeing several things I wanted to change. I have taken readers' suggestions very seriously. Steve Pensinger, the indefatigable editor of this and other writing books of mine, agreed that it was time for a second edition, and here it is.

I have rewritten the book from cover to cover—sometimes adding, sometimes subtracting, always aiming at greater clarity and usefulness. I have changed my mind about some things; my chapter on diction shows many surrenders to the flexible linguistic spirit of the times. I have thought through some matters anew; I hope my chapter on argument is now more complete and more in keeping with how our minds work. I have rearranged the order of the book, hoping to make it fit better with the expectations of readers familiar with other writing texts. Above all I have tried to be honest. What is American English today? How do published writers use it? What do students need to know about it? What rules should we observe as part of the courtesy that should inform all communication? What old rules in fact get in the way of effective writing?

The philosophy of the book is simple: we learn to write by writing essays and by thinking about what we have done. I have never found any utility in grammar drills or in exercises where students write fragments of essays. I do my best teaching by having my students write drafts of whole essays. I comment on those drafts, trying to help the student writers discover what they want to say and then to say it well. I read as many drafts of papers as my students care to write during a term. I have to write things again and again before I get them right; I try to give my students that same opportunity, and I have written this book to help all of us along our way.

As the examples in the book show, I have tried to see how good writers—those widely read and appreciated by the community of educated men and women—achieve their effects. I have quoted many modern American writers, and I have included even a few writers from Great Britain. The first edition of this book was widely used with the second edition of *Modern American Prose,* an anthology of essays edited by John Clifford and Robert DiYanni (Random House, 1987). I have keyed part of this edition to that work so that those who choose to use the two books together can do so easily. But the examples stand on their own, and I am confident that the principles set forth in this book can be verified by consulting any anthology of modern English and American prose.

I owe debts to many friends and friendly readers. Steve Pensinger is not only a canny editor, but he is also fun. Willis C. Tucker, my patient and generous journalism professor emeritus from the University of Tennessee, went through the first edition line by line making multitudes of comments—as he used to do in our editorial writing class at the University of Tennessee when the world and I were young. Michael Hennessy, Southwest Texas State University; Barry M. Maid, University of Arkansas at Little Rock; and Thomas Recchio, the University of Connecticut reviewed the first draft of the manuscript for this edition and made dozens of thoughtful suggestions, most of which I have incorporated into the book. My colleagues in the Expository Writing Program at Harvard make me think hard every day about what we do and how we do it, and many of their thoughts have found their way into the following pages. I am especially grateful to Linda Simon, Nancy Sommers, Pat C. Hoy, and our former associate John Holdren. Rod Kessler at Salem State here in Massachusetts and Nancy Anderson of Auburn University in Montgomery, Alabama, have shared with me in detail their experience of using the book in their writing classes, and we have lifted many a happy glass together.

Others from the past remain in beloved memory—my late
and dear mother, a dauntless newspaper woman at a time
when the profession was not thought ladylike, a woman who
read her children the King James Version of the Bible every
day and set its soaring cadences permanently in our hearts and
minds; my high school Latin teacher Myron V. Harrison, who
taught me how language holds together, Bill Bayne, editor of
the *Lenoir City News*, who suffered my early prose and even
paid me for it; John Lain who with Willis Tucker did his best
to cut out the adjectives when I wrote for him in the University of Tennessee journalism school; the late Sydney Ahlstrom
at Yale who valiantly tamed my prose for the academic world.

My wife Lanier Smythe and my sons Richard, Fred, and
John sustain me by their laughter—sometimes at me. My
brother John and my friends Ralph Norman and Milton Klein
endure through the years.

Richard Marius

A
Writer's
Companion

❖❖❖

Introduction

❖ ❖ ❖

I have written this book as an informal and friendly guide for writers. Fiction writers may find parts of it useful, but my main audience will be those writers who must write essays that explain ideas, argue cases, or tell stories.

Writing requires an astonishing array of complex mental and physical acts, many going on simultaneously as the writer writes. Mysteriously and wonderfully, we learn to write, coordinating many impulses and motions much as we do when we dance or sing or talk or play baseball or ride a bicycle. In this book, I consider the elements separately in the same way that a batting coach might give special attention to a player's wrists in swinging the bat, without assuming that the rest of the body remains still while the wrists snap.

My advice is descriptive; that is, I show how professional writers create their effects. Writing has very few rules; however, it does have principles created by those who have written the English language over several centuries, and here I have tried to define some of those principles from my observation of writers who appeal to large, educated audiences today.

Why pay so much attention to the writing of others? The French critic Roland Barthes has said that we can never write without taking into account what has been written. Writing takes place within a community of writers and readers and as part of an unfolding tradition. We are always—to use a fine phrase of Saul Bellow's—breaking bread with the dead. Readers approach any text with expectations picked up from a lifetime of reading. They are frustrated when the expectations are not met. They may tolerate a few lapses—a long, swirling sentence here, a misspelled word there, a breakdown in diction in another place. Frustrate them too often, and they will give up. The writer's job is to create an audience and to keep that audience interested to the end.

1

Writing must *communicate.* Communication holds communities together; language helps to make us members of communities, allows us to influence other human beings, and enables us to achieve some sense of who we are within the group. Communication follows conventions concerning the meanings of words, the forms of sentences, the shapes of various kind of discourse, the standards for evidence, and so on.

All of us belong to several "discourse communities," groups of shared knowledge and interests within which we communicate—communities wherein our language makes sense. The largest of these communities is the one that speaks English, especially American English. Within that large community are multitudes of subgroups—those who love computers, those who study the sixteenth century, those devoted to a sport such as baseball or a team such as the Boston Red Sox. Each community has its own language, its own patterns of communication.

We do not have to explain everything to readers in the discourse community for which we write or speak. If I write that the Red Sox beat the Yankees in the last of the ninth last night on a suicide squeeze, every serious fan knows exactly what I mean. But those outside the baseball discourse community will find the sentence opaque. Suicide squeeze? Did some Red Sox player kill himself so the team could win? The nonfan may wonder.

Fans understand the sentence. For starters, no Boston fan can imagine that any member of the Red Sox would make a personal sacrifice for the team. The sentence tells us rather that the teams were playing at Fenway Park in Boston, that the game was tied in the last of the ninth inning, that the Sox had a runner on third with no more than one out, that the manager ordered the batter to bunt, and that the runner on third started for home as soon as the pitcher went into his windup. If the batter had failed to bunt, the catcher would have easily tagged the runner out at the plate; but the batter made contact with the ball, hit it slowly along the ground in front of the plate, and the runner scored and the game was over. Can a nonfan understand even this explanation? Perhaps not. But any sports writer who set out to explain everything in every story would quickly lose his job on the newspaper. Writers assume a discourse community bringing knowledge to the writer's text. They try to make sense within that community, using what readers already know (here the rules of the game) to report something new (how the game came out).

We use the language our community understands. How does a particular audience use words? Good writers think about that question every time they write. Yet the community of language users is so large that it never completely agrees upon what all words mean or how they should be used. New words come into the language; old words pass away or change their meaning. How all this happens is mysterious. The task of the writer is to sort out effective usage from ineffective usage. I hesitate to say "good" usage or "bad" usage, for "good" and "bad" imply a moral judgment on language that I do not share. You are not a bad person if you say "ain't," and you are not bad if you say "between you and I." But those usages do not conform to the expectations about language shared by multitudes of educated readers, and those people will be offended because in using the non-standard usages you seem not to be part of their group. Foolish? Perhaps. But that is the way groups are. Baseball fans would be annoyed if a TV announcer wondered if the home team might punt in the last half of the ninth. Such a statement would tell them that he is pretending to be a member of a group to which he does not belong, and the discourse community of fans would hoot.

"Ain't" and "between you and I" are fairly obvious offenses against the discourse community of those who read and write; however, most questions of usage exist in a grey zone of uncertainty. No language is like the geometry of Euclid, which is a logical system based on unbreakable laws. Too many books and too many teachers have tyrannized beginning writers with the dictatorship of the rules. Many of these teachers are modern puritans, convinced that a corrupt world is about to topple and that only stern discipline can save us. In his angry book *Paradigms Lost* (the title is a heavy-handed play on Milton's *Paradise Lost*), critic John Simon asks why language changes. His answer: "Language, for the most part, changes out of ignorance."[1] Simon's fierce pages burn with denunciations of the "permissiveness" that descriptive books like this one inculcate in the young, and in a typical passage he assaults the National Council of Teachers of English (an organization to which I belong) as "a body so shot through with irresponsible radicalism, guilt-ridden liberalism, and asinine trendiness as to be, in my opinion, one of the major culprits—right up there with television—in the sabotaging of linguistic standards."[2]

For at least a couple of centuries doomsayers have predicted that civilization was about to collapse because the English language was dying; a grammatical Chicken Little somewhere is always proclaiming that the sky is falling. In *Grammar and Good Taste*, Dennis E. Baron tells us of the amusing frustration of the English grammarian Robert Lowth, who in 1762 wrote a book intended to provide a scientific understanding of good English style. Lowth conjured up a set of rules for writing—and then complained that Shakespeare, John Donne, John Milton, and the translators of the King James version of the Bible had violated them and had therefore fallen into poor writing![3]

That is the trouble with the frantic quest for absolute, scientific standards in English! Look around just a bit, and you will find good writers who violate them. Like the Puritans of old, our latter-day linguistic puritans find evil everywhere, even in those known to be good. John Simon mentions several writers he considers exemplary—but then cannot resist the temptation to point out their errors. In the end his book portrays an author who cannot be satisfied and who must therefore be miserable every time he reads.

Language is an art, not a science. It has "standards," but they change with life. Classical Greek and Latin do not change much; the people who used them are dead. They changed a great deal while the people who used them were alive. From Homer to Plato, the Greek language changed, and from Plato to the New Testament it changed yet again.

In our society the most important umpires of language are editors who decide what will be published and what not. Editors publish readable writing that others will buy. Editors who publish unreadable or uninteresting stuff get fired. Editors who can judge what the public will read keep publishing alive and themselves comfortable. Editors decide who will be our "professional writers"—writers who get paid for their work.

The flexible standard for this book is the work of professional writers published by editors. I call it "editors' standard," and I have tried to say what that standard is—or what it seems to be most of the time. Every writer occasionally breaks the rules. If your audience likes what you do and respects you for it when you break the rules, your risk has paid off. If you break too many rules, no editor will publish your work. The real "rules" of language are the expectations of readers.

Writing has always been difficult. The written words lie there, as Socrates told Phaedrus in a famous dialogue, without the help of a living person to explain them. They must speak for themselves. If we misunderstand them, no one speaks out of the writing to correct us. Words have histories; they have shades of meanings; they have contexts. Times change, and readers of different generations read into words thoughts that differ from what the writer may have intended. The same reader may see one thing in a text in youth, another in middle age, and yet another in old age—and all the interpretations may make sense.

All this makes communication difficult even when writers exercise great care. Readers have to make sense out of any text they read; the sense they make is an interpretation, and any text with enough thoughts in it gives rise to conflicting interpretations. English departments would die overnight if everyone agreed as to what all words mean. Writers must recognize the difficulty that the best writing gives readers; the careful writer works hard to minimize the difficulty of reading. Writing takes so much effort that the percentage of people who write well is always small—and therefore the good writer is always in demand.

Speaking is easier than writing. Speakers can misuse words yet still be understood because of their tone of voice, their gestures, and their expressions. They can repeat themselves until we get the point. Speaking is a democratic art; nearly everyone does it well enough to communicate. It may not always be pretty or clear or efficient; but it is communication. The movies, radio, and television have inundated us with speaking by all sorts of people who might find it difficult or impossible to write an essay. We hear the words they use and the forms of their sentences. Often the words do not have their traditional meanings; often speakers gallop all over the place like untrained horses forced to carry loose burdens on their backs. The talk on, say, the Johnny Carson show may be chaotic. Even so, out of such talk we construct meanings.

Readers have to construct meanings from texts. Texts do not have body language and intonations. They must stand alone. Writing usually represents more extended and more complicated thought than the thought expressed in most conversations. The writer develops ideas, one on top of another. That adds difficulty, for the reader must remember what has come before, be aware of what is there now, and be anticipating what will come in the next paragraph or on the next page.

For these reasons, the written language must be much more precise and more carefully organized than the spoken language. Professional writers—writers paid to write—succeed in communicating with readers. The best writers make readers enjoy their writing. What do they do? Here are some principles to keep in mind.

1. Professional writers begin by trying to interest readers. They never start by saying, "How can I avoid making mistakes?" They ask themselves questions like these: What do I have to say? How can I make people pay attention to what I am saying and take my writing seriously? How can I make them keep reading? Of course good writers want to be correct—just as the pianist playing a Beethoven concerto wants to hit all the right notes. But professional writers—and professional pianists—never assume that being correct is enough.

2. Professional writers are economical with words. They use as few words as possible to say what they want to say. They use short words rather than long ones when the short words express their meaning as well. They get to the point quickly. A doctor complain-

ing about the obscurity of writing in specialized medical books and journals sent me the following example of prose that no editor of a popular magazine would allow to see print. The writer was trying to show how the treatment of cancer affects community hospitals.

> The cancer burden and its financial ramifications have escalated to enormous proportions on the community level. Early diagnosis with open communication to the patient and cost containment are dominant in the perspective of community medicine. Bed space, operating room facilities, and therapy units are in desperate need of expansion but are curtailed by certificates of need. The burden of creative and imaginative utilization of existing advantages is projected back to the physician, and his personal role in directing a diagnostic maneuver, informing the patient of results, and accomplishing therapy is intensified.[4]

A professional writer would condense:

> The burdens of cancer have become enormous for community medicine. We want to diagnose the disease early, communicate honestly with the patient, and contain costs. We are short on bed space, operating rooms, and therapy units, and we lack the money to expand. The physician must take responsibility for using what is available and possible for diagnosis, for telling the patient the results, and for directing the therapy.

In the second version, 91 words have been reduced to 70. I do not believe I have cut anything essential from the first version, although I cannot understand parts of it. (What does the writer mean by "certificates of need"?) Professional writers prune away the nonessential as they revise their early drafts.

3. Professional writers are direct. They begin most of their sentences with the subject and tell us quickly what the subject does—or what happens to the subject. They don't write many long, looping dependent clauses between subjects and verbs. We read silently now, rather than aloud as people did until only a few centuries ago. We also read quickly. We can read faster if subjects are close to verbs and verbs close to direct objects.

In *The Philosophy of Composition*, E. D. Hirsch, Jr. illustrates the increasing directness of English style by giving several translations of the same text from Giovanni Boccaccio, the greatest of the fourteenth-century storytellers in Renaissance Italy. Hirsch shows that as the English translations come forward in time, they use sentences that are both shorter and more direct. Here is a version he gives from the sixteenth century:

Saladin, whose valliance was so great that not only the same from base estate advanced him to be Sultan of Babylon, but also thereby he won diverse victories over the Saracen kings and Christians; who through his manifold wars and magnificent triumphs, having expended all his treasure, and for the execution of one exploit lacking a great sum of money, knew not where to have the same so readily as he had occasion to employ it. At length he called to remembrance a rich Jew named Melchizedech, that lent out money for interest in Alexandria.[5]

An eighteenth-century version reads like this:

Saladin was so brave and great a man, that he had raised himself from an inconsiderable person to be Sultan of Babylon, and he had gained many victories over both the Saracen and Christian princes. This monarch having in diverse wars and by many extraordinary expenses, run through all his treasure, some urgent occasion fell out that he wanted a large sum of money. Not knowing which way he might raise enough to answer his necessities, he at last called to mind a rich Jew of Alexandria named Melchizedech, who lent out money on interest.[6]

An even more recent and more direct translation is the following:

Saladin, who was so powerful that he rose from an ordinary man to the rank of Sultan of Babylon and won countless victories over Saracen and Christian rulers, found that he had exhausted all his wealth, both in war and in the exercise of his extraordinary munificence. Now, by some chance, he felt the need of money, and a lot of it, too, and not knowing where he could get it as quickly as he wished, he thought of a rich Jew called Melchizedek who was a moneylender in Alexandria.[7]

We can understand the first version only if we read it slowly aloud. It is littered with cumbersome dependent clauses and participial phrases that come between subjects and verbs. We can understand the second version fairly well by reading it silently, and we can comprehend the third version even more readily. The first sentence in the third version has a dependent clause between the subject "Saladin" and the verb "found." The second sentence has two independent clauses, and in each of them the subject comes next to the verb—"he felt" and "he thought." They are much more direct.

4. Professional writers are efficient. Efficiency does not require only bland or simple thoughts. If you have complicated thoughts, you must sometimes use complicated language to express them. The general rule is to express complicated thoughts in language as simple and direct as the thoughts themselves will allow.

Unfortunately, many writers believe they must write obscurely to be taken seriously. So we get sentences like this:

> Individuals with a strong home defense orientation in living areas noted for multiple instances of criminal behavior in urban regions are most likely to practice the acquisition and continued possession of firearms.

The writer *means* that in city neighborhoods with a lot of crime, people buy guns to defend themselves and their homes. The interpretation just given is written efficiently; the original is not.

Efficient prose may not mean brevity. Sometimes a longer version of a thought is clearer—and more efficient—than a shorter version. The shorter version may abbreviate ideas so much that readers have a hard time following them. Here is a sentence from an article in a recent scholarly journal. The article analyzes what various groups of white people believe about opportunities for blacks in our society:

> The category of persons who see black opportunity as average and not greatly improved appears to contain a subtype who seem to be saying that opportunity for blacks has always been equal, denying the existence of past inequality of opportunity.

After reading the rest of the article, I think this sentence can be translated as follows:

> Some people think opportunities for blacks are about equal to those for whites and that there has been no great increase in opportunities for blacks in recent times. Some of these people seem to think that blacks have always had equal opportunity and that inequality of opportunity never existed.

The second version is longer, but it is more efficient because it is easier to understand. Efficient prose allows readers to move through a piece of writing without having to back up and read again. Efficient prose does not have to sound as if it belongs in a first-grade reader.

5. Good writers engage readers. They stimulate the imagination, especially the picture-forming ability of the mind. The children of my generation listened to radio drama and made pictures in their heads of what was going on. Ages before that, bards singing the epic tales of the tribe by the fire at night summoned up pictures from the minds of every person silently listening.

These pictures are painted by the experience of readers and listeners. A good writer describes a scene, providing a few telling details, and readers understand because those details call up something the readers have experienced. I tell a story, and if you are interested in it that is because the story somehow stimulates a flood of your own memories.

Here is a paragraph from an essay by Dr. Richard Selzer called "The Knife," describing how a surgeon holds his scalpel at the beginning of an operation.

> One holds the knife as one holds the bow of a cello or a tulip—by the stem. Not palmed nor gripped nor grasped, but lightly, with the tips of the fingers. The knife is not for pressing. It is for drawing across the field of skin. Like a slender fish, it waits, at the ready, then, go! It darts, followed by a fine wake of red. The flesh parts, falling away to yellow globules of fat. Even now, after so many times, I still marvel at its power—cold, gleaming, silent. More, I am still struck with a kind of dread that it is I in whose hand the blade travels, that my hand is its vehicle, that yet again this terrible steel-bellied thing and I have conspired for a most unnatural purpose, the laying open of the body of a human being.[8]

Seltzer uses our previous experience to make us share with him the moment when his scalpel cuts into a human body. How does he do this? Few of us have held a scalpel. Yet we know what it is to see someone hold the bow of a cello or the stem of a tulip, by the tips of the fingers, and we can imagine holding a surgical knife the same way. He likens the thin scalpel to a slender fish, and we can imagine how the fish moves quickly, darting, and as the blood comes up from the incision we can imagine the thin wake of red trailing the knife. We know the color red; we have seen blood. The yellow globules of fat beneath the skin may be vivid to us because we have seen yellow animal fat, and we can suppose that it resembles the fat beneath the skin of human beings.

Seltzer could have said, "I took my scalpel and sliced open the skin on my patient's stomach." Instead he put together words and phrases rich with sensory experiences we have had ourselves. He makes us recombine our memory of those experiences to understand better the experience he describes. Engaging writing reaches out to various vivid fragments of memory in the minds of readers and reworks those memories into images the writer wants us to have.

When teachers say, "Be concrete," or, "Be specific," they mean you should use the solid, sensory words good writers use to call up some memory, some experience, something readers have seen and heard and felt and smelled and tasted. Our most vivid memories are of sense experience—things we have seen, heard, smelled, touched, or tasted. All good writers give us details to help us make pictures in our minds from what we already know, and the most vivid details are those attached to sense experience.

You do not have to make pictures in every sentence. If your audience already knows a lot about your subject, you can be less vivid because you can assume a high degree of interest from your readers. For this reason many articles in specialized journals seem dull to outsiders; they are addressed to people already deeply interested in the subject and knowledgeable about it. Cancer researchers want to get quickly to the point in a technical article about cancer; they do not have time for vivid descriptions, though they may appreciate such descriptions when they are not reading an article solely for the information it can give them for their own research.

Even articles in specialized journals should use vivid examples now and then. Too many writers forget to keep the minds of their readers alert and responsive. A few years ago one of my students used the word *relationship* fourteen times in a three-page essay. When we talked about the paper, I said she should have tried to vary her writing a little more. The word *relationship* recalled no sharp memories of sense experience. My student believed this monotonous repetition should not be considered a flaw. "It makes sense," she said. "It's grammatical. I don't see why you criticize me when it's correct."

She had been taught that the aim of writing is to be correct, to obey the rules of grammar and syntax. No one had made her reflect on her own attitude when she reads, the swift judgments she makes as she decides whether a piece of writing is worth her time or not. I doubted that she would have been willing to read her essay if it had been written by someone else. Efficiency and vividness are precious gifts writers give to readers in a courtship where the readers are more fickle than modern professional athletes. Her attitude was, "It's correct! I don't care about anything else. Take it or leave it." Confronted with that sentiment, most readers will leave it.

I hope this book will help you win readers to your writing. If you read it carefully and apply its precepts to your prose, you can write more efficiently and vividly, and you may gain some other rewards as well. People will respect you for your writing, and you will be happier in doing it. You may even get to the point where writing becomes an addiction. Let me know if that happens.

A final piece of advice: Read. Read everything you can. Read day and night. Good writers are good readers. When they enjoy a piece of writing, they try to decide why they like it; when they dislike an essay, they think about the reasons for their dislike. If you make reading a habit of your life, think about the words and the structures you find in your reading, and try to imitate writing you love, you will be on the way to being an excellent writer.

One

Writing and Its Rewards

❖ ❖ ❖

*W*riting is hard work, and although it may become easier with practice it is seldom easy. Most of us have to write and rewrite to write anything well. We try to write well so people will read our work. Readers nowadays will seldom struggle to understand difficult writing unless someone—a teacher perhaps—forces them to do so. Samuel Johnson, the great eighteenth-century English writer, conversationalist, and lexicographer, said, "What is written without effort is in general read without pleasure." Today what is written without effort is seldom read at all.

Writing takes time—lots of time. Good writers do not dash off a piece in an hour and get on to other things. They do not wait until the night before a deadline to begin to write. Instead they plan. They write a first draft. They revise it. They may then think through that second draft and write it once again. Even small writing tasks may require enormous investments of time. If you want to become a writer, you must be serious about the job, willing to spend hours dedicated to your work.

Most writers require some kind of solitude. That does not mean the extreme of the cork-lined room where the great French writer Marcel Proust composed his huge works in profound silence. It does mean mental isolation—shutting yourself off from the distractions around you even if you happen to be pounding a computer keyboard in a noisy newspaper office. You choose to write rather than to do other things, and you must concentrate on what you are doing.

In a busy world like ours, we take a risk when we isolate ourselves and give up other pursuits to write. We don't know how our writing will come out. All writers fail sometimes. Successful writers pick themselves up after failure and try again. As you write, you must read your work again and again, thinking of your purpose, weighing your words, testing your organization, examining your evidence, checking for clarity. You must pay attention to the thousands and thousands of details embodied in words and experience. You must trust your intuitions; if something does not sound right, do it again. And again. And again.

Finally you present your work to readers as the best you can do. After you submit a final draft, it is too late to make excuses, and you should not do so. Not everybody will like your final version. You may feel insecure about it even when you have done your best. You may like your work at first and hate it later. Writers wobble back and forth in their judgments. Chaucer, Tolstoy, and Auden are all on record for rejecting some of their works others have found enduring and grand. Writing is a parable of life itself.

Many writers suffer writer's block at one time or another. They can't get going. If you have trouble putting words on paper—or on the computer screen—you are in good company. Nearly everyone does.

Writer's block is seldom a matter of sitting at a desk while words fail to come. Usually it is an unwillingness to commit ourselves to the desk, to the pen or typewriter and paper, to the computer, and to the time writing demands. We are impatient at our slow progress. We tell ourselves we will write in the evening and go to a movie after we have spent two or three hours at our desk. Then we decide to go to the movie first and write later. Later we decide to go to bed and try again in the morning. We put off writing as we put off a trip to the dentist. Procrastication is the worst writer's block.

It's almost always a bad idea to put off writing until you have to do everything in a night, spending hours and hours and hours at your desk or your computer. Even prolific writers seldom spend more than four or five hours a day writing. An inefficient writer who speaks of working all night long on a paper often measures not the time spent at the desk but the time from the beginning to the end of the writing task—including all the time spent watching the late news on television, talking on the telephone, and riffling through a magazine.

Measure the time you spend at the desk, your fingers on the keyboard or wrapped around your pen, forming words. Years ago, B. F. Skinner, the behavioral psychologist, rigged a clock to a light over his typewriter. When he sat down to write, he turned on the light, automatically starting the clock. When he stood up, he turned the light off, stopping the clock. He wanted to spend four hours a day writing. The clock told him when he had completed his task. Mechanical? Yes. But it worked. His little device drove him to concentrate on spending real time on real work, and he has been an astonishingly prolific writer, continuing to turn out books even in his eighties.

The first rule in writing is this: Sit down and do it. Stay at the desk. Keep going. We all get discouraged—especially when we start writing the first page of the day. We have trouble organizing our thoughts. We write a page or merely a paragraph or a sentence and immediately think we ought to change it. Writers love new beginnings, clean slates, new pages. We easily suppose that our previous effort has failed but that now, with a new start, we will get it right. But when we begin and begin and begin again, we deceive ourselves. We are only looking for an excuse not to get on with the task. The habit of starting again and again quickly makes us give up for the day, saying, "I'll do it tomorrow. I've made myself so nervous by all these false starts I can't go on today." So the game is lost.

Work in three- or four-hour-long periods every day. When you have put in that time, give yourself a rest. Do something else for a while. Get away from your work and come back to it the next day. Many writers tell me that they reward themselves somehow when they have done their daily stint; the anticipation of the reward keeps them at their task until the stint is done.

Your best bet is to get a complete draft on paper as soon as you can. No matter how terrible it is, no matter how disorganized, get through with it. Then you can revise. Revision is to me the chief joy of writing, for with my first draft in hand I have confidence that I do have something to say, and I can then set myself to the task of sharpening every sentence, measuring my words, thinking more about my subject, and tightening my organization so that the piece holds together.

Revision takes time. You must read your work over, pencil in notes to yourself, cross out some words and add others, and write new paragraphs on the backs of pages. Then you must write a new draft. Too many new writers deliver their first drafts with the air of weary people in a hurry to shed their dirty clothes at the end of a day. In the army's basic training program, sergeants regularly tell recruits about the unfired rifle in combat. Many soldiers in the thick of a fight refuse to fire their weapons, seemingly afraid of attracting hostile attention. A similar affliction curses new writers who cannot bear to look carefully at their work once it is done. They seem to be afraid of finding something wrong. They want to get rid of it as soon as possible.

It may be a comfort to know that professional writers suffer similar pangs. If anything, their unhappiness is greater because they make a living from words they put on paper, and their first drafts may persuade them that their children will soon go hungry and that the whole family may be thrown into the street because there's no money to pay the rent.

Battle-hardened professionals do not see a first draft as a final draft. They expect the first draft to be like a blob of clay that a skilled potter flings onto a whirling potter's wheel. Potential beauty resides in the blob; it can be brought out by the skilled and delicate touch of the potter's hand.

Writing is worth sacrifice. Believe that, and you can become a writer. You must reconcile yourself to slow improvement rather than instantaneous perfection. Sometimes you make sudden leaps; you learn to do something you could not do earlier. These are moments of soaring joy. Most of the time you labor with careful precision and concentrated attention on the small details that make the whole worthwhile. In the painful discipline of writing, you should be like a good pianist preparing to give a musical concert. Good pianists play every day, working hard on the pieces they will perform at last before audiences. Good pianists sacrifice for their music. Good writers do the same for their writing.

But for splendid rewards! Writing is one of the performing arts. The pleasures writers gain in pleasing an audience are similar to those enjoyed by pianists, ballet dancers, baseball players, lecturers, magicians, and trapeze artists. They are honorable pleasures, making us part of the human community, for our desire to please signifies that we value both ourselves and our audience.

Writing of all kinds—including student writing—would be much better if writers worked hard not merely to get things right but to give pleasure as well. Much of the fault here may lie with writing teachers, for they easily fall into the trap of thinking their task is only to correct papers. They may tell students only what is wrong with a piece of writing when they should be paying most attention to what the student is trying to say. They should then help that young writer to say it better. Many teachers would do well to praise more and criticize less.

The rewards of writing go beyond enjoyment. Most of us must write well if we are to do well at our jobs. Our society has moved from the industrial revolution to the informational revolution; about half the jobs in America involve the transfer of information, much of it by writing. The average engineer probably writes more every year than the average professor of English. Many people spend their workdays writing letters, memos, and reports. Technical writing—writing that explains how things work—is one of the biggest fields in American business. The explosive multiplication of copiers, computers, and fax machines shows one side of the demand for writing. No wonder some people speak of a writing crisis! No society in history has demanded as much writing as ours.

In our zeal to think of writing as communication, we may forget how much writing helps us know things—to arrange facts, to see how they are related to one another, and to decide what they mean. Nothing helps the mind and memory more than writing things down. Everyone who has taught a discipline such as history, literature, economics, or philosophy has had at least one student who protests, "I *know* it; I just can't *write* it." In fact, a person who cannot write about a discipline in the liberal arts rarely knows anything about it except a disconnected jumble of useless facts.

History, for example, does not come by divine inspiration or by the immediate intuition by which we know colors. We know history by knowing words—words written down in fading ink in archives, in attics, in cellars, or in libraries; words carved in stone or on clay tablets; words printed in books; words of teachers telling us about the past. We do not know the history of the American Revolution if we can only make the right identifications on a multiple-choice test. History is the story of human relations over time, and such relations are far too complicated and subtle to be captured by the common simplicities of a multiple-choice examination. To make sense of history, historians write carefully about it. Only when they can write about it do they know they know it.

When we write about our knowledge, we discover its limitations, and we have to go back to our sources and study some more. I frequently give my classes a collection of British and American firsthand accounts of the battles of Lexington and Concord that began the American Revolution on April 19, 1775. The assignment is simple. From what soldiers and civilians on both sides later wrote about their experiences on that day, my students write the story of what happened. They quickly learn that the sources contradict each other and leave many questions unanswered. The British said the Americans fired first; the Americans claimed the British fired first. The British and the Americans gave different accounts of the numbers engaged on each side. And so on.

My young student writers discover that they must read the sources with great care and that they must use common sense and their own experiences to tell a coherent story. As they write through successive drafts, they ask themselves more questions. They find some answers in the sources, but they cannot answer some important questions. They have to guess—and say they are guessing—or they have to draw up short before the perplexing silences of time. Telling this story makes them see how complex any human story is, and the experience of writing teaches them something both about the battles and the nature of history itself.

So it is about most disciplines in the liberal arts and for much of life: the best measure of our knowledge is how well we can write about it. Good letter writers reveal an understanding of their own experience lacking in those who never bother to express their thoughts and acts in writing. It is worth repeating a point I made in my introduction: writing cannot communicate everything. But writing reveals something essential, and when we write about ourselves we learn something fundamental about who we are.

Writing enlarges our minds in another way all writers find mysterious. As we write about a subject we know well, we think of more to write. Word pours out on word, idea on idea. Suddenly we see we have a piece we could not have predicted when we began. Young writers sometimes say they don't have enough thoughts to fill a five-page assignment. But if you observe carefully and write honestly and follow your own thoughts as you put them down, you will see quickly that you discover more and more things to say.

The best proof of how writing stimulates the brain is to try writing about something you know fairly well—perhaps a conversation you had with a friend this morning. As you write, you remember more and more of what went on—what she said, the tone she used to express herself, what you said to her, her responses, her sincerity, how you judged her as a person while you talked, what she was wearing, where you were, the light, the smells, the sounds coming from beyond.

When you see a movie or hear a lecture, write about it afterward. You will forget some things, and you will see how tricky memory can be. Even so you will get many things right. Your mind will create the moment anew, and once you have written your thoughts down, you will recall them much better. You will also find it instructive to realize that you cannot recall everything. When you make the discovery of what the mind resurrects as you write, you will want to write more, and you will enjoy writing in ways you never did before. Many people discover that keeping a journal and reading it frequently deepens the experience of life itself.

Perhaps the greatest rewards of writing lie in the pleasures of designing and preserving. I read once that writers remember details others do not notice—the fall of light after a storm on a summer afternoon, the smell of wet grass on a spring morning, the gesture someone made on hearing of a death in the family, the music of voices long still, the laughter of an aunt in the kitchen at Christmastime decades ago. Writers preserve moments in a world of relentless change. In setting their observations on paper, all writers create something—a design that fits the separate observations into a whole that makes sense, some coherent scheme that arranges details into an edifice of memory.

All writers create. I am annoyed to hear fiction and poetry called "creative" writing as if writing that explains, describes, and narrates should somehow be relegated to the basement of the writing enterprise. To assume that only fiction and poetry are creative is to imagine that fiction writers and poets are somehow superior to scholars, journalists, and others who report, explain, and describe. A good case may be made for the proposition that the most truly original and creative writers in our society today work in nonfiction. Nonfiction supports the publishing industry; readers buy more nonfiction books than novels. A friend of mine who happens to be a very good short story writer tells me that when he reads a book he has an insatiable thirst for facts—and that therefore he seldom reads a novel. His taste may seem quirky, but apparently many readers share it.

The art of the nonfiction writer is to make a design that joins disconnected observations and pieces of information, uniting them under some generalizations. That design requires as much creation as any novel. A biographer puts the relics of a life together to reveal a plausible human being, one we recognize as part of our experience, yet who stands out in a unique way in his or her own time and place. A historian makes connections between people and events that may not have been understood or even seen by those who lived during the period the historian describes. Readers take pleasure in seeing how the historical account corresponds to what they think they know of human existence—the play of rationality against irrationality, and the motivations, ambitions, evil, and goodness of the human race. The design of the story somehow belongs to the writer. Charles Darwin perceived the design of natural selection in biology and developed his theory of evolution, and although his uncounted disciples have worked more than a century to refine and correct his ideas, the theory somehow remains *his*—a creative act of observation, thought, and writing that endures.

On occasion, anxious students have told me they feared they might duplicate the thoughts and design of a writer they had never heard of and be accused of plagiarism. It is possible for two people, studying the same material and writing at the same time, to arrive at similar conclusions. Darwin and his fellow Englishman Alfred Russel Wallace worked independently of each other in the early nineteenth century on the theory of biological evolution by natural selection. Darwin published first—and spoke respectfully of Wallace in his preface. There are many other examples of writers who came on some of the same truths almost simultaneously, but it is impossible for two persons to write their conclusions in exactly the same language if they have not read each other's work. Minds are far more individual than snowflakes; no one else will ever quite duplicate the form you stamp on an essay or a report. Once you have created that form, it remains yours for all time.

With the design is always substance, and sometimes we surprise ourselves by discovering how interesting a subject can be in the light of the design we see in it. One of the best books I have read in recent years is David McCullough's *Mornings on Horseback*, a biography of Theodore Roosevelt that carries Roosevelt's story to his unsuccessful campaign to become mayor of New York City in 1886. The design of the book is not to tell about Roosevelt's political career. It is rather to tell of his development within his family, and that design makes McCullough notice the details of family life that a political biographer might have ignored—how the Roosevelts lived, the letters they wrote one another, the clothes they wore, the vacations they took, the diseases they suffered, and a huge number of other matters that make for an absorbing story. McCullough told me that once he arrived at his design, he began to see things about the Roosevelts that other biographers had slighted or else passed over in silence. His book is different from any other book on Roosevelt, although other writers studied the same materials. Our ideas of design, of purpose, affect how we see the world and may lead us to a new vision.

It is a vision that gets preserved—a preservation important for our private records and formal publications and even for papers we may write in college. Most writers take pleasure in thinking someone may read their works long after they themselves are dead. Writers great and small, modern and ancient, come alive whenever inquiring readers take their works from a shelf. A colleague of mine several years ago discovered he was dying of cancer. He sat calmly in my office one morning not long before the end, telling me with quiet pride that he knew he had written a book that would be valuable to others long after his death. I was moved by his soft rumination—and understood him perfectly. The thought was not morbid; it was rather a gentle counterattack against time and death that writers of all kinds make with their words.

Here is reason to keep a journal. You will learn to observe what happens to you, to sort out the important from the unimportant, whimsy from calculation. You will gain daily practice in putting observations into words and making sense of your life. Include in your journal thoughts you have about your reading, lectures you hear in class, and conversations you have with your friends, and you will have a record of the development of your mind—and you will help that development along. The daily practice of writing your autobiography will develop habits essential to anyone who wants to become a writer, including the habit of writing itself. In years to come you can redis- cover your life by seeing what you found worthy of preservation, and you will remember even more than you have recorded. The first task of the writer is to see; the second task is to record. The habit of re- cording will then help you see more than you ever dreamed possible.

Two

What Makes an Essay?

❖ ❖ ❖

Most readers of this book will be writing essays, extended pieces of nonfiction prose written to persuade readers to do something or believe something or to share with the writer an exploration of ideas. Essays differ according to the subjects they address and the audiences they assume. Every discipline has its own terminology and its own way of getting into a subject. Historians do not write exactly like literary critics; sociologists do not write like naturalists; physicists do not write like journalists. An essay in a scholarly journal differs from one in *Time*. Even so, all essays share some features, and these common features are the subject of this chapter.

The Definition of an Essay

The word *essay* was coined by a Frenchman, Michel de Montaigne, in the second half of the sixteenth century, to describe his written reflections on various subjects. His essays resembled public letters about his observations, his reading, and his ruminations. He rambled much more than essayists do now, letting his thoughts move from one idea to another. He was curious, as all good writers are, asking questions and seeking to answer them, and his rigorous honesty and quiet wit make disciples of his thought nearly four centuries after his death.

Montaigne's subjects were the experiences of daily life, which are still always worth writing about. He wrote with an independent mind, without accepting the prejudices of the crowd and without seeking favor from the powerful. His writing is natural, unaffected, simple. "I speak to the paper," he wrote, "just as I speak to someone I meet for the first time."[1] He never talked down to readers. Nor did he pander to their prejudices; he never feared to be in the minority. He tried to see things as they were, and his observations were surprising for their freshness. He proved that an honest observer always has something new to say.

He called his pieces "essays" from the French word meaning "attempts" or "trials." For him an essay was just that—an attempt to think clearly. He was far too humble to claim that he had established truth beyond all doubt. "I freely give my opinions on all things," he wrote, "even those that may go beyond my competence and on which I by no means claim to be an authority. And so my thoughts about them are only to reveal the extent of my vision and not the limits of things themselves."[2] He supposed that he had made an *essay* toward truth—observing honestly, marshaling his evidence, reflecting on his experience, interpreting it as fairly as he could. When he could not answer a question, he admitted his ignorance. He never claimed to have found all the truth about anything.

He knew his conclusions would not satisfy everyone. Still he advanced them tolerantly, serenely, without insulting his opponents, without heating his prose with passion except on the rare occasions when he condemned the religious wars burning across France in his time. He was confident without being arrogant. He did not believe he had to save the world. He believed that reason, clearly and gently set down on paper, would win its own battles. He did not try to crush his foes. He remained somewhat detached, like a man calmly taking us across a varied landscape, expertly pointing out features we otherwise might have missed.

Most good essays are akin to Montaigne's—civilized efforts to arrive at truth without rancor, without destroying those who disagree. Good essays appeal to the best in readers, to their sense of fair play, to their best emotions, to their wish to do the right thing, to their ability to think.

Now and then you may be tempted to write passionately for a noble cause. Resist the temptation. A few writers manage great passion for great causes, but success is rare in passionate writers because few writers control passion well. Angry passion easily becomes bombast and self-righteousness. Other passions can become cloying. Most readers hate prose dipped in syrup. Superheated prose is usually embarrassing.

A great essay of modern times is "Letter from a Birmingham Jail" written by the Reverend Martin Luther King, Jr., when he was jailed by a city government whose police chief had turned savage dogs on black citizens—including children—peacefully demonstrating for their rights. King's people had been whipped, beaten, bitten, maimed, and killed, and he had every reason to be furious. But his essay does not project fury. Instead it rises to a quiet eloquence and power just because it is so calm, so measured, so reasonable, and so fair. King had such confidence in the righteousness of his cause that he did not have to scream his convictions.

The best prose is tolerant and cool. If you are temperate and measured and reasoned, and if you treat your reader as a friend to persuade rather than a foe to slay, you will have a far better chance of carrying your point than if you dip your pen in fire and write to burn.

Qualities That Make a Good Essay

Here are some qualities of essays. Study them carefully.

1. Most essays are short enough to be read at a sitting.

Some books may be called essays since a serious, nonfiction book involves a sustained argument meant to make us accept the writer's view. In the more common meaning of the word, an *essay* is a shorter nonfiction piece that can be read at a single sitting. An essay is extended prose in that it is more than a sentence or a paragraph. Just how long you make an essay depends on your purposes and your audience, but all of us should recall the sound advice of Polonius in *Hamlet*: "Brevity is the soul of wit." Perhaps the Spanish writer Baltasar Gracian said it even better: "Good things, if short, are twice as good."

For new writers, an assignment to write a fifteen-page essay may seem monstrous. Experienced writers find the *short* essay far more difficult. They cannot fit all they know in the space available. They must decide what is most important in what they know and how to present it in the most striking possible way. Every word must count; every sentence must be just right. Every unnecessary word must be chopped out. That is hard work.

2. A good essay gets to the point quickly.

Readers want to know right away why they should read your work. Nothing annoys a reader like delay. "What is he trying to say? Why am I reading this?" Get to the point in the first two or three paragraphs; make the point clearly, and stick to it.

A good title can sharpen your purpose and state it at the beginning of your essay. Scholars are fond of titles with a colon in the middle: "My Hideous Progeny: Mary Shelley and the Feminization of Romanticism"; "History, Fiction, and the Ground Between: The Uses of the Documentary Mode in Black Literature." These two titles appeared in one issue of the PMLA (the Publication of the Modern Language Association), the major American journal devoted to studies in literature. This issue contains five articles; four have a colon in the middle. The title tells readers what to expect and motivates the writer to define those expectations in the first paragraphs.

Some inexperienced writers fail to give any statement of purpose to their essays. Others postpone it, not telling readers why they are writing until the fifth, sixth, or seventh page. Some writers love surprise endings. They want to tantalize readers, to delay the point of the essay until at last they reveal all, like a magician pulling a rabbit out of a hat. But writing is not a magician's trick, and such essays annoy us because they waste our time. They make us think that the writer is not so interested in informing us as in proving how clever he or she is. Readers quit reading such stuff; when readers quit reading, the writer has failed. Get to the point quickly; let your readers know the direction you want to take them.

WAYS TO BEGIN

No book can tell you all the ways to begin an essay. Your best bet is to study beginnings of essays by professional writers and to imitate them. Here are some common types.

Tell a story Lewis Thomas, scientist and writer, begins an essay on a small African tribe in the country of Uganda as follows:

> The small tribe of Ilks, formerly nomadic hunters and gatherers in the mountain valleys of northern Uganda, have become celebrities, literary symbols for the ultimate fate of disheartened, heartless mankind at large. Two disastrously conclusive things happened to them: the government decided to have a national park, so they were compelled by law to give up hunting in the valleys and become farmers on poor hillside soil, and then they were visited for two years by an anthropologist who detested them and wrote a book about them.[3]

Having seized our attention with this story, Thomas develops the story, enlarges it, and explains how the fate of the Ilks tells us something about human nature.

You can begin an essay with an anecdote that includes a puzzling fact that must be explained. Here is Annie Dillard:

> A couple of summers ago I was walking along the edge of the island to see what I could see in the water, and mainly to scare frogs. Frogs have an inelegant way of taking off from invisible positions on the bank just ahead of your feet, in dire panic, emitting a froggy "Yike!" and splashing into the water. Incredibly, this amused me, and, incredibly, it amuses me still. As I walked along the grassy edge of the island, I got better and better at seeing frogs both in and out of the water. I learned to recognize, slowing down, the difference in texture of the light reflected from

the mudbank, water, grass, or frog. Frogs were flying all around me. At the end of the island I noticed a small green frog. He was exactly half in and half out of the water, looking like a schematic diagram of an amphibian, and he didn't jump.[4]

A frog that didn't jump! This curious fact keeps us reading Dillard's essay. Why didn't the frog jump? She tells us in the next two paragraphs and moves on to a reflective essay on the horrors and mystery inherent in nature—and in our own lives.

We love stories, and they make good beginnings as long as we do something with them in the essay that follows. One caution: Don't represent a story as true when you have no evidence for the details. Don't make things up. For example, don't start a paper like this:

> It was night in the palace in Greenwich, and a sleepy silence hung over the dark corridors and the rooms where royal servants lay snoring abed. Only Henry VIII was awake, and he walked the floor aimlessly before the great fire that blazed on the hearth in his room. He could not sleep because he could not purge his mind of the greatest problem of his reign: How could he have a son?

You may imagine that Henry VIII had every reason for walking the floor at night, worrying about the succession to the throne of England. But no document gives any evidence that such a scene took place. You cast doubt on the rest of your essay on a historical event if you start by making up a story that has no basis in the evidence.

Describe a scene   Akin to telling a story is a description of a scene that arouses curiosity. The reader wants to know, "What is happening here?" Here is Joan Didion:

> The closed door upstairs at 120 South Spring Street in downtown Los Angeles is marked OPERATIONS CENTER. In the windowless room beyond the closed door a reverential hush prevails. From six A.M. until seven P.M. in this windowless room men sit at consoles watching a huge board flash colored lights. "There's the heart attack," someone will murmur, or "we're getting the gawk effect." 120 South Spring is the Los Angeles office of Caltrans, or the California Department of Transportation, and the Operations Center is where Caltrans engineers monitor what they call "the 42-Mile Loop." The 42-Mile Loop is simply the rough triangle formed by the intersections of the Santa Monica, the San Diego and the Harbor freeways, and 42 miles represents less than ten percent of freeway mileage in Los Angeles County alone, but these particular 42 miles are regarded around 120 South Spring with a special veneration. The Loop is a "demonstration system," a phrase much favored by everyone at Caltrans, and is part of a "pilot project," another two words carrying totemic weight on South Spring.[5]

What is happening? We sense that Didion feels scorn for whatever it is. Why? We read on and discover that the essay discusses bureaucratic bungling in electronic traffic management in Los Angeles.

Use a quotation   The essayist can begin with a provocative quotation, and then explain it and use the explanation to develop the thesis of the essay.

> "Reagan is going, the revolution stays." The billboards adorn the dusty roadways of Managua, a pitiful yelp of triumph in an exhausted country that has little else to celebrate. Yet the Sandinistas can cheer at least this: while Ronald Reagan will be just another private citizen in two months, Daniel Ortega Saavedra—the man Reagan once called a "dictator in designer glasses"—will remain firmly at the helm of a government that the White House terms an "outlaw regime."[6]

The springboard quotation may have a short introduction, telling where it is from:

> In the prelude to *Middlemarch*, George Eliot lamented the unfulfilled lives of talented women:
>
> > Some have felt that these blundering lives are due to the inconvenient indefiniteness with which the Supreme Power has fashioned the natures of women: if there were one level of feminine incompetence as strict as the ability to count three and no more, the social lot of women might be treated with scientific certitude.
>
> Eliot goes on to discount the idea of innate limitation, but while she wrote in 1872, the leaders of European anthropometry were trying to measure "with scientific certitude" the inferiority of women. Anthropometry, or measurement of the human body, is not so fashionable a field these days, but it dominated the human sciences for much of the nineteenth century and remained popular until intelligence testing replaced skull measurement as a favored device for making invidious comparisons among races, classes, and sexes.[7]

Begin with a simple, definite statement   Sometimes it's best to renounce all art and begin with a simple statement that provokes agreement or curiosity.

> Everyone must have had at least one personal experience with a computer error by this time. Bank balances are suddenly reported to have jumped from $379 into the millions, appeals for charitable contributions are mailed over and over to people with crazy-sounding names at your address, department stores send the wrong bills, utility companies write that they're turning everything off, that sort of thing.[8]

Ask a question   Occasionally the rhetorical question makes a good beginning. The writer answers it and proceeds to the rest of the essay.

> Is there a sporting event more inconvenient to watch than the World Series? Think about it. This year the Series was played entirely on the West Coast, and all of the games started at roughly 5:30 in the afternoon, Pacific Daylight Time. Now that's a swell hour for a California fan to head to the old ball yard. If he slipped out of the office early at, say, four o'clock and made it to his car a few minutes later, he was just in time to join the rush-hour multitudes on the freeways. If everything went smoothly, he was in his seat at the stadium by the third inning.[9]

A good beginning establishes a context and sets up a problem that the writer, in effect, promises to resolve by the end of the essay. We have all heard this beginning:

> Once upon a time there was a little girl named Red Riding Hood who lived at the edge of a forest. On the other side of the forest lived her grandmother, and in the forest lived a big, bad wolf.

Any child hearing this beginning knows that Little Red Riding Hood is going to meet up with that wolf in the woods. The writer includes those details to set a context; they imply a promise that the writer will do something with them. We would not know what to make of a story like this:

> Once upon a time there was a little girl named Red Riding Hood who lived at the edge of a forest. On the other side of the forest lived her grandmother, and in the forest lived a big, bad wolf. One day Little Red Riding Hood set out through the forest to take a basket of cakes to her grandmother. But just as she walked into the woods, she met a talent scout for the Dallas Cowboys, and he persuaded her to throw away her cakes and forget her grandmother, leave the forest, and come to Dallas to be a cheerleader, and she never thought about home or the forest or her grandmother again.

Any child who heard a story like this would cry out, "What about the big bad wolf? What about the grandmother?" A good story makes something out of the details at the beginning; so does a good essay. Its introduction includes some facts or ideas which by being in the opening paragraphs imply or promise that the writer will do something with them. The reader follows the writer into the essay to find out what happens to the details at the beginning.

BEGINNINGS TO AVOID

Here are some types of beginnings to avoid. Some of them don't introduce the essay; some are just boring.

The dictionary definition   Never begin an essay like this: "The dictionary defines *crisis* as 'a decisive or crucial time, stage, or event.' " Ugh!

The dictionary is an authority, and writers need authority. A dictionary definition contains a kind of outline that an inexperienced writer may follow; but as a beginning of an essay, it is trite and boring. Writing teachers see the tired old dictionary beginning hundreds of times—and groan each time.

You can write a good essay about a definition only in cases in which different people use the same important word in different ways. If people did not use the word in different ways, the essay would be unnecessary. What does *socialism* mean? You will not satisfy demanding readers if you begin an essay on socialism by referring to a dictionary. The dictionary definition offers only a hint of the astonishing diversity of interpretation that has marked the history of socialism. Your definition, derived from your own study, will make the substance of an excellent essay, but it will not be the bare-bones outline of a dictionary. It will be long enough to consider the important variations among the definitions of others. A Russian Communist will define the concept of socialism one way, a French member of the Socialist party another, and the president of the American Medical Association still another. Your essay in definition must take all these variations into account.

The historical background   The historical background beginning is another old standby that makes teachers groan:

> From the dawn of time forests have been preserves of wild animals often dangerous to human beings, especially to children, and numerous indeed are the tales of bloody encounters between wild beasts and little girls and boys. Certain predator animals seem to prefer human beings because humans are usually quite inadequate in their unarmed state to resist the attacks of beasts. At times human beings do foolish and careless things that expose them to unnecessary danger. Let us look at one example of this oft-repeated drama in real life by recalling an old fairy tale in which a young woman armed only with a basket of cakes encounters a wolf in the forest, with results that in most versions of the tale were extremely unpleasant for the little girl involved.

Another ugh! Many subjects require some historical background; for example, an essay defining socialism would have to take history into account. But don't provide a background merely to take up space. Beginning the story of Little Red Riding Hood with the history of animals would leave a child impatient and frustrated. Get to the point.

Students love to start with history. While they are giving the background, they can think of something to say in the essay. Maybe it is all right to get started this way on a rough draft. But spare your poor reader. Don't provide vague and unnecessary historical background.

The justification of the topic   Many inexperienced writers begin essays with a kind of apology. Their first statement tries to defend their choice of a topic: "Why should we discuss the minor characters in Shakespeare's *Macbeth*?" "The difference between the theology of Luther's sermons and his formal theological treatises has often been considered by scholars of the Reformation." They follow these opening statements with a long survey of previous scholarship, leaving themselves a tiny window through which they can scramble with their own contribution. The implied comment seems to be something like this: "You probably think nothing new can be said on this subject, but if you are patient, I can prove that I have a tiny contribution to make."

You don't have to have the permission of previous scholars before you can make your point. If you think Luther's theological treatises are different from his sermons, get to work and prove it. Don't uncoil a long and tedious list of previous scholarship. You may use other scholarship along the way. Indeed you should. Refute it, modify it, or use it to confirm your case. But don't begin with an uninteresting summary as if no one had the right to consider a subject without beginning with an account of all the scholarship that has gone before.

Real writers write to tell readers something. They don't apologize for daring to have an idea. Begin with something strong, something that will catch your readers' eyes and make them continue.

The blueprint beginning   The blueprint beginning runs something like this:

> In the following narrative, I am going to tell the story of a young woman named Red Riding Hood who got into trouble with a wolf in the forest. I shall tell how Red Riding Hood started through the forest to deliver cakes to her grandmother on the other side. I shall tell how she encountered the wolf, together with some details about the wolf's trickery and his unpleasant disposition. I shall discuss the method by which the wolf consumed Red Riding Hood's grandmother, and I shall tell many interesting details of the conversation the wolf, disguised as the grandmother, had with Red Riding Hood before he consumed her. I shall conclude with some observations of the difficulties of animals who talk to people.

Ugh and double ugh! Such a flat, tedious announcement may attract someone already passionately interested in your subject, and it may be legitimately used in some professional journals whose readers are specialists in the topic and want nothing but the facts. You may wish also to write such an introduction as a first draft to help you get started. However, such beginnings fail to attract those not already interested. Professional writers work harder, coaxing their imaginations to come up with something more appealing. Imagine how startled you would be to read the following introduction to an article in *Sports Illustrated*:

> This story will tell you about the World Series. It will announce the contesting teams, provide some background about their seasons and their victories in the playoffs, describe their coaches, their players, and the players' families, especially their adorable children, and make some remarks about their fans. It will include a summary of events about each of the games, and it will conclude with the results as well as with some comments made by coaches, players, and fans after the Series was over.

You know—almost unconsciously—that this kind of beginning is deadly and that reading the story to follow will be like wading through knee-deep mud in running shoes. Don't use it.

The man from Mars   Variations on this beginning include the man from another planet, the archaeologist from a future civilization, or the person awakened from the dead of an earlier epoch to look at our own time. "If a man from Mars were to visit our nation today, he would be astounded to discover how much time Americans spend in their automobiles." In fact if a man from Mars were to visit our planet, he would be such a celebrity that he would not have time to think much about Americans in their automobiles. These are tired old beginnings. If they once had verve, they lost it long ago. Don't use them. Thousands of uninspired writers have worn them out.

3. A good essay stays with its subject to the end.

A good essay develops a major theme. It may explore the theme from several different angles. It may develop subthemes. A good essay shows the writer thinking, thinking, thinking. It may develop some thoughts only to reject them. Even so, the good essay is finally about one principal and identifiable subject. You must check everything you put into an essay to be sure it supports the matter at hand. A good essay does not wander into long digressions. It stays on course.

Inexperienced writers often produce incoherent essays because they try to stuff too much into them. Often they think of themselves as test-takers and concentrate on proving that they know "enough."

They throw everything they can think of into the piece, and it becomes a verbal hash in which none of the tastes is identifiable.

Digression may help you write a first draft, for when you put your first words on paper, you may wander all over the place, like a dog sniffing from one scent to another in a broad field. But by the time you write your final draft, you should have decided what you want to say and take your reader directly to it. Look at each sentence, each paragraph, to be sure it fits your purpose. If it does not, cut it out.

4. A good essay makes internal connections.

This point is closely related to the last. An essay with one thesis, one point, will be made of parts that build towards the support of that thesis. Be sure those parts are connected by transitions to help readers move easily from one part to another. The verbal signs of such transitions are words such as *because, furthermore, therefore, thus, but, and*, and *nevertheless*. You seldom write these words to make the transitions, but you may imply them in various ways. In a good piece of writing, a reader senses the connections and uses them to move easily from one part of the essay to the next.

Here again the good essay resembles a good story. In telling a story, we construct a chain of cause and effect. We say, "This happened; and because this happened, this next thing happened; and because that next thing happened, another thing happened." Were we to leave out a step, the rest of the story would be confusing or incomprehensible. Good fiction involves such a connected series, beginning with the first cause and proceeding until the last effect.

A good essay proceeds in much the same way. The essayist may say something like this: "A is true. Because A is true, B is also true. Because A and B are true, C is also true." Sometimes the connections are more tentative. "A is true. If A is true, B also may be true. If A and B are true, C may also be true." Whether the connectives are certain or tentative, they exist, and they hold the parts of the good essay together. One thought leads clearly to the next. Readers are not left wondering how the writer got here from there. Good writers read their own work carefully. When you read yours, see if you can separate it into distinct parts. Be sure to connect each part to the next.

A brief example may demonstrate the principle. Suppose you write an essay on the political thought of Thomas Jefferson. It might follow a pattern like this:

Thomas Jefferson believed all men are created equal.

Furthermore he believed that all men had a capacity to reason and to make decisions about their own lives.

Therefore he rejected kings and the supposition that some men were created to rule over other men.

Therefore he believed that only a republican government based on majority rule could claim to be virtuous.

Furthermore he believed in freedom of speech, the press, religion, and assembly because only if people were free to present opinions and information could reason be free to operate.

Therefore he granted the right of monarchists in the United States after the Revolution to say that the new American Republic was a mistake.

Transitional words indicate the bridges between one thought and the next. In writing your essay on Jefferson's concept of politics, you may not need to include these transitional words. You may be able to write with such a clear sense of connection that readers can supply the transitions, seeing easily how the parts of your essay are connected. Be sure you connect each part of your essay to the next.

5. A good essay subordinates some of its parts to others.

This point is related to the requirement that every essay have a purpose and to the requirement that there be transitions between the separate parts of the essay. The parts of an essay have to be integrated; your points must add up to something. Never leave your readers saying "So what?" when they have read your essay. If they are to understand why you wrote the essay, you have to integrate your writing and make a distinction between minor points and major ones.

Frequently my students give me what I call the "museum tour" essay. They are the guides; I am the visitor. "Here is a painting," the guide says. "Here is another painting. And here is another. And look, there is another." But I ask, "What does all that mean? Why are you telling me these things? What do you make of all this?" You must make readers see why you think the parts go into the whole and how the parts are related to each other. Some of these parts must be subordinated to other parts.

During the 1988 presidential campaign, I asked my students to read *The Boston Globe* and *The New York Times* each day to see what the candidates were saying. I asked them to write an essay on the vision of the electorate of either George Bush or Michael Dukakis. Who does Bush think the voters are at heart? Who are the Americans in Dukakis's mind? The task was to infer the answer to those questions by studying what the candidates said and to build the inferences into an essay. I asked my students not to become mired in the question of whether the candidates were right or wrong. I did not want a campaign speech; I wanted an analysis.

One student wrote a draft that might be outlined like this: George Bush thinks Americans distrust liberals; he also thinks Americans want a strong defense; he also assumes Americans do not want to pay any more taxes; he also assumes Americans are patriotic; he assumes, too, that Americans are afraid of crime. This student's paper was a museum tour: first this, and then this, and then this. The paper did not present any clear subordination of one part to another; every point seemed equal to every other point.

After some discussion, the student and I came up with a more defined thesis:

> George Bush has made his campaign an effort to label Michael Dukakis as a liberal and to blame liberals for many problems that make Americans uneasy.

> For
> He paints liberals as weak on defense.
> He blames liberals for high taxes.
> He makes liberals seem unpatriotic.
> He says liberals are soft on crime.

My student subordinated the other points in his rough draft to the first one. The subordination drew the essay together, unified it, and made it flow more easily from part to part.

When you have an essay that seems to be a loose collection of facts, unify it by subordinating some of your points to others. To subordinate, study your work to see which parts belong to a broader, more embracing category. Make a distinction between your main points and the evidence or arguments that support them.

6. A good essay includes evidence to help readers relive the experience the writer writes about or to relive the process of thought by which the writer arrives at a conclusion.

Beginning writers often forget that their job is not merely to summarize their conclusions but to help readers relive the writer's thoughts.

Storytelling is again a model for the principle. You do not read a story just to see how it ends. You ruin a mystery novel if you read the last chapter before you start reading the book. You read to share the excitement of the story itself, and in reading fiction for pleasure, you want to arrive at the end with the characters, having lived their lives with them in the pages of the book. In an essay, you get the reader to live with you through the thinking that led you to your conclusion.

The following paragraph gives evidence that helps the reader to relive the writer's experience:

> John has a violent temper. I beat him at chess last night, and he threw the pieces into the fire, tossed a beer bottle through the window, turned over the refrigerator, tore the chessboard to pieces, yelled at

> me, and told me that I was an arrogant amateur who won only by dumb luck. Then he told me that if I didn't come back again tonight to play and give him a chance for revenge, he would stop being my best friend.

By the time we finish reading this little tale, we agree that John has a violent temper. The writer has helped us relive the experience he had with John. We have evidence to prove the case.

An essay without evidence is sound and fury. Avoid the attempt to support one empty generalization with another. "Latin should be taught in all public schools because people who know Latin write English better than people who do not." Both these statements are opinions. How do we know that people who know Latin write English better than people who do not? Has there been a test of the writing ability of those who know Latin and of those who do not? The results of such a test would be evidence. But without evidence, we have only a couple of opinions, and we have no reason to accept them. Many people have said that knowing Latin helps one write better English; no one to my knowledge has ever proved the assertion. Until someone conducts some sort of test, the assertion remains empty.

What is evidence?

Experience is evidence. If you write an autobiographical essay, a detailed account of your experience will support the generalizations you make about your life and times. Obviously the experience of an individual is not necessarily final evidence for generalizations we might make about all people or about large groups of people. An account of personal experience may be prejudiced and unreasonable. Someone may say, "I was in Paris last year, and all the French were rude; none of them spoke English." Someone else who speaks French well may discover that the French in Paris are extremely generous and polite.

Yet thoughtful accounts of personal experience carry much weight. A few years ago *The New York Times* writer Hedrick Smith published a splendid book called *The Russians* based on his personal experiences with Russian people during his years as bureau chief for the *Times* in Moscow. Philip Caputo's *A Rumor of War*, his account of his military service in Vietnam, provides a moving statement of what it was to be an American soldier in that war. Both books are filled with personal anecdotes. Those of us who have never been to either Russia or Vietnam can feel that we possess important knowledge about both places because we have relived the experience of two gifted writers through their words.

Statistics provide evidence. Medical statistics show that cigarette smokers are much more likely to die of lung cancer and heart disease than are nonsmokers. Baseball statistics show that left-handed hitters are much more successful against right-handed pitchers than against left-handed pitchers. Statistical data have to be interpreted fairly and intelligently; someone has said that statistics don't lie but that liars use statistics. Even so, statistics represent evidence, and they can strengthen your essay.

Quotations provide evidence. If you are going to tell what a literary or historical or scientific text means, you have to quote from it, providing the exact words that help us hear a voice and catch a tone.

Vladimir Nabokov, teacher and author of many popular books, including *Lolita*, used to tell his students to begin their study of a novel or story by noting exactly what the writer said. This close reading, this intense preoccupation with exactitude, should guide the careful writer in the search for evidence. Study the text and see exactly what it says. Quote from it to prove your point—not long block quotations but short, pungent statements.

Authorities provide evidence. A renowned medical researcher who says that he thinks blood cholesterol is not as dangerous to the heart as most medical scientists think is an authority. You can use his comment as evidence—but not conclusive evidence. The opinion of an authority is only another opinion, respected because we assume that the authority has done something worthy of the respect he enjoys. Authorities can be wrong. It is best to mention an authority after you have given other evidence that supports the position you and the authority take.

7. A good essay on a controversial subject includes evidence that may seem to contradict the point the writer makes.

If you write on a controversial subject, you must consider contrary evidence and opinions. Careless or dishonest writers ignore contrary evidence. They imagine they will weaken their case if they mention the arguments on the other side of the issue. The reader who discovers such a deceit quickly loses respect for the writer.

Every year thousands of writers in college courses argue important issues without considering contrary evidence and often without acknowledging that any contrary evidence exists. They will, for example, write a paper attacking proposals for a military draft, pretending that everyone favoring the draft is an ignoramus, an imperialist, a militarist, or a tyrant. Those favoring the draft will, in a similar spirit, argue that foes of the draft are pampered youths, kooks, or cowards who refuse to give anything of themselves to their country.

Controversial issues seldom have all the good guys on one side and all the bad guys on the other. Papers that assume such a moral division convince only the naïve; they do not change the minds of those in the thoughtful audience looking for guidance, the audience you should be trying to persuade. If you persist in writing as if every opponent is a knave or a fool, fair-minded readers will dismiss your work.

One of the greatest writing problems my students face is within themselves. They want to believe that knowledge is a seamless garment, that all its parts fit so closely together that there is no room for disagreement. But knowledge is seldom so tidy. Knowledge comes with rough edges and holes, and honest writers acknowledge them.

Concede the truth of contrary evidence when you believe it is true. You may argue that it does not damage your case. Or you may argue that it has been misinterpreted by your foes. If, for example, you argue for a military draft, you must consider whether such a draft discriminates against young men since young women are not drafted for combat duty. Do you concede that this discrimination will exist but that it must be accepted as a lesser evil in a society that needs conscription? Or do you argue that past discrimination against young men does not mean that women should now be exempt from the draft and combat duty? You have to decide. Whatever you decide, be fair.

Never be too proud or too frightened to make a concession. To concede a point gives the appearance of fair-mindedness and confidence—an appearance valuable in persuasive essays. Strategic concession has been recognized since the orators of ancient Greece as a major strength to both speaking and writing. A writer might include in an essay the following concession:

> Yes, I concede that the bottle bill will be a pain to all of us. We can't toss the bottles out any more. We will have to pay more for Cokes and beer. We will have to haul the bottles back to stores to collect our deposit. The bottle bill will cost all of us more time and money than we like.

Such a concession allows the writer to come back with a stronger argument for the essay's posistion:

> But the bottle bill may save some money, too—money now spent in cleaning up the litter tossed along our streets and highways, money spent in repairing the damage done to tires and sometimes to bare feet by broken glass. For the experience of other states with bottle laws is that litter is dramatically reduced when people have some financial incentive to return bottles to the store rather than toss them away when they are empty. Once people experience a cleaner environment, they may decide that the little extra time and money they spend because of the bottle bill are well worth the cost.

Those who argue vehemently and blindly for a cause sound like fanatics. Only fanatics listen to fanatics. Your aim should be to attract another kind of reader.

8. A good essay is written with its audience in mind.

Remember your audience, the people you expect to read your work. We have already posed some important questions about audience. What do your readers know? What do you share with them? What will interest them? How can you get them to read your work and respect you?

Share your writing with your friends. Get them to tell you what you have said. Don't ask them what they think of your writing, for most of them will say it's good. When you ask them to tell you what you have said, you put another kind of obligation on them, and you may learn much more about your prose.

Most professional writers share their work with another person or with a small group of friends. An acquaintance of mine says he writes for about five people he knows—all of them critical but tolerant. I write for my editor. She is a woman of taste and intelligence, and I believe that if I can interest her, others will be interested, too.

Writing for an audience does not mean dismissing your sincere thoughts in favor of a hypocritical effort to please at any price. You have your own opinions, your own knowledge, your own ambitions for your writing. Try to express them to please and persuade people you know. You can take pride and pleasure in making someone you admire say, "You have done a good job on this; you have convinced me, and I like the piece."

My editor is a good person who loves to read. She will not let me insult people or make sweeping generalizations. She will not let me be silly or vague or bad-tempered. Writers writing about things they care about may make all these errors in their early drafts. My editor marks them; I know now what she is likely to mark, and I keep her in mind as I write, trying to avoid the flaws that irritate her. I do not always succeed. But she is my audience, and my sense of her as a person makes my writing better than it would be without her.

Respect your audience. Make your audience respect you. Wayne C. Booth, a noted authority on writing, has said that every piece of writing has an "implied author," someone your readers find standing behind the words on the page. Your implied author may be the opposite of the person you think you are. Students are sometimes amazed and hurt to discover that the impression of themselves they convey in writing is not what they want readers to think about them. Your own implied author should be sincere, humane, convincing, tolerant, interested, fair-minded, and honest, showing confidence in the intelligence and fair-mindedness of your readers.

Don't be cute or silly, but be lively. Write naturally. Use simple words rather than complicated ones—unless your thoughts can only be expressed by the more complicated words. Don't qualify statements too much; you should not sound wishy-washy. Write as if you like your readers and trust them to have good sense. Don't show off. Don't condescend. Be honest and forthright, simple and direct.

9. A good essay is mechanically and grammatically correct and looks neat on the page.

Telling a writer to use correct grammar, punctuation, and spelling is like telling a pianist to hit the right notes. The mechanical conventions we use in writing have developed historically, sometimes without much logic. English spelling seems especially illogical, and whether you spell well or not has nothing to do with basic intelligence. Some people are bad spellers, and all that means is that they are bad spellers. Even so, the mechanical conventions are essential symbols of communication, and you must observe them. Otherwise readers will struggle with your prose. If you do not observe the conventions, most readers will suppose you are careless, illiterate, or even stupid.

Type your papers, or do them on a word processor. If you don't know how to type, learn. Compose at the keyboard. You can do it. The convenience of doing so will help you all through life.

Mark up your early drafts. But when your work goes out to readers, it should be neat and clean and correct. If your work shows that you do not respect it, you can hardly ask others to take it seriously. If you can't spell, get help. Ask friends to read your work and correct your spelling. Use the dictionary. I am a terrible speller, so I have at least one dictionary—and sometimes four or five—at every desk and table where I work at home or in my office. Word-processing programs now have spell checkers; use them. Think of your readers; misspelled words and other violations of conventions make reading very hard. To observe the conventions is a form of courtesy.

10. A good essay concludes swiftly and gracefully.

Conclusions are difficult, and many writers have trouble with them. You can conclude in many ways. In your conclusion, your final paragraphs should reflect the thoughts presented in your first paragraphs. Don't make your last paragraph a blueprint summary of what you have said:

> I have now shown that little girls who carry baskets of cakes into woods where lurk big, bad wolves are likely to come to a bad end.

The mutual reflection of first and last paragraphs should be more subtle than that. Subtle or not, the connection between your beginning and your end should be discernible.

Here is the last paragraph of Joan Didion's essay "Bureaucrats." We have already seen the first paragraph on page 25:

> The circle seemed intact. Mrs. Wood and I smiled, and shook hands. I watched the big board until all lights turned green on the Santa Monica and then I left and drove home on it, all 16.2 miles of it. All the way I remembered that I was watched by the Xerox Sigma V. All the way the message boards gave me the number to call for CAR POOL INFO. As I left the freeway it occurred to me that they might have their own rapture down at 120 South Spring, and it could be called Perpetuating the Department. Today the California Highway Patrol reported that, during the first six weeks of the Diamond Lane, accidents on the Santa Monica, which normally range between 49 and 72 during a six-week period, totaled 204. Yesterday plans were announced to extend the Diamond Lane to other freeways at a cost of $42,500,000.[10]

You can read the first paragraph and the last and see all sorts of reflections—"board," "Santa Monica," "120 South Spring Street," and others. Although you do not know everything Joan Didion has said in her essay, you can tell that she thinks the "Diamond Lane," whatever it is, is an idiotic boondoggle. That is one of the advantages of having this mutual reflection in first and last paragraphs: readers see everything being knit together at the end, of having the promise made in the first paragraphs kept by the last. Joan Didion tells a little story to begin and another to conclude. The stories cohere.

Now we can look at the beginning and end of the essay by Lewis Thomas we looked at earlier called "To Err Is Human." Here again is the beginning:

> Everyone must have had at least one personal experience with a computer error by this time. Bank balances are suddenly reported to have jumped from $379 into the millions, appeals for charitable contributions are mailed over and over to people with crazy-sounding names at your address, department stores send the wrong bills, utility companies write that they're turning everything off, that sort of thing.[11]

Here is the end:

> We should have this in mind as we become dependent on more complex computers for the arrangement of our affairs. Give the computers their heads, I say; let them go their way. If we can learn to do this, turning our heads to one side and wincing while the work proceeds, the possibilities for the future of mankind, and computerkind, are limitless. Your average good computer can make calculations in an instant which would take a lifetime of slide rules for any of us. Think of what we could gain from the near infinity of precise, machine-made miscomputation which is now so easily within our grasp. We could begin the solving of some of our

hardest problems. How, for instance, should we go about organizing ourselves for social living on a planetary scale now that we have become, as a plain fact of life, a single community? We can assume, as a working hypothesis, that all the right ways of doing this are unworkable. What we need, then, for moving ahead, is a set of wrong alternatives much longer and more interesting than the short list of mistaken courses that any of us can think up right now. We need, in fact, an infinite list, and when it is printed out we need the computer to turn on itself and select, at random, the next way to go. If it is a big enough mistake, we could find ourselves on a new level, stunned, out in the clear, ready to move again.[12]

Here are a set of statements that effectively conclude an argument whose outlines we can grasp without reading the rest of the essay. Somehow Thomas finds something positive in computer error. Mistakes with computers are common, and Thomas finds that they open up a way to progress. To follow this wry argument, we need to read the whole essay. Even so, we can gain something from reading the first and the last paragraphs.

Like Thomas, you may end by drawing some conclusions suggested by the argument you have presented in the rest of your essay. The whole essay adds up to what you do at the end. The last paragraph here is a little like the sum of a column of figures you might add in an arithmetic problem. This is the total of all the points you have made so far.

Quotations make good conclusions, just as they make good beginnings. When a quotation stands at the start of an essay, it demands to be explained by the rest of the essay. When a quotation stands at the end of an essay, it reflects the conclusion the essay has made, sometimes summing it up.

Here is the last paragraph of Stephen Jay Gould's essay "Women's Brains." (We looked at the first paragraph earlier, on p. 26.)

> I prefer another strategy. Montessori and Morgan followed Broca's philosophy to reach a more congenial conclusion. I would rather label the whole enterprise of setting a biological value upon groups for what it is: irrelevant and highly injurious. George Eliot well appreciated the special tragedy that biological labeling imposed upon members of disadvantaged groups. She expressed it for people like herself—women of extraordinary talent. I would apply it more widely—not only to those whose dreams are flouted but also to those who never realize that they may dream—but I cannot match her prose. In conclusion, then, the rest of Eliot's prelude to *Middlemarch*.

> The limits of variation are really much wider than anyone would imagine from the sameness of women's coiffure and the favorite love stories in prose and verse. Here and there a cygnet is reared uneasily among the ducklings in the brown pond, and never finds

the living stream in fellowship with its own oary-footed kind. Here and there is born a Saint Theresa, foundress of nothing, whose loving heartbeats and sobs after an unattained goodness tremble off and are dispersed among hindrances instead of centering in some long-recognizable deed.[13]

Write a conclusion that reflects the beginning of your essay without mindlessly repeating it. Don't bring in a new argument or send readers off in a strange new direction. Bring them to a sense of end, a conclusion that keeps the early promise you have made to them.

Concluding Remarks on the Essay

We take for granted our amazing ability to recognize different forms of literature when we read them. We know that we are reading poetry when we read a poem; we know that we are reading fictional prose or a play when we read those texts. We may not know at first whether we are reading a short story or a novel if we take a page at random from the whole. But we know we are reading fiction unless the author has made a deliberate attempt to deceive us into supposing that he or she is writing about truth. (George Orwell never shot an elephant, although he wrote a celebrated account of this supposed deed, and he never helped hang a condemned prisoner in India, although he also claimed to have done so.) Fiction usually tells us by its form that it is fiction.

We also know quickly when we are reading nonfiction, even if we pick up a piece and start in the middle without having any idea as to the title or the author. We may not know whether we are reading an essay or a book, but we know that the author has an intention of making us think we are reading something that is "true" or "real."

The essay has its form in the general family of nonfiction. Readers begin essays with certain expectations. If they do not find them fulfilled, they stop reading. I have tried to summarize these expectations in this chapter. Check your own essays by my list and see if they conform to it. If not, think your essay through again to be certain that your deviation is worth the risk you run in denying to readers their own hopes for your writing.

The essay form will be useful to you throughout life as you write memos, business letters, reports, and articles. Develop the habit of studying essays you find enjoyable and informative. Check the advice in this chapter by sitting down with any good essay to see how it is put together. As you become more aware of the habits of good writers, you will develop these habits yourself. Your prose will reflect what you read carefully. Be a good reader, and you will not need this or any other book about writing to help you write well yourself.

Three

The Writing Process

❖ ❖ ❖

*N*ow that we have our goal—the essay—in mind, we can think of how to reach it. It is not an easy road. Shakespeare is said to have written his plays without erasing a line. The rest of us are not like him. Most writers revise and revise and revise. They cross out and write variations in the margins of their manuscripts. They rearrange the parts of their work. Those who work without a computer may cut drafts apart with scissors and paste them together again in a new arrangement.

Computers with word-processing programs have made the physical labor of writing less burdensome. Computers cannot improve writing. They can make revision more rapid, but you must still do the work, and it takes time.

How much time you spend on your writing depends on how serious you are about it. For the serious writer, writing is a way of life, an everyday habit. Writers work at their craft like disciplined athletes training for the Olympics or pianists practicing for concerts in Carnegie Hall.

Part of the time must be spent in preparation. Writers must know things. Battered old writing teachers curse their fate when they read student papers filled with sweeping generalizations and preachy emotionalism. Such papers betray student writers who have not looked anything up, not read any books or articles, not asked any hard questions. The first step in writing is knowledge. It would be good for writers to do the first drafts of their papers in the reference rooms of libraries. Access to reference books makes it simpler to get the names and dates right and to get background information. When you read up on a topic, you often find the data falling into what lawyers call "fact patterns." That is, the facts start pointing to conclusions. For example, to prepare to write a paper on the character Horatio in *Hamlet* you may read every speech Horatio gives and the attitudes toward him expressed by other characters in the play. As you investigate, the facts begin to add up to a conclusion: Horatio may be the only unambiguously good person in the play.

Write about what you know; that is a familiar piece of advice given to students learning to write. The backside of this aphorism is that you cannot write well about anything you *don't* know. Many inexperienced writers can write fairly well about themselves. The reason is simple: they know a lot about themselves. You can write well about many subjects if you take the trouble to learn something about them. Keep notes on your reading; write down your thoughts about your reading as you go along.

When I get a writing assignment, I begin filling notebooks. I can look up from where I sit writing at my computer and can count seventeen notebooks on my bookshelf; another lies in my shoulder bag that I carry on my daily bicycle commute to and from my office. Two others lie on my desk in my little cell in the library where I work every afternoon. Whenever I go on a trip I have a notebook at hand. I am always scribbling ideas, trial sentences, and random thoughts in them. Like a prospector digging through mud and sand for gold, I sift my notes for quotations and thoughts for everything I write—including this book.

Find your own writing process. Mine is wrapped up in notebooks; I urge them on you. A notebook is portable, durable, and efficient since you are unlikely to lose pages bound together. A friend of mine carries a small pack of 3 × 5 cards in his shirt pocket. The cards are hard on his shirts but good for his mind and memory. Vladimir Nabokov, an American novelist and poet, wrote his notes in pencil on such cards, and later someone typed his manuscripts from them. If you prefer to carry 3 × 5 cards around with you, do it. You can hold them together with rubber bands, and later you can arrange them in the approximate order in which you might use them in writing an essay.

If you use a notebook, don't be afraid of letting it get messy and disorganized. It's your private property, your fenced-in garden where you play with your thoughts. No one else will see it. Jot down ideas as they come into your head. Professional photographers throw away fifty shots for every one they keep; you can toss away the ideas that you cannot use later on. You will find that the habit of writing keeps your mind working, and out of that work will come some things you can use.

Learn to paraphrase and summarize information because some of your notes will be about what you read. (The best reading is done with a pen or pencil in hand and a notebook open beside the book or magazine on your desk.) A paraphrase puts in different words the

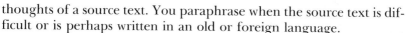

thoughts of a source text. You paraphrase when the source text is difficult or is perhaps written in an old or foreign language.

Thomas More, the English scholar and saint who died as a martyr to his Catholic faith in 1535, wrote vigorously against Protestants when they first entered England under the reign of Henry VIII. Here is a text from one of More's works:

> I here also that Tyndale hyghly reioyceth in the burnyng of Tewkesbery / but I can se no very grete cause why but yf he reken it for a grete glory that the man dyd abyde styll by the stake when he was fast bounden to it. For as for the heresyes he wolde haue abiured them agayne wyth all hys harte, and haue accursed Tyndale to, yf all yt myghte haue saued hys lyfe. And so he gaue counsayle vnto one Iamys that was for heresye in pryson wyth hym. For as Iames haty synnys confessed / Tewkesbery sayed vnto hym, saue you your self and abiure. But as for me bycause I haue abiured byfore, there is no remedy wyth me but deth. By whych wordes yf he had not ben in dyspayre of lyfe / it well appereth he wold wyth good wyll haue ones abiured, and ones periured agayne.[1]

As you can readily see, this text, written in sixteenth-century English, would be difficult to copy in a notebook *verbatim* (word for word). A reader can, however, paraphrase it, and in reviewing it in his notebook recall More's thoughts. Here is an acceptable paraphrase:

> Protestant William Tyndale, translator of the New Testament into English, praised martyrs to Protestant faith in England, but More mocked these claims, saying of a man named Tewksbury, who had been burned at the stake, that the only thing praiseworthy about his death had been that once bound to the stake he remained there. Tewksbury, More says, had been accused of Protestant beliefs once, had recanted and come back to the Catholic faith, but then had gone again into Protestantism and had been arrested again for heresy. English law held that a person found guilty the second time of heresy had to be put to death without mercy. More says Tewksbury would gladly have recanted if he could have saved his life again but that Tewksbury knew this was not possible. However he did advise another accused Protestant whom More calls James to recant and save his skin. James later gave testimony to the authorities about Tewksbury's statement. More's point is that a Protestant "martyr" died because he had to die, not because he bravely sacrificed himself, and that he cannot be claimed by Tyndale as a proof of faith unto death.

Note that the paraphrase is somewhat longer than the text that is paraphrased. The paraphraser, perhaps a student of More, wants to give a full explanation of what is going on in the source—good practice for any researcher. This explanation takes time and space, and this writer takes as much of both as is necessary to be sure he has written down a clear understanding of the text.

A summary would be much shorter. Here is a summary of this text from More:

> More mocked Tyndale for claiming one Tewksbury as a martyr. Tewksbury would have saved his life if he could have, says More, but since he had already been condemned once as a heretic, the second condemnation brought an automatic death sentence under English law. Tewksbury advised a fellow prisoner, condemned only once, to recant and save his life.

We might imagine this summary in an even shorter form. For both paraphrase and summary, the student can note down the page number and title in More's works where the text is located. He can easily look it up again if he has some questions from his own notes, but if he has taken the notes carefully, he will probably not have to do so.

Summaries are great time-savers in research. Occasionally you will want to quote word for word to capture a colorful phrase or a succinct sentence full of important meaning. But don't waste time copying every word; a summary is much quicker and, if it is accurate, will serve you just as well as the exact quotation. If you decide you need an exact quotation, you can always go back to the source for it.

When you do quote word for word, use quotation marks to help you recall what you have done. When you summarize an idea, make a note of the source to use in your footnotes or endnotes. Plagiarism—the most serious offense a writer can commit—may result from poor note-taking. Take care to avoid even the appearance of stealing ideas and language from others which can occur when you fail to attribute your sources. To avoid confusion and plagiarism, some people write direct quotations, summaries, and paraphrases on one page and their own comments, thoughts, and questions on the facing page. Whatever you do, make some clear difference between your thoughts and the thoughts of others.

Comment as you read and take notes. Make a list of questions about any subject you want to write about. Part of knowledge is being aware of your ignorance. Unanswered questions drive you to seek more information, and if after a search you still cannot answer a question, you will have learned something important about the limitations of general knowledge on a subject.

Inventing

Keeping a notebook helps form the habit of respecting your own thoughts. Most people have interesting thoughts, but they usually do nothing with them. A major difference between creative and uncreative people is that the creative people take their own ideas seriously enough to linger over them and think about where they may lead.

Jotting down ideas helps you remember and develop them. Out of these jottings may come the subject of an essay. Many beginning writers and some experienced writers have a hard time thinking of things to write about. Scribbling ideas helps to define subjects you may use for essays. Sometimes a cause of writer's block is the failure to define a subject precisely enough to start writing about it. Responding to your reading by writing comments as you go along may help you avoid freezing up when you start to write the draft of an essay.

Always choose a limited and defined topic. You cannot do an elaborate psychological analysis of Henry VIII in five pages. You cannot use the simple title "Luther" for a ten-page library paper; it would imply that you intended to consider every aspect of Luther's life and thought in a ten-page essay. Limit your topic to something you can do well in the space at your disposal. When you are considering a topic, try out different versions of it in your notebook.

QUESTIONS TO HELP YOU INVENT

As you study your evidence, ask yourself the following questions. Write them down and try to provide answers to them.

1. What do you see? In looking at a text, this question becomes, What exactly do the words say?

A close reading is the first step toward understanding a text. I have mentioned earlier the writing assignment many students have prepared for me about the battles of Lexington and Concord on April 19, 1775. Most of us have read Henry Wadsworth Longfellow's poem which portrays Paul Revere making plans for his midnight ride and saying:

> And I on the opposite shore shall be
> Waiting to ride and spread the alarm
> Through every Middlesex village and farm.

Longfellow gives us several verses showing Revere doing just that—standing by his restless horse and waiting to see the lanterns posted in the steeple of Old North Church, across the Charles River in Boston, to signal that British troops were on the march out into the countryside of Middlesex County to seize arms and gunpowder the Patriots had stored at Concord. The first time I gave this assignment, one of my students, a biology major, in reading Revere's recollections of that night saw that Revere had ordered the lanterns to be posted *before* he had himself rowed across the Charles so he could ride through the dark and warn the Minutemen that British troops were coming. Revere feared he might not get safely across, and he had the lanterns posted to warn others who might carry the message in his place. Most of us have taken our idea of Revere's ride from Longfellow; my student took it from Revere himself—a superior source.

Students commonly believe that all possible truth has been squeezed out of familiar texts. In fact a delight in scholarship lies in the power of texts to yield new truths to those who study them diligently. Read carefully yourself, and you may well discover that previous students have been wrong in their interpretations because they have not read the text as carefully as you have. It is seldom sufficient to read the text only one time. Truly creative thinkers may read a text a dozen times, coaxing their minds to see it anew. They are like the fictional detective Sherlock Holmes, studying clues that may suddenly reveal some truth that the casual observer may have overlooked entirely.

If you write about personal experience, you may jot down a simple story of something that happened to you. Study that experience as you might study a text. What happened? What do you remember? What do you not remember? Any good narrative is a chain of cause and effect. This happened, and that caused this other thing to happen. That in turn caused something else to happen. Little Red Riding Hood lived on the edge of a great woods. Her mother gave her a basket of cakes to take to her grandmother. That cause had the effect of taking Little Red Riding Hood into the woods. That effect became another cause; the wolf met Little Red Riding Hood and asked her where she was going; the effect was that Little Red Riding Hood told him she was going to visit her grandmother. That effect became a cause, making the wolf run ahead and get to her grandmother's house ahead of Little Red Riding Hood. One thing leads to another— a simple enough statement but one on which the entire art of storytelling depends.

Examining the causes and the effects in your memory of your own life serves much the same purpose as examining a text carefully. Looking at memory closely enough, sorting out the connections, and understanding insofar as possible exactly what happened can make you see past experience as revelation or epiphany. Something happened to you; a sudden flash of insight created by your concentration on the happening reveals a story that may enlighten others about their lives.

2. Are there patterns in the evidence?

Many writers return to the same themes over and over again, perhaps using the same words to describe them. Pay attention to these repetitions. Original essays often grow out of the discovery of patterns in texts. William Faulkner, the Mississippi writer and Nobel Prize winner, wrote about families in many of his books and stories. Why? Martin Luther talked continually about "faith." What did he mean by the word? Karl Marx wrote frequently of the "bourgeoisie." What was it?

It's surprising and disappointing to see how often inexperienced writers use some of the important words in a text as if everyone knows what the words mean. As I have mentioned elsewhere, we do not all agree on the meaning of words. Interpretations vary. You can write an excellent essay by defining a common word in a text. Thomas Jefferson wrote much about "liberty" and "reason." What did he mean by those words? Who had liberty? Did everybody have equal reason? That is, were all people equally intelligent? If not, how much reason did Jefferson think people possessed?

In the book *Profiles in Courage*, ghostwritten for John F. Kennedy, Kennedy told the story of eight senators who showed great courage at various points in their public careers. But what did courage mean exactly to Kennedy—or to his ghostwriter? Why did he extoll this virtue? Looking at the stories in the book, we can pick out a particular kind of courage, not the same as other kinds of courage we may know. In the sense of difference lies the topic of an essay.

The second amendment to the U.S. Constitution says, "A well-regulated militia, being necessary to the security of a free State, the right of the people to keep and bear arms shall not be infringed." What does "militia" mean? "Right of the people"? "Infringed"? Does the sentence mean that government cannot regulate the ownership of pistols by private citizens? These are more complicated questions than they may first appear to be. We can arrive at plausible answers only by carefully comparing the uses of these various words in several contexts by the writers to whom they were important. A good writer cannot perform this task off the top of her head; she must work hard, studying and thinking and writing until she comes to a conclusion.

Some patterns may be negative. That is, you may find an interesting topic for an essay in noting the silence of writers and speakers on certain issues. What did Franklin D. Roosevelt say about blacks, about Jews, and about women in his speeches? Almost nothing. Why? The silences of texts often shout at us when suddenly we think to pay attention to them. A little more research may explain why Roosevelt said so little about those who suffered so much.

3. What can you infer from the evidence?

When we infer, we bring previous knowledge and experience to help understand something new. Inference is basic to all reasoning. It is the skill of Sherlock Holmes on a murder case and the skill of the medical researcher looking for a cure for cancer or AIDS. Without inference we merely report facts. Inference suggests to us what the facts mean. We see smoke and infer fire. We see a woman smile and infer that she is happy; we see a child cry and infer that he is not happy. We see two men shouting at each other in the street, and we infer that they are angry. Past experience tells us that people smile when they are happy, cry when they are not, and shout at each other when they are angry—at least sometimes.

We infer from statistics. Eighty-three percent of the men who die from lung cancer are cigarette smokers; we infer that cigarette smoking causes lung cancer.

We infer from texts. "The Lord is my shepherd," reads the Twenty-third Psalm. "I shall not want. He maketh me to lie down in green pastures; he leadeth me beside the still waters." We infer that this psalmist lived amid sheep and shepherds and that the first people who heard his song understood him because they were children of a life among pastures and herds.

The more we know about a subject, the more reliable our inferences. If a scholar has carefully read again and again the thousands of pages left to us by St. Thomas More, I trust his inferences about More's character much more than I do the inferences of someone whose only knowledge of More comes from the movie "A Man for All Seasons" or from various pictures of More drawn or painted in his lifetime.

Our inferences may be wrong, even if we are careful scholars. That is why some students and other inexperienced writers fear to infer. Nobody likes to be wrong. Yet knowledge advances as we test inferences. And it's almost impossible to write an interesting essay without inference.

Suppose your teacher tells you to write a seven-page paper on Shakespeare's *Macbeth*. You will bore her into a trance if you summarize the plot. She's read the play a hundred times. She's seen it on the stage and in the movies. She knows what happens to all the characters. Papers that tell readers only what they already know are doomed to be as forgettable as last year's TV sitcom. The assignment is to write a paper. We write papers to tell readers something they don't already know or else to make them see in a new way what they know. We write to share our thinking, our reasoning. By summarizing the plot, students make a subtle and lethal change in the assignment. Now it has become an examination. We take examinations to prove to others that we know something. Not many readers sit down in their chairs at night and say, "Well now, I think I'll relax and improve my mind by reading a few examinations."

When you begin to infer, you start thinking. For example, look at these lines from the poem "Sunday Morning," by Wallace Stevens:

She hears, upon that water without sound,
A voice that cries, "The tomb in Palestine
Is not the porch of spirits lingering.
It is the grave of Jesus, where he lay."

You can infer that such lines with such a title indicate a poem with some religious significance. What? Why? The questions send you on your way to the topic of an essay.

A geologist observes a boulder resting on the naked granite of a mountain in New Hampshire and sees that the boulder is unlike the granite and unlike any other stone in New Hampshire but that it is like the stone in a part of Canada to the north. She infers that the strange boulder has been carried to this place by the ice sheets that once covered New England, pushing huge loose stones down from the north. Indeed, since no one in historical memory ever saw these huge layers of ice cover New England, the entire theory of an ice age rests on the inferences of geologists. A particular inference stands until someone can come up with one that seems more valid.

Inference is a powerful tool. Be brave enough to infer when you write, and be aware of your inferences when you make them.

4. What will the journalistic questions tell me?

Writers ask questions and answer them; I have made that point several times somewhat casually in this book already. Journalists ask these five questions of every subject they study, and they seek to answer them in their work: who, what, where, when, and why. Something about the human mind cries out to have them answered. We hear that one of our friends has had a car wreck. What happened? Who was driving? Who was hurt? Who was responsible? Who saw it? When did it happen? When did the police get there? When did the ambulance come? Where did it happen? Where were the injured taken? Why did it happen? Why did we not hear about it sooner?

The same questions can help you see a text more clearly and help you define topics for a paper. For example, you may ask the question "Who?" of the short story "A Rose for Emily," by William Faulkner. Who is Miss Emily Grierson?

She is a woman grown from beautiful youth to ugly old age in a changing Mississippi town.
She is the only daughter of a protective and tyrannical father.
She is a member of a family that takes pride in its reputation and does not want her to marry beneath her station.
She is a woman with little money.

She is lonely.

She is unloved.

She is a monument and a curiosity in the town.

She is a failure in all her personal relations except that with her black servant.

She is a murderer.

The list can go on. As you write down all the responses you can think of to the question "Who?" you begin to see things in the story you may have overlooked or misunderstood in your first reading. The same process would work for the four other questions. As you write down the answers to these questions, you begin to see other questions you have not thought of before.

5. What connections can I make between what I observe or read and other things I know?

When you read a short story or a novel, ask yourself how you can bring other parts of your knowledge or experience to bear on your reading. Creative people have a kind of mental scanner in their heads, playing the entire range of their knowledge when they study any subject, illuminating that subject by what they have learned elsewhere.

The comparative quality overlaps that of inference. You may read Hemingway's *For Whom the Bell Tolls* and look carefully at the strong woman character Pilar, wife of Pablo, the guerilla leader in the hills during the Spanish Civil War of the late 1930s. If you have read other Hemingway novels, you may naturally compare Pilar with other women in Hemingway's tales. Or you may compare her with women portrayed by other authors. How does she compare with women in Faulkner? With women in the fiction of Henry James? What would a modern feminist say about Pilar?

By comparing one thing with another, you may see both things more clearly. You integrate your own experience and understand it better. You may know vaguely that you like Faulkner's women better than the women in Hemingway's work. (Or you may discover the reverse.) Working out your reasons for this preference can make for a fascinating paper.

I love reading the papers of those rare students who bring knowledge of other disciplines to bear on papers they write for me—the woman who brings some knowledge of religious studies to bear on Hamlet or the man who uses something he learned in an economics course to illuminate a point about Thomas Jefferson. My students don't do this sort of thing very often. My colleagues in other disciplines encounter the same one-track thinking. The student in a history course does not think a reference to literature belongs in a history paper; the student in an economic course believes that what she has learned in history does not relate to economics. If you try to bring knowledge from various disciplines to the papers you write, you will be a more interesting writer.

Scanning everything you know to illuminate the topic at hand is a form of comparison. The faculty of comparison is called into action when you study the changing reputation of a character, a work of art or literature, or a social attitude. In some sense we are always interpreting our present experience by comparing it with other experiences we have had, and we are always interpreting the past—our own or a historical past—by what we know from our experience.

Remember that *experience* includes our reading, study, and research. Experience is not something that happens to you just on the outside. You have experience by reading, by reflection, by conversation. In an important way, your experience in writing is as intimate as any other. It is your ceaseless effort to make sense and to communicate sense to others.

6. What contradictions exist in the evidence?

Most interesting topics if probed far enough reveal contradictions and paradoxes. Some things don't add up. Every good reporter learns to interview people with an ear open to contradiction. In a good press conference the reporters will ask questions that get the speaker to consider the contradictions: "Mr. President, how do you reconcile your statement that you support education with your budget cuts for schools and student loans?"

Contradictions are not necessarily moral flaws. They are simply part of human character. Ralph Waldo Emerson said in his celebrated essay "Self-Reliance," "A foolish consistency is the hobgoblin of little minds, adored by little statesmen and philosophers and divines. With consistency a great soul has simply nothing to do." The good writer recognizes the inconsistencies of character and takes them into account. They may be good; they may be bad. They are always there in a human being. To ignore them is to write untruly.

You can also find contradictions in written evidence, and the contradictions may be just the place where careful study may fuel a good paper. In *Utopia*, published in 1516, Thomas More had his mythical Utopians practice religious toleration. They demand only that people believe God exists, that He rewards and punishes men and women in an afterlife for deeds done on earth, and that He guides the world by his providence. Utopia is an imaginary island off the coast of the New World, and many readers through the centuries have assumed that here More expresses a plan for an ideal society. But when the Protestant Reformation burst on the European scene and spread to England, More wrote many books vehemently demanding that Protestants be put to death, and while he was lord chancellor of the realm, he was responsible for having several Protestants burned alive for their religious beliefs. What do we do with the contradiction between what More wrote in *Utopia* and what he wrote and did when the Protestants later started making converts in England? We cannot write as if the contradiction does not exist. To be honest, we must try to explain it. When you find contradictions in your evidence, you must at least admit that they are there. If you can reconcile them, you're in luck. If you cannot, you must at least point them out and puzzle over them. Such puzzling can help make an excellent paper. Writers are not required to perform the superhuman task of explaining everything.

Another sort of contradiction occurs when different writers disagree with each other. One of my students once did a fine paper comparing essays written through the years on *The Age of Jackson*, by Arthur Schlesinger, Jr. My student showed that when the book came out in 1945, scholars all over America praised it. But after this first enthusiasm cooled, other scholars took a second look and began to argue that the work was badly flawed. My student read about ten reviews of the book written over a period of some twenty years and sketched his findings in an interesting and original paper. Most interesting topics create arguments; if you survey these various arguments and try to discover the reasoning behind them, you may make an important contribution to knowledge.

Take contradictions in the evidence into account. Knowledge of any subject is partly clear, partly obscure, and partly perverse. Too many writers are like bad mechanics who, when a part does not fit, solve the problem by finding a bigger hammer. If you try to pound all you know into a scheme where everything fits perfectly, you are almost certain to distort the evidence and to give a false picture of reality. Be bold enough to face contradictions squarely when you meet them, and be truthful enough to admit defeat when you cannot reconcile them.

7. What resulted or may result from the subject of inquiry?

We love to know how things turn out. Good papers establish chains of cause and effect and sometimes try to point at the end to some enduring result of an action, a book, a battle, a treaty, a court case, a critical appointment, a presidential election, or whatever. Sometimes you may wish to speculate about what might happen if a certain course of action were to be adopted. As you will see in the chapter on argument, the relation of cause and effect is often more difficult than it may seem at first glance. The difficulties should not deter you from trying to sort out both cause and effect, for such speculations may enlighten us about the events we study.

In 1898 the United States fought a war with Spain. What were the consequences? We became more deeply involved in Asia. We took over the Philippine Islands and Puerto Rico. We made Cuba independent. We reunited our own country, which had been emotionally split by the Civil War. We created a crisis of conscience in our theory of democracy because a great part of the American tradition had been against imperialism, a crisis heightened when the Philippine people took up arms against the American soldiers who came to "liberate" them. So it goes. You can extend the consequence from any important event into a list and convert the list into an essay.

Sometimes questions about cause and effect may stir up "what if" papers. What if the British had won the American Revolution? What if the United States had not made the Louisiana Purchase from Napoleon? What if Shakespeare had died in 1600? What if Ernest Hemingway had been a woman? What if Martin Luther had been killed by the lightning storm in 1505 that frightened him so much that he became a monk? We can never answer the "what if" questions to our complete satisfaction. Asking them may help us see more clearly what did happen. Virginia Woolf has a great "what if" piece in her book *A Room of One's Own*. She poses the question, "What if Shakespeare had had a sister as gifted as he and as ambitious as he was to be a playwright?" The question allowed Woolf to make a vital critique of how women have been traditionally treated in Western society.

The "what if" question is a good, playful one to ask when you are preparing to write a paper. It may make you rearrange old forms fixed in your mind. The creative person frequently has a playful mind, the ability to ask questions that may at first seem nonsensical but then can be used to open a serious inquiry. Never imagine that genius must be somber.

THE PLAY OF WRITING

All these questions involve a kind of play of the intellect. You can play with ideas in your notebook, perhaps creating disorganized, even chaotic streams of ideas. As you play, your mind organizes your ideas better than you may imagine in advance. The mind does not always work by calculation. If we are willing to trust our own brains, we will find that they may work brilliantly without our trying to force them along. You can help free your thoughts and liberate your mind from uncreative restraint by being willing to play with words and ideas. Writers must overcome the inhibitions that rise up whenever we think of exposing our thoughts to a public. The notebook is a good private place to play without fear of mockery. It may be a mess, but it can be an original mess, giving you much good.

Writing Drafts

Finally the moment comes when you sit down to begin your first draft. It is always a good idea at the start to list the points you want to cover. A list is not as elaborate as a formal outline. In writing your first list, don't bother to set items down in the order of importance. List your main points and trust your mind to organize them. You will probably make one list, study it, make another, study it, and perhaps make another. You can organize each list more completely than the last. This preliminary process may save you hours of starting and stopping.

Write with your list outline in front of you. Once you begin to write, commit yourself to the task at hand. Do not get up until you have written for an hour. Write your thoughts quickly. Let one sentence give you an idea to develop in the next. Organization, grammar, spelling, and even clarity of sentences are not nearly as important as getting the first draft together. No matter how desperate you feel, keep going.

Always keep your mind open to new ideas that pop into your head as you write. Let your list outline help you, but don't become a slave to it. Writers often start an essay with one topic in mind only to discover that another pushes the first one aside as they work. Ideas you had not even thought of before you began to write may pile onto your paper, and five or six pages into your first draft you may realize that you are going to write about something you did not imagine when you started.

If such a revelation comes, be grateful and accept it. But don't immediately tear up or erase your draft and start all over again. Make yourself keep on writing, developing these new ideas as they come. If you suddenly start all over again, you may break the train of thought that has given you the new topic. Let your thoughts follow your new thesis, sailing on that tack until the wind changes.

When you have said everything you can say in this draft, print it out if you are working on a computer. Get up from your desk and go sit in a chair somewhere else to read it without correcting anything. Then put it aside, preferably overnight. If possible, read your rough draft just before you go to sleep. Many psychological tests have shown that our minds organize and create while we sleep if we pack them full before bedtime. Study a draft just before sleep, and you may discover new ideas in the morning.

Be willing to make radical changes in your second draft. If your thesis changed while you were writing your first draft, you will base your second draft on this new subject. Even if your thesis has not changed, you may need to shift paragraphs around, eliminate paragraphs, or add new ones. Inexperienced writers often suppose that

2nd draft
- rearrange ideas
- add new ideas
- put in or cut out

revising a paper means changing only a word or two or adding a sentence or two. This kind of editing is part of the writing process, but it is not the most important part. The most important part of rewriting is a willingness to turn the paper upside down, to shake out of it those ideas that interest you most, to set them in a form where they will interest the reader, too.

I mentioned earlier that some writers cut up their first drafts with a pair of scissors. They toss some paragraphs into the trash; others they paste up with rubber cement in the order that seems most logical and coherent. Afterward they type the whole thing through again, smoothing out the transitions, adding new material, getting new ideas as they work. The translation of the first draft into the second nearly always involves radical cutting and shifting around. Now and then you may firmly fix the order of your thoughts in your first draft, but I find that the order of my essays is seldom established until the second draft.

With the advent of computers the shifting around of parts of the essays has become easy. We can cut and paste electronically with a few strokes of the keyboard. We can also make back-up copies of our earlier drafts so we can go back to them if we wish. But as I said earlier, computers do not remove from us the necessity to think hard about revising.

Always be firm enough with yourself to cut out thoughts or stories that have nothing to do with your thesis, even if they are interesting. Cutting is the supreme test of a writer. You may create a smashing paragraph or sentence only to discover later that it does not help you make your point. You may develop six or seven examples to illustrate a point and discover you need only one.

Now and then you may digress a little. If you digress too often or too far, readers will not follow you unless your facts, your thoughts, and your style are so compelling that they are somehow driven to follow you. Not many writers can pull such digressions off, and most editors will cut out the digressions even when they are interesting. In our hurried and harried time, most readers get impatient with the rambling scenic route. They want to take the most direct way to their destination. To appeal to most of them, you must cut things that do not apply to your main argument.

In your third draft, you can sharpen sentences, add information here and there, cut some things, and attend to other details to heighten the force of your writing. In the third draft, writing becomes a lot of fun (for most of us). By then you have usually decided what you want to say. You can now play a bit, finding just the right word, choosing just the right sentence form, compressing here, expanding there.

I find it helpful to put a printed draft down beside my keyboard

3rd draft - polish words/ sentences, add, delete

and type the whole thing through again as a final draft, letting all the words run through my mind and fingers one more time rather than merely deleting and inserting on the computer screen. I wrote four drafts of the first edition of this book; I have preserved the final draft of that edition on computer diskettes. But I am writing this draft by propping the first edition up here beside me and typing it all over again. By comparing the first draft and the second draft, one can see how many changes I have made, most of them unforeseen until I sat down here to work.

I have outlined here my own writing process. It works for me. You must find the process that works for you. It may be different from mine. A friend tells me that his writing process consists of writing a sentence, agonizing over it, walking around the room, thinking, sitting down, and writing the next sentence. He does not revise very much. I think it unnecessarily painful to bleed out prose that way, but he bleeds out enough to write what he needs to write. Several of my friends tell me they cannot compose at a typewriter; they must first write with a pencil on a yellow pad. These are the people most likely to cut up their drafts with scissors and paste them together in a different form. They also tend to be older. Most young writers are learning to compose at a keyboard, and they cannot imagine another way to write. Neither can I—though on occasion yet I go back to my pencil for pages at a time.

The main thing is to keep at it. B. F. Skinner has pointed out that if you write only fifty words a night, you will produce a good-sized book every two or three years. That's not a bad record for any writer. William Faulkner outlined the plot of his Nobel Prize-winning novel *A Fabel* on a wall inside his house near Oxford, Mississippi. You can see it there to this day. Once he got the outline on the wall, he sat down with his typewriter and wrote, following the outline to the end. If writing an outline on a kitchen wall does the trick for you, do it. You can always repaint the wall if you must.

Think of writing as a process making its way toward a product—sometimes painfully. Don't imagine you must know everything you are going to say before you begin. Don't demean yourself and insult your readers by letting your first draft be your final draft. Don't imagine that writing is easy or that you can do it without spending time on it. And don't let anything stand in your way of doing it. Let your house get messy. Leave your magazines unread and your mail unanswered. Put off getting up for a drink of water or a cup of tea. (Never mix alcohol with your writing; true, lots of writers have become alcoholics, but it has not helped their writing.) Don't make a telephone call. Don't straighten up your desk. Sit down and write. And write, and write, and write.

Four

Making Arguments

❖❖❖

Most writing involves argument. A good term paper, an M.A. thesis, a dissertation, or a book is seldom a mere report of facts. More often a piece of writing argues that the facts should be understood in a certain way—the writer's way. Good writers interpret the facts, and all interpretations are arguments. Some have said that all writing argues that we should believe something or do something.

In this chapter I lean toward the more traditional meaning of argument—the effort to make readers accept the writer's point of view rather than another. How do you build arguments where some real issue is in dispute, where there are choices, and where you explicitly call on readers to take your side? This chapter will help you answer this question.

Some people dislike the word *argument* because it sounds pugnacious. But it is a civilized term; we make arguments instead of war. We persuade people rather than beat them into submission. The democratic process depends on argument. Candidates argue that they are more qualified than their opponents; elected representatives argue that their policies are better than the alternatives. Lawyers and judges argue about what the laws mean. Without argument, democracy would die.

Many arguments are explicit. A lawyer making a case for a client accused of robbery argues either that the client is innocent or that mitigating circumstances require judge and jury to consider this no ordinary robbery.

If your company sends you into the field to look at possible sites for a new branch office, you must make an argument for the one you think best. If you want your university to sell its stock in companies doing business with South Africa, you must do more than carry signs and shout slogans; you must make an argument that divestiture (as getting rid of such stocks is called) will bring progress to South Africa, and in such a charged affair, you must take up the arguments of your opponents and show where you think they are wrong.

If you review a book, you must argue that it is good, bad, or mediocre, and you must tell why. You have to quote the book, describe its presentation of the evidence, and defend or attack its conclusions. If you disagree with the author's interpretation, you must take the time to present your case. You cannot merely denounce the author as a fool, leaving readers to assume that you possess an infinite wisdom and knowledge that you do not care to display.

You cannot argue well about issues no one disputes. Few activities bore a college teacher more than reading papers that argue positions so safe that no one disagrees with them: "Economics is important to society." "Shakespeare wrote some interesting plays." "Dickens often treated poverty in his novels." "Abortion is a much debated issue in our society." Few things please readers (including teachers) more than a paper that makes an original and unexpected argument: "Some people may be allergic to exercise." "King Lear got what he deserved." One caution here: don't make unexpected arguments when you have no evidence to support them or when the subject is frivolous. I once had a student argue that if the Roman Empire had had electricity, it never would have fallen. There was no way to disprove his argument—and arguments that offer no possibility of being disproved are usually frivolous or at best tedious.

College teachers are paid to read anything students write. Teachers are usually kind and generous people. (At least they start out that way.) Sometimes they become so tired from grading dozens and dozens of papers during a course that they let themselves be bullied into giving a paper a good grade if the information in it is reasonably accurate and the paper is written reasonably clearly, no matter how dull it is or how removed its argument is from its evidence. The reality every writer must face is that once out of college, we find few readers as patient as our teachers. We gain a worthwhile audience only if we are interesting, challenging, disciplined, and coherent. We waste the time we put into writing and lose the reward for our work if we produce arguments so pointless that no one will read them.

Making a Good Argument Paper

Here are steps in making a good argument paper. Read them carefully and check your own arguments by them.

1. Begin on ground the writer and readers share.

Never begin an argument assuming that everybody agrees with you already or that no one agrees with anything you say. Don't condescend, and don't scream in outrage. Don't treat your opponents like fools or criminals. The best arguments assume that writer and reader share some values, some information, some purposes.

We have already considered briefly one of the greatest modern arguments—Dr. Martin Luther King's "Letter from a Birmingham Jail" written on April 16, 1963, when King had been arrested for leading nonviolent demonstrations against racial segregation in Alabama. A group of white ministers of religion had publicly objected to Dr. King's tactics that had provoked mass meetings, demonstrations, and reprisals by white policemen who used big, vicious dogs against peaceful black men, women, and children.

Dr. King might have begun his response to these ministers by denouncing the hypocrisy of any religious leader who supported segregation even tacitly. Instead he began by calling attention to the religious heritage that he shared with them. From those common values, he argued that they should share his goal—equal justice on earth for all God's people.

Always look for the common ground. Inexperienced writers often suppose that they impress readers by outrageous or insulting introductions. Yet time and again experience has shown that most people hate shrill, discourteous, and angry arguments. Even if your readers agree with you, most will feel uncomfortable with a diatribe. Remember that people want to believe that something in you, the writer, is akin to them. Not many of us want to believe that we are mean and ugly, ungenerous and spiteful. We like to think that we are reasonable, civil, and generous.

The tone of your beginning is all-important. Many speakers show their common ground with an audience by beginning with a joke. Laughter immediately unites audience and speaker and disposes the audience to listen to the rest of the speech. Writers seldom begin with jokes. But as I showed in Chapter Two, they often begin with stories, quotations, and statements of intention that make readers say, "This person and I share something; we are alike; I want to go on with this."

When you begin well, you dispose your audience to consider your position, and your argument is half won. If at any time in your writing you break the bond between yourself and your readers by making offensive remarks, you will lose them unless your evidence and your arguments are so compelling that they must keep going. You can insult anybody and write outrageously if your essay proves beyond any doubt that you have discovered a cure for cancer or the secret of eternal youth. Otherwise stay calm. You may lose your audience if you don't.

I have spent so much time on this issue because in my experience, incivility is the single greatest flaw in the arguments of inexperienced writers.

2. Declare your argument early and define its major terms.

The same rule applies here that governs any essay: get to the point fast. Make sure you know what you want your readers to do or believe. Don't argue merely to make a fuss. Once you know what you want, say what it is, and do it early in your essay.

Always define your terms. The definition helps put you and your readers on common ground. Arguments often go astray because readers misunderstand important words. Usually the misunderstanding is the writer's fault. When you define your terms, you help yourself and your readers understand your foundations.

On one level, definitions are simple. A definition classifies a term and sets it off from other members of the same class. The ninth edition of the Merriam-Webster *New Collegiate Dictionary* defines *lemon* as "an acid fruit that is botanically a many-seeded pale yellow oblong berry and is produced by a stout thorny tree." *Lemon* is shown to belong to a class of similar things called *fruits*. It differs from other members of that class by its acidity, its pale yellow coloration, its being produced by a stout thorny bush, and its being botanically a berry.

Definitions in essays go beyond the bare bones of a dictionary definition—a major reason dictionary definitions are seldom sufficient for the leading terms of essays. Words have histories, and essayists must consider the details of those histories much more fully than writers of dictionaries are required to do. Writers must recognize that a word like *liberalism* or *reason* or *socialism* or *fascism* or *romanticism* has *historical* connotations, and good essayists strive to be clear about which of those connotations they use in their essays.

In universities the study of literature is divided by both periods and genres. The period of a piece of literature denotes the time in which the piece was written; genre takes into account the kind of literature a piece is—poetry, essay, short story, novel, nonfiction book. Someone writes, "Machiavelli's little book *The Prince* was a typical product of the Italian Renaissance." But what was the Italian Renaissance? The writer who sets out to answer that question will realize that so many people give so many different definitions of "Renaissance" that it is impossibly vague to say that any book was a "typical product" of the period. Here is a way that the obligation of a writer to define may change the writer's mind about the argument. Broad, sweeping generalizations that use words in all-embracing ways usually make bad arguments.

Yet we see such arguments all the time—often presented by people who should know better. Why? We love to label things, believing in an almost primitive way that giving something a label somehow makes it manageable. Ancient religions held that when you named something, you controlled it. We often speak and write as if we believe that superstition. Yet a label may be misleading, and when labels become misleading, writers must define them carefully. Often the best definition involves ambiguities and other difficulties, and writers have to take these slippery matters into account in the same way that someone walking on a frozen street must take into account the ice. Professor Gilbert Allardyce introduces his article "What Fascism Is Not: Thoughts on the Deflation of a Concept" with some ruminations about a definition. He explains why his article undertakes a more precise definition of a much used word:

> "Perhaps the word fascism should be banned, at least temporarily, from our political vocabulary," S. J. Woolf wrote in 1968. Historians who have confronted the problem of defining this mulish concept may sympathize with this modest proposal. Unfortunately the word "fascism" is here to stay; only its meaning seems to be banned. Nevertheless, the German philosopher-historian Ernst Nolte is probably correct in stressing that historians do not have the responsibility to invent new terms simply because the existing ones seem inadequate. But they do have the responsibility to confess how truly inadequate the term fascism has become: put simply, we have agreed to use the term without agreeing on how to define it. This article is concerned with the reason for this unfortunate state of affairs.[1]

Take care to define your use of broad and general terms. General words originate as ways of describing qualities shared by a class of things or people—works of art, essays, novels, political views, rulers of states, or whatever. Soon the general word assumes a life of its own, a kind of phantom existence that provokes writers to suppose that they have said something important if they apply it to anything they choose.

Many of us recall the 1960s, when various radicals hurled the term *fascist* at anyone they hated, whether a university dean, a scholar, a police officer, or a parent. Everybody was a "fascist" who believed in the exercise of authority. Others, calling themselves conservatives, used the word *radical* to describe anyone who opposed American involvement in the Vietnam War, and some found themselves berated as being radical merely because they believed in the freedoms of speech and assembly guaranteed by the United States Constitution. Earlier the words *red* and *communist* were used as a devastating weapon against people devoted to liberal and humanitarian causes. During the McCarthy period of the early 1950s, words like *communist, red, fellow traveler*, and *un-American* developed a strange power just because no one bothered to define them.

The need of precise definition—especially in argument—is always with us. When words take on lives of their own, writers should put them under the microscope. Do enough individuals within a group share enough qualities to permit any general word to describe them? Before you start using any sweeping collectives like *socialism*, *democracy*, *romantic*, *liberal*, *conservative*, *humanistic*, and others, ask yourself what you mean by them, and put your definitions before your readers.

Be fair. If some disagree with you, take the disagreement into account. You do not have to discard your definition merely because others disagree with it, but you help yourself and your readers if you describe the disagreement and give your own views forthrightly. If you define your words unfairly or in sharp opposition to their common usage, you can lose your audience quickly. "Any American who wants the United States to stop supporting military governments in South America really wants the entire continent to go communist." Come now! It's not that simple, and fair-minded readers know it.

Define your assumptions. All arguments begin from premises, from convictions the writer (or speaker) assumes she shares with her audience. "We all agree that A is true," we say. "Because we agree that A is true, I want to show that we must also believe that B is true." Before we can accept such a chain of reasoning, we must know what A is so we can decide if indeed we all believe it is true.

Allan Bloom, a professor at the University of Chicago, has argued that this generation of students is ignorant because it is unacquainted with the western tradition that he associates with the "great books." These include works by Plato, Aristotle, Kant, Marx, and many others. On examination, Bloom's list of "great books" includes only white male authors, only four of whom are American. His critics have rejected his premise that one is ignorant if unfamiliar with the works of Plato but one is educated if one knows the "great books"—and yet knows nothing of black American woman writers such as Toni Morrison, Maria Angelou, Alice Walker, Nikki Giovanni, and a host of others. Bloom's critics argue that education cannot be defined by a single book list, and so they say that he has misconstrued the entire cultural situation he addresses. They define his assumptions and attack them and reduce his book to absurdity. If you do not define your own assumptions, you may suffer the same fate.

In making your own arguments, you must know your premises and state them clearly enough to make your readers understand them at the beginning. In arguing against other arguments, you must define the assumptions of your opponents. To do both these tasks, you must sometimes think hard and go beneath the easy surface generalizations that may give the appearance of authority while having none.

3. Use evidence.

Here we return to a point I made in Chapter Two, "What Makes an Essay?" Writers must know things. You cannot toss good arguments off the top of your head, without study and without a pondering of the evidence. You must stuff your mind with facts to be a good writer. Lawyers speak of "fact patterns" in the evidence for a trial. That is, at a given moment, the facts begin to point to a conclusion, to mean something. A lawyer points out to judge and jury that the facts do tend in that direction.

I have mentioned that we look for patterns in what we observe. These patterns, once discovered, reveal connections between data. Paul Fussell, in his remarkable book *The Great War and Modern Memory*, noticed that soldier-poets in World War I wrote continually of the sky—dawn, sunset, the stars. He realized that they wrote of the sky because they spent seemingly interminable months looking up at it from the trenches stretched across Europe where the opposing armies faced each other in a bloody stalemate. Often there seemed to be nothing else to look at, and Fussell argues that the confinement of the trenches made them choose the sky as the surface in which they saw their experience reflected. He noted that in World War II, British soldier-writers avoided large descriptions of the sky. He reasons that they did so because World War II was a war of motion. Here is a pattern. Fussell saw it; we now say, "Of course." But he had to see it before we could agree.

Such patterns exist in everything we read and in everything we observe. The trick is to see them and to express them. We see the facts, the basic data. (Somehow the word *fact* seems inadequate to what I am trying to express.) We seek to relate those facts to one another and to some underlying pattern or principle that explains or connects them. Our explanation should account for as many of those facts as possible. The failure to account for some facts indicates that some new explanation or at least some further explanation is necessary.

The discovery of the planet Pluto in our solar system is a model for the discovery of patterns and connections and meaning. In the nineteenth century, astronomers had discovered the planet Uranus and then the planet Neptune, both unknown to the ancient world. By the end of the century it appeared that neither planet followed a regular orbit about the sun. Something seemed to be slowing them down at times, speeding them up at others, making them wobble just a bit. Astronomer Percival Lowell became convinced that there was yet another planet out there, causing those variations in orbit. In 1930, long after Lowell's death, another astronomer discovered tiny Pluto, vindicating Lowell's opinion.

Very often we discover some fact that does not fit our previous explanations, and so we must devise another explanation. We have to know a lot to get to that point. In argument as in every other kind of writing, knowledge is the writer's indispensable friend.

The writer of a paper on English literature makes arguments in much the same way as does the scientific theorist. Each gathers information by careful study, and each feels that she sees something in it that others have not noticed or that she can put the information together in a plausible way that has not been discovered by others. If the writer and the scientific theorist work hard at assembling their data—and perhaps if they have a bit of luck—they come to a creative moment, an instant of illumination, where they see a pattern of connections that makes everything make sense.

Charles Darwin observed small differences between the beaks of birds on the Galapagos Islands and their cousins on the distant mainland of South America. What caused those variations? The birds' beaks were by no means the only biological problem that he found on those blackened volcanic islands, but they loomed large in his mind. He decided that at some distant time birds on the islands had been identical to birds on the mainland. But through generations of isolation in a different environment, a new species had evolved, similar to the species on the mainland but differing from them in many features, including beaks. Species were not fixed eternally; all living things were in continual change through the generations.

His next step was to assume that some changes aid survival, and so the living things that acquire them have a better chance of passing them on to their progeny. These were the building blocks he put together finally in *The Origin of Species*, one of the most revolutionary books of all time. It is also a readable book, in which Darwin presents a staggering quantity of data in a style that allows readers with little scientific knowledge to understand his theory. Inspiration comes out of knowledge. Our most creative moments come from our wrestling with what people have created before us and with our own experience.

But how does the insight come? What makes all the information come together in a pattern in the writer's mind? No one can give a precise answer. "The light dawned" is a common cliché to describe the feelings we have when an insight strikes us. Always the light dawns after a period of hard work—observing, assembling data, thinking, worrying, proposing various patterns to see what seems to embrace most of the data and what theory provides the most plausible explanation for what we observe.

The investigative reporters who wrote about the Watergate burglary of June 17, 1972, put together details until they had a theory that accounted for most of them. They thought that the burglary had been planned by high White House staff members and that Richard Nixon knew about it either beforehand or soon afterward and had tried to cover up the involvement of his associates. Their case was *plausible*. That is the key word. It could be believed because it fitted the facts. No one else could come up with another case that was equally plausible. Had these reporters spun out their theory without the long, difficult, and perhaps dangerous work of gathering data—evidence—no one would have paid any attention to them.

The great literary scholars have followed much the same process in studying and writing about poets, playwrights, and other writers in our tradition. These scholars first read the text—not once but again and again and again. Then they make notes. They ask questions. They make comparisons. How does this work of this writer compare with her other works? How does this writer compare with other writers in her own time? How does this writer compare with writers before her? After her? How have opinions about this writer changed from her own time until now? How does the technique of this writer fit the techniques of other writers, perhaps in different genres?

Cleanth Brooks, studying William Faulkner's novel *Absalom, Absalom!* early in the 1960s, realized that it is a mystery story and that Faulkner does not tell us exactly what brought about the doom of his character Thomas Sutpen. Two college boys, Quentin and Shreve, sitting in a cold dormitory room hundreds of miles from Mississippi, go over the fragments of the story and try to make them fit together into a plausible whole. But Brooks pointed out that we do not know finally if their solution is the right one, and one might design other plausible arrangements of the facts we know.

Most of us reading *Absalom, Absalom!* for the first time probably overlook the significance of how the story is told. Brooks thought of another kind of story he had read—the detective story. He put the two experiences together and published them in a brilliant critical essay in the Spring 1962 issue of the *Sewanee Review*.

One of the saddest recognitions of a college teacher is that students seldom bring together the various disciplines they are studying. (I have touched on this issue in my chapter on the writing process.) They write as if all their experiences can be compartmentalized like a catalog of courses. If they are writing a paper in English, they do not imagine that they might inform that paper by drawing on something they have learned in sociology or economics. If they are writing a paper in history, they do not think that they might make a comparison between an important historical character and a novel written at the time she lived. Good writers scan all their experience—what they have done themselves, what they have read, what they have heard from others—to see what might be in it to illuminate the subject they happen to be writing about.

Effective arguments always rest on evidence. In this book, my evidence is the collection of quotations from other writers to support my analysis of what writers do. You must present evidence to support *your* arguments; otherwise, you will be reduced to making naked assertions. If you have a reputation as a great authority in the field about which you write, your assertions may be worth something. But most of us lack the authority to carry an argument by the weight of our assertion alone. We convince readers only by adducing evidence.

The Rhetoric of Argument

Evidence is a collection of facts that support an argument. What we do with the evidence may be called the rhetoric of argument—how we present the evidence in a persuasive way. Much of the rhetoric of argument is inference. If A is true, we may assume that B is true. In reading a text, we see the surface meaning of the words, and we infer some other conclusions about them.

In my chapter on the writing process, I have drawn attention to one of Wallace Stevens's early poems, "Sunday Morning." He includes these lines:

> The day is like wide water, without sound,
> Stilled for the passing of her dreaming feet
> Over the seas, to silent Palestine,
> Dominion of the blood and sepulchre.

From the title "Sunday Morning" and these lines we can infer immediately that somehow this poem is about religion or the religious consciousness. We read the whole work. On a Sunday morning, when she has not gone to church, the woman in the poem is caught up in contemplation of all that religion once meant to her and to perhaps the world at large. Throughout we can feel nostalgia and regret, as if she longs for a faith she no longer has. Stevens does not have to tell us outright that this poem is about religion. He trusts us to have had enough experience with life and faith to infer his meaning.

We may use different modes of inference, and these modes are the subject of the following sections of this chapter. We call these modes *arguments* because they represent techniques of argumentation. In an argumentative essay, the arguments you use will be parts of the whole.

THE *A FORTIORI* ARGUMENT

A fortiori is a Latin term that means "to the stronger." Stripped down, the *a fortiori* argument reads like this: "If we know that A is true, it is even more likely that B is true." The argument gains power if the first proposition seems improbable. In Chaucer's *Canterbury Tales*, the "poor parson of a town," explaining his longing for virtue, used this metaphor: "If the gold rust, what shall iron do?" He counted the priests as gold in English society, the lay people as iron. Priests had to be pure to keep the people pure. He implied that it is not probable that gold should rust, but if it does, how much more likely it is that iron should do the same.

We use the *a fortiori* argument often in daily life. If cigarette smokers run a much higher risk of cancer of the mouth than non-smokers, cigar smokers run an even higher risk of the same cancer because cigar smoke is so much stronger.

Lawyers frequently use the *a fortiori* argument in court. If a lawyer has proved that the witness lied in making one statement, it is much easier to make a jury believe the witness has lied in making other statements as well. "We have seen that the accused lied when he said he was not having an affair with the victim's wife; isn't it likely that he also lied when he testified that he shot the victim by accident?"

The *a fortiori* argument turns up in advertising. A computer software company advertises that its update of a word-processing program includes 500 new features. The implied argument is this: If the program was good before, it should be much better now.

The *a fortiori* argument influenced the course of the Vietnam War. Some U.S. Air Force generals argued that American air power could be used to bomb the North Vietnamese into submission. Foes of the bombing pointed to the failure of heavy British and American bombing to break the will of the Germans in World War II or even to halt German war production. Many studies concluded that the bombing of German cities only increased the German will to resist. Therefore, they argued, it was unlikely that bombing could reduce the will of the North Vietnamese. The *a fortiori* argument was this: If heavy bombing failed to break the will of a concentrated urban population in World War II, it is much more unlikely that heavy bombing can break the will of a rural population living in widely scattered hamlets.

The *a fortiori* argument is essential to the inferences necessary in writing history. The evidence historians rely on is always fragmented and maddeningly incomplete, and history itself is a process of assembling a puzzle made up of broken and missing pieces. Historians fill in the blanks by making intelligent speculations drawn from inferences. They can know some things with a fair degree of certainty: for example, South Carolinians subdued Fort Sumter with artillery in April 1861. Other things remain forever uncertain. Did Lincoln deliberately provoke the South Carolinians into becoming aggressors?

Did he move quickly to trigger war because he feared that the British might recognize South Carolina's "independence"? Did he think that faced with armed conflict the South Carolinians might draw back from war?

Historians assemble all the evidence they can and try to frame it into a plausible, coherent picture. Historian Barbara Tuchman describes this process of inference from her own research:

> If the historian will submit himself *to* his material instead of trying to impose himself *on* his material, then the material will ultimately speak to him and supply the answers. It has happened to me more than once. In somebody's memoirs I found that the Grand Duke Nicholas wept when he was named Russian Commander-in-Chief in 1914, because, said the memoirist, he felt inadequate to the job. That sounded to me like one of those bits of malice one has to watch out for in contemporary observers; it did not ring true. The Grand Duke was said to be the only "man" in the royal family; he was known for his exceedingly tough manners, was admired by the common soldier, and feared at court. I did not believe he felt inadequate, but then why should he weep? I could have left out this bit of information, but I did not want to. I wanted to find the explanation that would make it fit. (Leaving things out because they do not fit is writing fiction, not history.) I carried the note about the Grand Duke around with me for days, worrying about it. Then I remembered other tears. I went through my notes and found an account of Churchill's weeping and also Messimy, the French War Minister. All at once I understood that it was not the individuals but the *times* that were the stuff for tears. My next sentence almost wrote itself: "There was an aura about 1914 that caused those who sensed it to shiver for mankind." Afterward I realized that this sentence expressed why I had wanted to write the book in the first place. The "why," you see, had emerged all by itself.[2]

Aside from being a splendid account of the role of inference in the writing of history, this paragraph gives us the *a fortiori* argument: Because we know that so many brave men wept in 1914, may we not assume that the Grand Duke Nicholas wept not out of a sense of incompetence but out of a sense of impending doom?

The *a fortiori* argument can be falsified—as all good arguments can. No baseball fan would make this statement: Since Dwight Evans hit a meaningless home run in a game the Red Sox were winning 10–0 at the end of the season, was he not more likely to hit a home run in the World Series? And courts generally rule out this argument in rape trials: Since we know that this woman willingly had sexual intercourse with several men before the alleged rape, may we not assume that she consented on this occasion, too? A *non sequitur* is involved in both instances. That is, the conclusion does not follow (*non sequitur* is Latin for "it does not follow") from the first statement. Evans does not control his home-run hitting by his will alone, and no matter what a woman has done in the past, it is still possible that she was raped.

THE ARGUMENT FROM SIMILITUDE

The argument from similitude holds that because people or events or things are alike in some ways, they must be alike in others. It is an argument that allows certain predictions to be made about groups, and it is frequently used in polls. It is indispensable for some research in the social sciences, but it can also lead to dangerous inaccuracies and prejudices.

A study a few years ago revealed that Volkswagen owners were likely to be further to the left politically than were owners of Fords and Chevrolets. The same study showed that the owners of Swedish-made SAABs and Volvos were likely to be the furthest to the left on the American political spectrum. The study did not claim that every Volvo owner was a political radical; it made its conclusions about groups rather than about individuals. No one argued that *because* someone bought a Volvo she would be to the far left in politics; that argument would be absurd. If the study had any validity, it was only to show that a willingness to break with long-established American custom might express itself in both car buying and politics.

Some life insurance companies offer lower rates to nonsmokers. Nonsmokers live longer as a group than smokers. But no one would argue that *every* nonsmoker will live longer than every smoker. A few nonsmokers die every year from lung cancer, and a few people may smoke two packs of Camel straights every day and die at age 85 when they are run over by trucks while they are jogging. Comparisons that classify people by groups offer only probability to the individuals within each group; they do not rigorously predict what will happen to each individual.

The argument from similitude can be used fraudulently when someone claims that because the people or things being compared are alike in some ways, they are alike in all. When Richard Nixon, a skilled rhetorician, ran his first campaign for the U.S. Senate in 1950 in California, he faced Helen Gahagan Douglas, a member of the U.S. House of Representatives from California. Nixon was eager to paint Douglas red at a time when the tirades of Senator Joseph McCarthy, the Korean War, and the terror of Stalinism in Russia made Americans fear anything that smacked of communism. Nixon compared the voting record of Douglas in the House with that of Vito Marcantonio, a radical congressman from New York. Marcantonio had supported the Soviet Union's foreign policy through its every slippery twist. In domestic policy he had supported price controls, public housing, civil rights, and health insurance. But most people knew him only for his hysterical speeches in support of the Soviet Union.

Nixon's associates found 353 votes in which Douglas and Marcantonio had been on the same side. These votes had nothing to do with the Soviet Union, but Nixon went doggedly from the indisputable fact of these 353 votes to a fallacious conclusion: If Helen Gahagan Douglas had voted with Marcantonio on so many occasions, she must agree with him in everything else.

Frank Mankiewicz, a Douglas campaign worker, pointed out that Nixon himself had voted with Marcantonio 112 times in four years. Even the most vigorous anti-Communist might, on reflection, doubt Nixon's implication that 353 bills submitted to the House of Representatives were Communist-inspired. But few people paused to reflect on much of anything in those mad times, and Nixon won the election—and a reputation for deceit that dogged him until his resignation from the presidency in 1974.

THE ARGUMENT FROM CAUSE TO EFFECT

The argument from cause to effect or from effect back to cause is one of the most common in human discourse, one of the most necessary, and one of the most dangerous. We want to know why things happened—why war was declared, why cancer struck, why the economic recovery came, why a novel was popular, why crime increased, why the President was elected.

On the surface the argument from cause to effect appears simple, but the supposed simplicity can be misleading. Why do black players dominate professional basketball? One school of thought holds that blacks have a muscle mass that enables them to jump higher and with greater agility than most whites. The argument—which to some seems racist—is supported by some respectable researchers. But another school of thought holds that basketball is the only sport open to the poor urban child. It requires little space and simple equipment. Black children start playing it early and play it often while white suburban children are doing other things. With more black children devoting much more time to basketball, more of them grow up to be professional basketball players.

This debate illustrates the difficulty of cause-and-effect reasoning: the causal relation between two events is often almost impossible to establish beyond any doubt. When the argument is emotionally charged—as any argument about race may be—the difficulties are all the greater.

Some causes can produce more than one effect; it is misleading to isolate only one cause and pin all the effects on it. No reputable historian would dare argue that World War I was caused only by the assassination of the heir to the throne of the Austro-Hungarian Empire in 1914 or that the Civil War was caused only by the election of Abraham Lincoln in 1860. We may say that the assassination and the election were precipitating causes, the immediate causes that made people act decisively. Good historians know that the great crises in history build up like gas escaping slowly and steadily from a house. Then some accident provides a spark, and an explosion results. Without the accumulated gas, the spark would remain only a spark, quickly passing away.

To make effective arguments from cause and effect, you must assemble data carefully and make your argument measured and cautious. Avoid sweeping generalizations that claim much more than your evidence can support. Support what you do claim by continual reference to the data that support your views.

We yearn for certainty about cause and effect, but certainty seldom exists. In the last century Louis Pasteur discovered that by heating milk to a temperature slightly less than the boiling point, harmful germs would be killed. Here is a clear relation between cause and effect; pasteurization caused safer milk.

We would like certainty in everything, but human events offer much less of it, and informed readers become annoyed when they believe that a writer claims much more for a cause than seems plausible. Nearly everyone who has taught the history of western civilization has had a student who believes that the Roman Empire fell because the Romans used lead pipes and died of lead poisoning. Many others have worked out to the finest details why they think President John F. Kennedy was murdered in 1963. The Mafia did it. The Cubans did it. Anybody did it but Lee Harvey Oswald, so the various arguments run. If you make that kind of argument, you may feel smug because *you* have not been deceived, *you* stand above the ignorant masses, and *you* have managed to see everything with simple clarity. Such explanations appeal because they seem to make the great mysteries of human existence more manageable and less subject to chance. But they are almost always false; readers recognize them to be false, and most of them scorn the writers who make them.

It is all right to suggest possible causes and effects for which you do not have final proof. Many great scientific theories have been put together because careful observers have supposed that the facts could be accounted for if one assumed something unproven or even unprovable. The notion of black holes—stars that have collapsed into tiny points of matter so dense that their gravity prevents even light from escaping from their surface—fits the theory that physicist Albert Einstein developed to explain many forces in the universe. But no one has ever seen a black hole with a telescope, for by definition a black hole *cannot* be seen.

Historians often suggest cause-and-effect relations between events, although they cannot finally prove them to the satisfaction of everyone. In his best-selling *The Rise and Fall of the Great Powers*, historian Paul Kennedy argues that the cause of the decline of the great powers in modern times has been their excessive military spending. Both the United States and the Soviet Union, he thinks, have fallen into the trap of spending more for the military than their economies can afford. Kennedy compiles a great deal of data, and his conclusions seem plausible. But he knows that he cannot prove his case beyond any doubt, and he has vigorously attacked those who interpret his book as saying that the United States is in an *inevitable* decline.

Again the counsel is to be cautious and not to claim that you have proved beyond any doubt the cause-and-effect relation you may see in the data. Present the truth as you see it as carefully as possible, but leave room for other interpretations.

Cause-and-effect reasoning abounds in fallacies. One of the most common of the fallacious arguments is called *post hoc; ergo propter hoc*, a Latin phrase meaning that because one thing happens after another, the first is the cause of the second. A few years ago I read in a newspaper a passionate letter to the editor arguing that sex education in the public schools had caused an increase in violent sex crimes in recent years. The writer argued that before sex education was instituted, sex crimes were less frequent, and therefore sex education had caused these crimes. Someone quickly replied that this kind of argument could prove that the demise of the television program "Leave It to Beaver" was the real culprit; it could be demonstrated, this writer said, that sex crimes dramatically increased after that program went off the air.

It is easy to spot fallacies like these since the relation between cause and effect is so nebulous. But many fallacious arguments are much more complicated and subtle, and many people—even the writers who use them—may be deceived. Honest writers examine the evidence with care to see if it proves what they want to prove. If the evidence does not support the case, good writers will say so; if the evidence may be interpreted several different ways, honest writers will say that, too. We may yearn for simple answers, but truth is always best served when we see how complicated some events are, how difficult they are to explain, and how mysterious they often remain even when we have done our best to understand them.

Despite all its obvious dangers, the argument from cause to effect or from effect back to cause is indispensable in every field of thought. Strange indeed would be the essay without at least one paragraph devoted to it.

In writing such essays, you must infer—a process we have frequently examined in this book already. To infer, you observe something carefully, compare it with your other experiences or knowledge, and try to think out a pattern of cause and effect to explain the observation.

One of my favorite writing assignments early in a course is to have students look at the popular advertising of clothing in newspapers and magazines at various times in the past hundred years and then to ask them to speculate on the roles of men and women as implied by those ads. What did people think of women and their place in the world in a day when fashion ads showed female models so laden with clothing that we wonder how they had strength to walk? The assignment is an exercise in cause and effect. The effect is obvious—the pictures of the clothing itself. But what was the cause? To answer this question, students must use inference imaginatively.

Once I had students in a writing class visit a funeral of their choice to write an essay on the event, making inferences about the social function of the practices they observed in burying the dead. What is the social function of a eulogy? Why do we usually pray at funerals? What scriptural texts are read, and why are these texts chosen? What does a funeral tell about the people to whom it is addressed or at least about the view of the person in charge? The questions are endless, and most of them involve some speculative use of the cause-and-effect argument, inferences that will lead from the obvious to the less obvious.

Inferences may not be provable. Good writers always advance arguments drawn from inference in a spirit that is confident without being arrogant. What seems to be a perfectly plausible cause-and-effect relation to one person may seem implausible to another. Trust your readers. If your inference is sound, thoughtful readers will consider it and will probably accept it.

An early point is worth repeating: you make the cause-and-effect argument best when you pile up evidence to support your case. The argument from cause to effect or from effect back to cause works best when you present it one step at a time, making your arguments, explaining them, and giving examples to support them. Avoid sweeping generalizations. Avoid simplistic assertions. Advance confidently but not arrogantly; infer carefully; and always keep in mind the skeptical readers, the good man and the good woman who must be convinced if they are to believe that your reading of cause and effect is correct.

THE ARGUMENT FROM NECESSITY

The argument from necessity holds that no choice exists in a matter requiring action. The writer or speaker says, in effect, "Things are as I say they are, and you cannot do anything other than what I say you must do." It is an argument intended to make people do something without holding back, without second thoughts. It is almost always the argument of those who lead nations to war, for if we had a real choice, most of us would prefer to remain at peace.

On Monday morning, December 8, 1941, President Franklin D. Roosevelt made a great speech to Congress asking for a declaration of war against Japan. He began by presenting an undeniable fact in an unforgettable way:

> Yesterday, December 7, 1941—a date which will live in infamy—the United States of America was suddenly and deliberately attacked by naval and air forces of the Empire of Japan.

Roosevelt moved from this statement of fact to the argument that the United States now had no choice but to declare war on Japan. The Congress and the American people believed him.

A more modern version of the argument from necessity arises from various ecological issues. Many believe that the greenhouse effect—which results from the pouring of pollutants into the atmosphere—is increasing concentrations of carbon dioxide and warming the world's climate. If the warming continues, the polar ice cap will melt, and the consequent rising oceans will drown coastal cities all over the world. Many concerned people argue that we must take dramatic measures to cut down atmospheric pollution or else face catastrophe.

The argument from necessity is always vulnerable from two angles. An opponent can always say, "But the facts are not as you present them," or, "Even if your statements are true, your conclusion about what is to be done is false."

During the Vietnam War, President Lyndon Johnson argued that if South Vietnam fell to communism, all Asia would then go communist in a so-called domino effect, as if these countries were a row of upright dominoes that must all fall when one was toppled. Therefore, he said in speech after speech, the United States had to win the war by continuing to send in American troops and American supplies. Opponents countered that the domino effect was a myth and that even if other Asian countries should become communist, they could not act in concert to harm any vital interest of the United States. In effect, Johnson's opponents countered Johnson's argument from necessity by saying there was no necessity.

The argument from necessity embraces a contradiction. It assumes a choice; yet the argument is that no choice exists. I am asked to choose war and am told at the same time that I have no choice but war; I am asked to vote for a candidate who promises a balanced federal budget, and I am told that if I do not want the country to fall into ruin, I have no choice but to vote for such a candidate. The argument works only if the audience believes that the necessity does exist and assumes that people will do willingly what they are compelled to do anyway. This type of argument has the potential to backfire and damage both the credibility and the reputation of those who use it carelessly.

THE ARGUMENT FROM AUTHORITY

Aristotle called the argument from authority the "ethical" argument. He did not mean that the good ethical argument was more moral than the bad ethical argument. He meant the term *ethical* in the Greek sense, meaning character. The ethical argument is based on what we think of the person making the argument.

We believe some people because they exude an aura of authority. We believe them not merely for the logic of their discourse but for the force of their personalities and for their reputation. We believe them because they tell us vividly about something that happened to them. We trust them. So the argument from authority may be the least logical of all arguments in rhetoric; but it also may be the most believable. Certain religious groups that depend on testimony often demonstrate great vitality. At their communal services, people arise to tell—often with great emotion—stories of what God has done for them or shown them. Their hearers believe them, and the religion makes converts.

The argument from testimony may be the decisive argument in issues of historical writing. Historians sometimes assume a kind of logical explanation for past events that, on examination of the testimony of participants, proves to be untrue. Sir Thomas More, the "Man for All Seasons," died heroically for his Catholic faith during the rule of King Henry VIII of England in 1535. More was witty, courageous, and affectionate. He also vigorously opposed Protestantism in England. In 1935, a biographer of More assumed that More feared Protestantism not out of "religious bigotry" but because he thought Protestants would bring civil disorder to England. This biographer's logic went something like this: A witty, courageous, and affectionate man cannot oppose the religious convictions of others merely on the grounds of religion alone. If More opposed the Protestants, there must have been some reason beyond religion. The biographer's logic does not hold, however, for an examination of the thousands of pages More wrote against Protestants shows well enough that More thought

Protestants ought to be burned alive at the stake because their doctrines led people into the everlasting torments of a burning hell. He said so again and again and again, dozens if not hundreds of times. Modern, "rational" explanations of his behavior are wrecked by his own testimony.

The argument from authority or testimony reveals circumstances that may be in doubt. Fidel Castro of Cuba has often said that he holds no political prisoners and that such prisoners as are held in his jails are well treated. I know a doctor who spent fifteen years in one of Castro's prisons, and he has described conditions there in detail. These details include torture, near starvation, isolation, and daily humiliation. I believe his testimony, and I do not believe Castro.

The argument from authority or testimony often plays a great role in matters of taste. Academics are especially prone to use the argument themselves and to accept it from others. I once heard T. S. Eliot say in a lecture that the three most important authors in his literary education had been Dante, Donne, and Hawthorne. He did not argue for the greatness of any of these writers; he merely asserted that they were great. Those in the packed assembly listening to Eliot in Wolsey Hall at Yale University believed him—at least for that moment—because we knew Eliot's reputation and supposed that if he made a literary judgment, it must be true. I went home and started reading Dante's work—something I had scarcely done before.

To use the argument from authority, you must satisfy several requirements. You must have had sufficient experience to be taken seriously. A former prisoner in one of Castro's jails has had enough experience to tell us about them. You must speak in a tone that makes readers think you are judicious and unprejudiced. My friend, the former Cuban prisoner, spoke without bitterness, without even anger of his experience. His calm account of details made him a believable witness. If you use hysterical language in describing your experience, readers may suppose that you are irrational, and we are not disposed to believe obviously irrational people. You always do best if you write with confidence, gentleness, and detailed certainty. Make people respect you by the tone you use and by the credentials you bring forward, and they will believe you.

Always try to be an authority yourself. Study the subjects you write about. Learn the pros and the cons of every issue. Be able to defend your position with the facts. Nothing is so stultifying as to read prose whose author has been so uncertain about making conclusions that no firm word of his own comes through anywhere.

You should also freely use the authority of recognized experts. Lawyers call on experts to support their cases in trials. You can quote

books, articles, interviews, and other sources. When you write a literary essay about a novel, you can help your cause by finding an article
by a well-known critic who agrees with you. If you argue that Castro's
government in Cuba has destroyed the civil liberties of the Cuban
people, you can quote someone like my friend who spent those years
in one of Castro's jails. If you believe that the United States should
not give military aid to El Salvador, you can submit the testimony of
people who have suffered at the hands of the government the United
States support there. If you are making an argument about an event
in history, quote an eminent historian who has worked in the area
you are writing about.

The opportunities for testimony are limitless, and good testimony
for your side can help you convince readers. Work hard to dig out
supporting testimony. Be sure your witnesses are fair and truthful.
Quote them accurately. Be confident without being arrogant.

Arrangement of Arguments

I have chosen to call *arrangement* what others have traditionally
called types of reasoning. These types are deductive reasoning and
inductive reasoning. I find it valuable to think of deductive and inductive reasoning as ways of putting arguments together and arranging the evidence. Some evidence and some forms of argument fit naturally into deductive reasoning; some others fit better into induction.
Your decision to use one or the other at a given moment depends on
the evidence you possess and the way you decide to use it. You will
use both deduction and induction in almost every good argument
paper.

DEDUCTIVE REASONING

Deduction is the process of going from something we know for a fact
to a conclusion about something else. It involves inference—a means
of thinking we have frequently discussed in this book. Deductive reasoning goes on in a form traditionally called the syllogism. Syllogisms
involve three parts—a major premise, a minor premise, and a conclusion. The major premise is a statement of fact. The minor premise is
another statement of fact. The conclusion involves a comparison or a
reading of those two statements so that an additional statement of
fact may be made about the minor premise. You can get lost in a technical discussion of syllogisms, but an example can quickly clarify
things. The following syllogism has been used for centuries to illustrate the form:

Major premise:	All men are mortal.
Minor premise:	Socrates is a man.
Conclusion:	Socrates is mortal.

Such an example makes deductive reasoning seem neat and easy. In practice, however, such reasoning may be more complicated. Yet a little study will often reveal a syllogism in an argument, and it is good practice to look for such syllogisms in your reading. Astronomers in search of the planet Pluto made an argument something like this:

Major premise:	The gravitational pull of a nearby planet may cause variations in the orbits of other planets.
Minor premise:	Uranus and Neptune show variations in their orbits.
Conclusion:	There must be another planet out there that we have not yet discovered.

Another syllogism might run like this:

Major premise:	People write about those topics that most concern them personally.
Minor premise:	Ernest Hemingway wrote again and again of men who sought to prove their manhood and courage.
Conclusion:	Hemingway probably felt a great need to prove his own manhood and courage.

Even such cautious statements of syllogisms may seem a bit awkward when the syllogism is arranged in the bare-bones way that I have used here. Yet it is essential for the writer to be able to find such syllogisms in the framework of his or her thought and in the thought of others. Once we have reduced a line of deductive argument to a syllogism, we can check the terms to see if we can believe the conclusion or not.

Perhaps most of the time in deductive arguments, the major premise is not stated; it is only implied. A presidential candidate will attack his opponent for being inexperienced in matters of foreign policy. The implied major premise is that no one should become president without having made decisions about issues in foreign policy. A scholar may object to another scholar's use of Freudian psychology to interpret someone's life in the past. The implied major premise is either that Freudian psychology is invalid or that it cannot be used to psychoanalyze the dead (or both). The scholar may make his point without developing it, and we are left to work it out for ourselves.

❖

Deductive reasoning offers some obvious problems. The major premise may be wrong or at least disputable. The presidential candidate who claims vast experience in foreign policy may have had no influence on events, or if he did, he may have bungled and blundered on five continents. A look into history may cast doubts on syllogisms used in the present. Harry S. Truman, who as vice president of the United States succeeded Franklin Roosevelt on Roosevelt's death in 1945, had had virtually no experience in foreign policy when he took office. But by general consensus modern historians rate him high on achievements such as the Marshall Plan that aided European economic recovery and his quick response to counteract the Russian blockade of Berlin by creating an airlift to ferry in supplies across Russian lines to the former capital of Germany. Is the premise valid then that a presidential candidate experienced in foreign policy is necessarily superior to an inexperienced candidate? Perhaps not.

Deductive reasoning must take observation into account. Deduction is crippled when it ignores observation and works only off principles someone thinks are logical when in fact those principles do not fit the facts. The ancient Greeks are often credited with the discovery of modern science, but in fact they were more apt at working out logical systems than they were at observing nature, and some of their conclusions were contrary to the facts. Centuries afterward the prestige of Greek philosophy stood against the birth of a true modern science based on observation. When in the seventeenth century Galileo tried to prove that the earth moved, he ran into the Greek logic of his adversaries. Among other propositions, they put forward the following syllogism:

Major premise: People feel motion when they are moving.
Minor premise: We do not feel the earth move.
Conclusion: Therefore the earth does not move.

Those who lacked Galileo's mathematical skill and his experience with the telescope were reduced to a Greek "logic" that has long since been proved wrong.

Yet many people continue to uphold ideas that fit certain false premises in their own minds that they refuse to correct by observation. "Liberals are unpatriotic; Jones is a liberal; therefore Jones is unpatriotic." "The Marlboro Man smokes cigarettes and looks handsome and tough; I want to look handsome and tough; therefore I will smoke Marlboros." "No sensible person can be religious; Smith is religious; therefore she cannot be a sensible person."

Despite its abuses, deductive reasoning is an essential tool in the arrangement of arguments, and we both encounter it and use it continually. "Computers are extremely sensitive to slight changes in electrical voltage; surge protectors keep voltage changes from damaging the computer to which they are attached; computer owners should own a surge protector." "College graduates nearly always get better-paying jobs than non-college graduates; Jones wants a job that pays well; Jones should get a college education." "Democracy depends on the freedom of people to acquire information wherever they can find it; reading is one of the most important means of acquiring information; therefore democracy depends on a free press."

INDUCTION

We have already encountered induction in our discussion of fact patterns in an earlier section of this chapter. Induction is the process of observing facts until we perceive some kind of relation between them that allows us to draw some sort of conclusion about them. Induction has been at the heart of modern medical research. Pasteur observed that certain bacteria were present in milk and that people who drank that milk were often afflicted with disease. He concluded that the bacteria caused the disease—and his conclusion changed modern medicine for all time.

By the same sort of induction, researchers in this century have noted that lung cancer afflicts cigarette smokers at ten times the rate that the disease afflicts nonsmokers. Researchers have concluded that cigarettes cause lung cancer, though as yet they are not sure just how smoke works on the lungs to do so.

In literary studies you may notice that certain themes come up again and again in a writer's work. You may be justified in drawing some conclusions from this recurrence. Many critics have noted that women in John Updike novels appear to exist chiefly as sexual objects for Updike's male characters. Feminist critics attack him for the limited view he takes of women in his work.

Archaeologists discover identical Greek pottery ware in southern England, Spain, southern France, Egypt, and Palestine. They conclude that Greek trade extended all over the Mediterranean and as far north as England at the time the pottery was manufactured.

In using inductive logic, we assemble clues that add up to the solution of a detective story. To use inductive reasoning we take stock of our experience and try to make sense of it. For the writer, induction requires careful collection of facts and careful thought about how those facts hold together—if indeed they do.

Induction and deduction may go hand in hand. By induction researchers have determined that nonsmokers who live in the same house with a cigarette smoker run a much greater risk of heart disease and cancer than do those nonsmokers who live in a smoke-free house. Lawmakers in various cities have deduced from these findings the conclusion that nonsmokers have the right to a smoke-free workplace and smoke-free areas in restaurants and other public areas. Once induction leads us to a conclusion, we are free to deduce other conclusions from it.

Logical Fallacies

No discussion about argument can be complete without a few words about logical fallacies. An honest writer will avoid fallacious reasoning; a good reader will recognize bad logic when she sees it.

FALLACIES OF DEDUCTION AND INDUCTION

We have already noted fallacies of deduction. A fallacious deduction may arise when the major premise is wrong or when the connection between the major premise and the minor premise is faulty. We will look at some more examples of faulty deduction when we consider the logical fallacies below.

Fallacies of induction most commonly occur when we try to draw conclusions from too few instances. An American fortune-teller predicted the assassination of John F. Kennedy in her list of predictions for 1963. A great many people, including the editors of many newspapers, thought that she might have some real psychic powers, and for years at New Year's she was paid well to make predictions about what was going to happen in the next twelve months. In time her predictions proved to be so far off the mark so frequently that they became ridiculous, and she dropped into obscurity. The confidence originally placed in her arose from her one "lucky" guess about a national calamity. Her case is special, but it makes the point that even good writers and thinkers may be led astray by drawing conclusions from too little data.

STRAW MEN

A *straw man* is an argument one claims one's opponents are making when in fact they are not making that argument at all. One attacks this imaginary argument instead of facing the real issue. The setting up of straw men that can easily be burned or otherwise disposed of is an affliction of current political discourse. It is a curse of our times. Someone opposes prayer in public schools, and advocates of school prayer accuse him of being against religion. Someone opposes book censorship by school boards, and someone else accuses her of loving pornography. Someone opposes abortion, and someone else accuses him of wanting to keep women in a subservient position. Someone favors abortion, and someone else accuses her of being immoral. A college president points out the hazards and the uncertainties of divesting university-held stocks in corporations doing business in South Africa, and students accuse her of racism. A presidential candidate supports the United States Supreme Court decision that children may for religious reasons refuse to pledge allegiance to the flag, and his opponent claims he is unpatriotic.

In serious writing, setting up straw men is an immoral act, and readers with their wits about them will disdain this cowardly practice. Writers who set up straw men fear to face the arguments of their opponents at their strongest points. Examples of straw men have been almost endlessly multiplied in this society. Notice the practice in others, and avoid it in your own writing.

THE AD HOMINEM ARGUMENT

The words *ad hominem* are Latin for "against the man," and the fallacy called by this name is an attack on a person rather than a serious effort to deal with that person's arguments. The attack assumes that a bad person cannot produce a good program or a worthwhile thought. Like the straw-man fallacy, the *ad hominem* argument is all too common in political campaigns in this country. It has now become rare for candidates facing one another in an election to treat each other as honorable human beings.

The *ad hominem* argument usually represents faulty deduction.

> My opponent is a homosexual; therefore nothing he says about national politics can be trusted. I, on the other hand, consort only with members of the opposite sex; therefore my sentiments about national affairs are almost infallible.

Most people would recognize the obvious faulty reasoning in the above example. But what about in this one?

> My opponent was expelled for cheating when he was in college thirty years ago. Therefore you cannot trust anything he says about foreign affairs.

This argument assumes that because the speaker's opponent did something dishonest thirty years ago, he is still dishonest, and that dishonesty taints everything he says on any subject, including foreign affairs. It does not consider the opponent's life since the dishonesty, and it ignores any other statements about foreign affairs that might have been sensible and farsighted. It assumes a syllogism like this:

Anyone who cheats once in school will always be completely dishonest.

My opponent cheated thirty years ago.

My opponent is completely dishonest now.

Reduced to these terms, the *ad hominem* argument can seem absurd, but it is a serious matter for many of us. People long for goodness as well as for truth, and they have trouble believing that bad people can have good thoughts. Attacking the character of one's opponent can take the weight of an argument off the issues and put it on personalities that may have little to do with the wisdom or foolishness of a policy.

The *ad hominem* argument can be valid. A political candidate with a notorious record of lying and theft in school and during all the years afterward is not a good bet for high office. But anyone writing about any issue should be sure to define the issue and debate it without seeking to make those on the opposite side of the issue seem like criminals (unless there is obvious evidence to the contrary). Too often the *ad hominem* argument is the rhetorical refuge of a scoundrel.

THE BANDWAGON ARGUMENT

According to the bandwagon argument, since everybody is doing something we should do it, too—regardless of the knowledge or the character of all those people who are doing it. It is, alas, another argument that flows through American political discourse. A candidate may use public opinion polls to show that his victory is assured and in so doing try to win the votes of people who have not yet decided to cast their votes for that supposedly assured victor.

The strength of the bandwagon argument lies in our human propensity to seek the company of our own kind and to be sociable beings. We do not like to be isolated. Most of us hate to speak out against strong public opinion. If everybody is doing something, our social nature tells us that we ought to be doing it, too. The bandwagon mentality makes some people hesitate to express an opinion until they know what others are thinking. A group of college students discussing a movie will often wait cautiously for someone to express an opinion; then they will all agree with that opinion, no matter what they really think. Likewise, their professors will often be loathe to express dislike for any of the great literary classics because they are afraid of being thrown off the bandwagon of academe. I greatly admired the courage of one of my English department colleagues for admitting to me one day that he found *Moby Dick* one of the most boring books ever written.

The bandwagon argument is often fallacious. Although public opinion supports a war or a political candidate or a social program or a piece of legislation relating to some moral issue, public opinion may be wrong. It may be that some brave writer or speaker must get off the bandwagon and try to wave it to a stop before it rolls over a cliff. The strength of the United States Constitution and our democracy rests on the freedom to stand alone, and the mere statement of near unanimity of views does not necessarily argue that those views are correct.

The bandwagon argument does have some proper uses, even though it is often used improperly. If, for example, all the authorities in a discipline are fairly well agreed about something, you may give their testimony in an argument. A student of mine wrote a paper a few years ago advocating a constitutional amendment that would give the president a single six-year term. He supported his argument brilliantly by showing that the last four presidents of the United States had advocated a similar idea. This was an argument from authority—the authority of people who had held the office he was writing about. In a sense he was calling on his readers to get on the bandwagon.

Yet the general connotation of the bandwagon argument is that people emotionally take up a position merely because others have done so, whether they know anything about the argument or not. The bandwagon argument is often associated with the *ad hominem* argument because people who preach the bandwagon frequently pass on to the declaration that their opponents are foolish and even dispicable beings. It is worth remembering that bandwagons may turn into stampedes and that stampedes rarely do anybody any good.

Concluding Remarks on Argument

Argument is essential to democracy, to public discourse, to scholarship, and to daily life. From the smallest meetings in our communities to the greatest debates of the Congress of the United States, argument helps us see our way, make choices, and abide by them. It is a high mark of civilization, and when people lose the ability to argue well or to follow the arguments of others, all our democratic institutions are threatened. Never be afraid to argue; but always be prepared to argue well.

Always be honorable in your arguments. Admit it when all the evidence does not stack up in your favor. In arguing we come to recognize that knowledge rarely holds together in perfect symmetry. Life is not that easy, and that is why we argue. Concede points when the evidence requires concession. If the preponderance of the evidence supports you, a concession will not ruin your argument. Failure to concede obvious weakness will give you a reputation for dishonesty or for lack of ability. Treat your opponents with respect, as if they were erring friends, not evil enemies. Marshal your evidence. Remember that the solution to many arguments is neither this or that but some of both.

Here it is worth repeating something I have said in various ways throughout this book. Knowledge seldom has neat edges that all fit together. It comes with ragged corners, with missing pieces, and with uneven sides. We make our best arguments by assuming a confident humility.

Five

Paragraphs

❖❖❖

*P*aragraphs are a modern invention. Greek and Latin writers did not divide their works into paragraphs. Until the nineteenth century, written English scarcely noticed them. The word *paragraph* originally meant a mark placed at the head of a section of prose to announce that the subject of the discourse was changing slightly. After the mark, the section might go on for several pages. Eventually the paragraph mark was replaced by an indented line. Even then the indentation might introduce a long section of unbroken prose. The paragraphs of John Stuart Mill and Charles Darwin, both great nineteenth-century prose writers, often went on for several pages. Only gradually did the paragraph assume its modern form—a fairly short block of prose introduced by an indentation, organized so that every sentence in it contributes to a limited subject.

Paragraphs help writers and readers alike. They order our thoughts and make writing easier to follow. They break our ideas down into manageable units that we can treat efficiently. They let us arrange an essay one step at a time, and they allow readers to follow our thoughts along the stairway we have built for them.

Paragraphs give readers a sense of pace: from paragraph to paragraph we see that the prose is going somewhere. They also provide relief for our eyes. The unbroken columns in an early nineteenth-century newspaper look dark and forbidding to today's historian. (Indeed, the most probable cause of the paragraph's popularity was the expansion of literacy fed by the penny press. Ordinary people—sometimes not well educated—wanted their newspapers to be more readable, and editors wanted their stories to be more flexible for inserts and deletions that helped fit a story neatly into the space available.) We hesitate to start reading unparagraphed material because we subconsciously believe we cannot get through it. By breaking down a piece of writing into small blocks, paragraphs give us confidence that we can absorb the piece block at a time.

The Structure of Paragraphs

A lot of nonsense has been written about paragraphs; much of it is not only wrong but harmful. Much of the nonsense arises from the false notion that every paragraph is a short essay and that the thesis for the essay should be expressed in a *topic sentence*. Some books teach that a topic sentence may be at the beginning, the middle, or the end of a paragraph. Many teachers command students to underline the topic sentence, and students dutifully obey whether the paragraph has a topic sentence or not.

The topic sentence is said to be a general statement that is supported by the evidence in the rest of the paragraph. A good topic sentence is supposed to develop paragraph unity.

No doubt, paragraph unity is important. In our reading we do not like to be jerked around from thought to thought without seeing any connections between those thoughts. Smooth-flowing paragraphs take us from thought to thought, from detail to detail. Sometimes a paragraph does develop an idea stated in a general statement that fits the standard textbook definition of the topic sentence. The other sentences in the paragraph provide some reason to accept the generalization. Such paragraphs usually explain things. In most other paragraphs, no textbook topic sentence can be found.

Let's consider the textbook topic sentence first in a paragraph that explains something. Here is a paragraph from Loren Eiseley, a scientific writer of great breadth and rhetorical power:

> Yet Darwin did not compose the theory of evolution out of thin air. Like so many great scientific generalizations, the theory with which his name is associated had already had premonitory beginnings. All of the elements which were to enter into the theory were in men's minds and were being widely discussed during Darwin's college years. His own grandfather, Erasmus Darwin, who died seven years before Charles was born, had boldly proposed a theory of the "transmutation" of living forms. Jean Baptiste Lamarck had glimpsed a vision of evolutionary continuity. And Sir Charles Lyell—later to become Darwin's confidant—had opened the way for the evolutionary point of view by demonstrating that the planet must be very old—old enough to allow extremely slow organic change. Lyell dismissed the notion of catastrophic extinction of animal forms on a world-wide scale as impossible, and he made plain that natural forces—the work of wind and frost and water—were sufficient to explain most of the phenomena found in the rocks, provided these forces were seen as operating over enormous periods. Without Lyell's gift of time in immense quantities, Darwin would not have been able to devise the theory of natural selection.[1]

Eiseley's paragraph starts with a general statement—which we may call a topic sentence—and the rest of the paragraph builds on it.

The sentences in the paragraph that follow the initial sentence give reasons to believe the first general statement. Eiseley expands on the topic, provides details, and develops thoughts from one sentence to the next.

But many paragraphs—most paragraphs, in fact—are not introduced by general statements. Here, for example, is a paragraph from James Baldwin's "Notes of a Native Son":

> On the 29th of July, in 1943, my father died. On the same day, a few hours later, his last child was born. Over a month before this, while all our energies were concentrated in waiting for these events, there had been, in Detroit, one of the bloodiest race riots of the century. A few hours after my father's funeral, while he lay in state in the undertaker's chapel, a race riot broke out in Harlem. On the morning of the 3rd of August, we drove my father to the graveyard through a wilderness of smashed plate glass.[2]

We could summarize the paragraph above in a general topic sentence such as this: "Several interesting things happened on the day my father died." Such a sentence would be tedious and unnecessary. As Baldwin tells us what happened, event by event, we easily follow along. We see the unity of the paragraph as we read it.

But how do paragraphs work? What do paragraphs with general topic sentences have in common with paragraphs that lack such sentences? Paragraphs have unity. But how do writers attain this unity?

I believe that we write with a sense in our heads of when we are going to make a slight shift in the subject we are treating. When we wish to move on to another point, another idea, another incident, we indent and write a sentence. The first sentence of the paragraph contains some ideas we wish to expand in the next sentence. We pick up one of those ideas and use it in that next sentence. We connect the two sentences by some repetition—a word, a pronoun, or a synonym for an idea in the first sentence.

Let's examine that process in the paragraph from James Baldwin.

> On the 29th of July, in 1943, my father died.

Think for a moment of all the possibilities in this sentence. We have several key thoughts—"29th of July," "1943," "my father," and "died."

Baldwin picks up the thought of the date and the thought of the father. The important topic here is "when." He develops them in this sentence:

> On the same day, a few hours later, his last child was born.

"On the same day," is a synonym for "On the 29th of July, in 1943," and "his" refers to "my father." Baldwin develops a thought of what happens on July 29, 1943. Now he develops a further thought, also related to the question "when."

> Over a month before this, while all our energies were concentrated in waiting for these events, there had been, in Detroit, one of the bloodiest race riots of the century.

Two thoughts are picked up here. "Over a month before this" develops the thought of "On the 29th of July, in 1943," and "On the same day." "While all our energies were concentrated in waiting for these events" relates to the ideas of the death of Baldwin's father and the birth of the father's last child.

Baldwin continues in the next sentence to develop the idea of "when," also referring to his father's death by mentioning the funeral:

> A few hours after my father's funeral, while he lay in state in the undertaker's chapel, a race riot broke out in Harlem.

Again referring to his father's funeral, and also referring to the race riot mentioned in this sentence, he develops the next sentence:

> On the morning of the 3rd of August, we drove my father to the graveyard through a wilderness of smashed plate glass.

This sentence concludes the paragraph. We see in these sentences a network of interlocking thoughts that begin with the first sentence. That first sentence is not a general topic sentence; it is a simple declaration of fact. The other sentences are similar declarations of fact, but they are all tied to the first sentence by the words they use. Every sentence picks up some words or ideas from the previous sentence and adds something new.

These are qualities of all paragraphs, whether they have a general topic sentence or not. They reflect the writer's mind. If the writer had other interests, the paragraph would have gone off in another direction, but it still would have been carefully laced together by this network of interconnections. Suppose someone else had written this:

> On the 29th of July, in 1943, my father died. I scarcely had time to notice the event because on that day I was ordered to fly yet another raid against Hamburg, and we had to take off within an hour after I received the telegram from home. I was the navigator on our B-24 "Liberator" bomber, and had to fly the mission because there was no one to replace me. It was our second raid on Hamburg in four days, and I was so tired I did not have the energy to grieve for a loss so far away.

Again we have the tight interconnections between sentences—each sentence after the first one both reaching back to pick up a previous word or idea and extending the thoughts, adding new information. What makes the two paragraphs different? The different purposes of the writers. But the structure in each is the same—a looking backward and a moving forward in each sentence.

The first sentence is all-important to any paragraph. The writer, setting down that first sentence, makes a commitment to develop some word or phrase in it as he or she proceeds to the second sentence, to the third, and to the fourth. You will begin many paragraphs with general topic sentence containing ideas that must be supported and developed in the rest of the paragraph. Always the best way to preserve unity in the paragraph is to be sure to connect the first sentence to the rest by this network of repetition and development that I have here demonstrated.

Baldwin's paragraph and the one that I have constructed from his first sentence are both typical narrative paragraphs, used in all storytelling. Here is a paragraph from Alice Walker's "Beauty: When the Other Dancer is the Self ":

> My father is the driver for the rich old white lady up the road. Her name is Miss Mey. She owns all the land for miles around, as well as the house in which we live. All I remember about her is that she once offered to pay my mother thirty-five cents for cleaning her house, raking up piles of her magnolia leaves, and washing her family's clothes, and that my mother—she of no money, eight children, and a chronic ear-ache— refused it. But I do not think of this in 1947. I am two and a half years old. I want to go everywhere my daddy goes. I am excited at the prospect of riding in a car. Someone has told me fairs are fun. That there is room in the car for only three of us doesn't faze me at all. Whirling happily in my starchy frock, showing off my biscuit-polished patent leather shoes and lavender socks, tossing my head in a way that makes my ribbons bounce, I stand, hands on hips, before my father. "Take me, Daddy," I say with assurance. "I'm the prettiest."[3]

I have drawn lines from sentence to sentence in this example to show you the connections, the way sentences after the first sentence in the paragraph pick up previous words and ideas, repeat them, and build on them. This paragraph does not have a general topic sentence, and it does not need one. We follow it easily because of the connections between the sentences.

All good paragraphs develop in much the same way. The first sentence presents several thoughts. The second picks up the one the author wishes to develop and goes on. Sometimes student writers forget to carry that development from the first sentence through the following sentences in the paragraphs. They write a kind of shorthand that leaves out some necessary thoughts, some essential connections. Readers are left to leap from sentence to sentence like agile children jumping from stepping-stone to stepping-stone over a stream. Readers want a smooth bridge that will carry them to their destination without causing unnecessary strain. The most frequent cause of unnecessary strain within a paragraph is the lack of development from sentence to sentence. Always review your sentences to see that each sentence in a paragraph picks up and develops an idea mentioned in a previous sentence. If you discover a sentence that lacks a proper connection with what comes before it, you probably have a disorderly paragraph.

Always the first sentence is key to the rest. Sometimes paragraphs begin with a broad, general statement as a first sentence, then follow it with a second sentence that limits the general statement. The rest of the paragraph builds on the second, limiting sentence. Most textbooks call the limiting sentence the topic sentence because it expresses the idea developed by the rest of the paragraph. But it seems far more sensible to think of the first sentence as setting the stage for the rest. When you read such paragraphs, you can easily imagine the writer setting down the first sentence, then committing herself to developing the most important thought she finds in it. Here is such a paragraph, as historian Barbara Tuchman describes the Anarchist movement in America in the late nineteenth century:

> Men who were Anarchists without knowing it stood on every street corner. Jacob Riis, the New York police reporter who described in 1890 *How the Other Half Lives,* saw one on the corner of Fifth Avenue and Fourteenth Street. The man suddenly leaped at a carriage carrying two fashionable ladies on an afternoon's shopping and slashed at the sleek and shining horses with a knife. When arrested and locked up, he said, "They don't have to think of tomorrow. They spend in an hour what would keep me and my little ones for a year." He was the kind from which Anarchists of the Deed were made.[4]

The first sentence makes a general statement; the second limits the general idea to a particular incident; and the rest of the paragraph provides details of that incident. This kind of paragraph occurs often in professional writing. The first sentence provides a general introduction; the second sentence focuses on something more specific; and the rest of the paragraph builds on the ideas of the second sentence. But even here, the second, limiting sentence depends on some idea expressed in the first sentence.

Unity and Disunity in the Paragraph and the Essay

I have described the way a paragraph *tracks,* the way it moves from thought to thought smoothly, keeping the later parts in harmony with the earlier parts. An essay tracks on the same principle. Every sentence after the first sentence in an essay looks back to something that has gone before and looks ahead to something that will come after. In a good essay you can draw lines of connection all the way through from sentence to sentence, as I have done in the paragraph above written by Alice Walker.

Disunity in paragraphs often leads to disunity in the essay, for if a paragraph jumps the track, it may derail the rest of the essay that comes after it. Such disunity usually occurs because the later sentences in a paragraph do not flow naturally from the first sentence.

Writers stumble into disunity when they are not sure what they want to say or when they have lost track of what they have said already. Sometimes they write a first sentence, wait a long time to write the second, and in the interval forget what they said in the first. If you have trouble with paragraph unity, check your first sentence carefully. See what ideas it contains. Then see if your next sentence takes up one of these ideas and develops it. Read your work aloud; I repeat this advice again and again to my students. Your ear helps you edit when your eyes fail you.

You may check the unity of some paragraphs by trying to leave a sentence out. This is especially true in paragraphs that argue, explain, or narrate. Such paragraphs usually build sentences into something like a chain, each sentence a link depending on the link behind it. Leave a sentence out, and the chain breaks. The paragraph comes apart. Here, for example, is a narrative paragraph from Loren Eiseley. Eiseley tells of the voyage Darwin made as naturalist on His Majesty's Ship *Beagle.* That voyage made Darwin start asking himself what accounted for the differences between various species of plant and animal life that seemed remarkably similar to one another— questions that led him to develop his theory of biological evolution by natural selection. See how these sentences are chained together by their subject matter. Ask yourself if you can leave a sentence out or change its order in the paragraph.

They sailed from Devonport December 27, 1831, in H.M.S. *Beagle,* a ten-gun brig. Their plan was to survey the South American coastline and to carry a string of chronometrical measurements around the world. The voyage almost ended before it began, for they at once encountered a violent storm. "The sea ran very high," young Darwin recorded in his diary, "and the vessel pitched bows under and suffered most dreadfully, such a night I never passed, on every side nothing but misery, such a whistling of the wind and roar of the sea, the hoarse screams of the officers and shouts of the men, made a concert that I shall not soon forget." Captain Fitzroy and his officers held the ship on the sea by the grace of God and the cat-o'-nine-tails. With an almost irrational stubbornness Darwin decided, in spite of his uncomfortable discovery of his susceptibility to seasickness, that "I did right to accept the offer." When the *Beagle* was buffeted back into Plymouth Harbor, Darwin did not resign. His mind was made up. "If it desirable to see the world," he wrote in his journal, "what a rare and excellent opportunity this is. Perhaps I may have the same opportunity of drilling my mind that I threw away at Cambridge."[5]

Take a few minutes to trace the linkages in this paragraph. The first sentence looks back to a previous paragraph with the opening pronoun "They." "They sailed from Devonport December 27, 1831. . . . " The possessive pronoun "Their" that begins the next sentence extends the reference made by "They" in the first sentence. "The voyage" that begins the third sentence looks back to the action expressed in the first sentence by the words "They sailed. . . . " So it goes through the paragraph, one sentence looking back to the last and all of them falling into a chainlike order that can scarcely be changed, thought building on thought. We could leave out the sentence "Captain Fitzroy and his officers held the ship on the sea by the grace of God and the cat-o'-nine-tails," although it adds vigor to the whole. Otherwise, if we leave out a sentence, the meaning of the next one is suddenly difficult. The paragraph runs, carrying us along, repeating nothing unnecessarily but including enough backward glances to help us see easily the relation of each sentence to the previous sentence and to the next one.

You cannot always test paragraph unity by leaving out a sentence. Some paragraphs make a general statement in the first sentence and follow it with a list of detailed statements that support the generalization. You can change the list around or even leave part of it out, and the paragraph will still hold together. Descriptive paragraphs often have this quality. Let's take a look at a couple of descriptive paragraphs Eiseley wrote in an essay called "The Judgment of the Birds."

It was a late hour on a cold, wind-bitten autumn day when I climbed a great hill spined like a dinosaur's back and tried to take my bearings. The tumbled waste fell away in waves in all directions. Blue air was darkening into purple along the bases of the hills. I shifted my knapsack, heavy with the petrified bones of long-vanished creatures, and studied my compass. I wanted to be out of there by nightfall, and already the sun was going sullenly down in the west.

It was then that I saw the flight coming on. It was moving like a little close-knit body of black specks that danced and darted and closed again. It was pouring from the north and heading toward me with the un-deviating relentlessness of a compass needle. It streamed through the shadows rising out of monstrous gorges. It rushed over towering pinna-cles in the red light of the sun or momentarily sank from sight within the shade. Across that desert of eroding clay and wind-worn stone they came with a faint wild twittering that filled all the air about me as those tiny living bullets hurtled past into the night.[6]

As in all paragraphs, the first sentence in each of these is of essential importance in setting the stage for what comes later. But the sentences after that first sentence can be rearranged in almost any order; the para-graph will maintain its sense. Every sentence reaches back to the first sentence of the paragraph to amplify the thought expressed there.

Some paragraphs organize material in clumps of sentences that follow the first sentence. The sentences in each clump are closely re-lated to each other. But the clumps themselves may be rearranged or even eliminated without disturbing the harmony of the whole. (In a well-written paragraph, the elimination of a clump of sentences would reduce the richness and dilute the thought.)

Here is a paragraph organized in clumps of sentences broken down in a schematic way. The paragraph comes from William Manchester's survey of American history from 1932 to 1972, *The Glory and the Dream*, and it describes the journey of John Glenn, the first American astronaut to orbit the earth in a space capsule:

The temperature in the capsule had risen to 108 degrees, he noted, but the air-conditioning in his suit kept him cool.

He had been instructed to explain his every sensation—the audi-ence, after all, was paying for the trip—and he began by reporting that he had no feeling of speed. It was "about the same as flying in an airliner at, say, 30,000 feet, and looking down at clouds from 10,000 feet."

Over the Atlantic he spotted the Gulf Stream, a river of blue in the gray sea.

Over the West Coast he made out California's Salton Sea and the Imperial Valley, and he could pick out the irrigation canals near El Centro, where he had once lived.

His first twilight was awesome: "As the sun goes down it's very white, brilliant light, and as it goes below the horizon you get a very bright orange color. Down close to the surface it pales out into a sort of blue, a darker blue, and then off into black." The stars were spectacular. "If you've been out on the desert on a very clear, brilliant night when there's no moon and the stars just seem to jump out at you, that's just about the way they look."

Approaching Australia he radioed, "Just to my right I can see a big pattern of light, apparently right on the coast." From a tracking station below, Astronaut Gordon Cooper explained to him that this was the Australian city of Perth. Its 82,000 inhabitants had turned on all their light switches, to welcome him and test his night vision." Glenn replied, "Thank everybody for turning on, will you?"[7]

The clumps of sentences in the preceding paragraphs are arranged chronologically. You could leave any clump out without substantially damaging the unity of what is left. You could even rearrange some of the clumps without making readers feel that they had lost anything.

We can summarize the two common ways to organize paragraphs with a couple of diagrams:

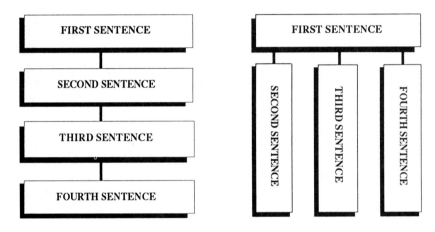

Transitions between Paragraphs

Paragraphs should not only hold together within; they should also allow smooth passage from one paragraph to the next. To ensure this smooth flow, pay attention to the transitions within your paragraphs. Transitions are words or phrases that look backward, tying the paragraph to what has come before, and that look forward, binding the first sentence of your paragraph to what comes afterward. Good transitions make reading easier for readers; transitions also help writers with their own thinking by setting up relations within prose that are essential to its shape and unity.

Two kinds of transitions are available. The more obvious and somewhat more clumsy are the clear, transitional words that tell your reader in no uncertain terms that you are moving from one idea in your paper to another. Words like *therefore, however, moreover, furthermore, nevertheless,* and many others say to your reader, "This is the way; come with me."

At times we all use these unambiguous transitions. But before we write one, we should pause. Must we use it? These transitions are careful, plodding words, words that leap quickly to mind when we are stuck. When we use them too frequently to hold an essay together, they leave the rivets showing.

We can become addicted to such transitions. They are so easy! They do the job! But the best transitions rarely call attention to themselves. As always, you can study the work of professional writers to check my advice. You can go for pages and pages without seeing a *thus* or a *therefore* in the pages of *The New Yorker, Popular Mechanics, Sports Illustrated*, or *The Atlantic*. In a good, lively book on a serious topic, you will rarely find such words. You don't see the rivets in the writing. You see paragraphs smoothly welded together so that you don't feel the bumps and the cracks. How do good writers achieve these effects?

A good device in making transitions is to choose a word in the last sentence of one paragraph to repeat in the first sentence of the next. Look at the following example, taken from John McPhee's essay called "The Swiss at War." Here are the first two paragraphs of the essay:

> It seems likely that the two most widely circulated remarks ever made about Switzerland's military prowess were made by Napoleon Bonaparte and Orson Welles.
>
> Welles said, "In Italy for thirty years under the Borgias, they had welfare, terror, murder, bloodshed—but they produced Michelangelo, Leonardo da Vinci, and the Renaissance. In Switzerland, they have brotherly love, five hundred years of democracy and peace, and what did that produce? The cuckoo clock."[8]

We have two transitions here. The primary transition is the word "Welles." It appears at the end of the one-sentence opening paragraph of McPhee's essay. It begins the next sentence, the first sentence in a two-sentence paragraph. (McPhee's essay originally appeared as an article in *The New Yorker*, a magazine that prizes the short paragraph.) The second transition is the word "Switzerland." It appears in the first paragraph and reappears in the second sentence of the second paragraph. These repetitions of nouns weave the paragraphs together and provide us with an unbroken tapestry of thought.

You can make a transition by repeating a verb in the first sentence of a new paragraph that you have used in the last sentence of the preceding paragraph. Here is the last part of a paragraph by Annie Dillard followed by the first couple of sentences of the next paragraph:

> It is dire poverty indeed when a man is so malnourished and fatigued that he won't stoop to pick up a penny. But if you cultivate a healthy

poverty and simplicity, so that finding a penny will literally make your day, then, since the world is in fact planted in pennies, you have with your poverty bought a lifetime of days. It is that simple. What you see is what you get.

I used to be able to see flying insects in the air. I'd look ahead and see, not the row of hemlocks across the road, but the air in front of it. My eyes would focus along that column of air, picking out flying insects. But I lost interest, I guess, for I dropped the habit. Now I can see birds.[9]

The verb "see" makes the transition between paragraphs. Once Dillard decides to pick up that word in the beginning of the second paragraph above, she explodes into new ideas about seeing. She uses the verb "see" three times quickly so that we unconsciously realize how important the word "see" is in the last sentence of the first paragraph that I have quoted. We move easily from one "see" to the next.

Sometimes a noun in the last sentence of a paragraph will be represented by a pronoun in the first or second sentence of the next. Here is Lewis Thomas writing about "Late Night Thoughts on Listening to Mahler's Ninth Symphony":

I took this music as a metaphor for reassurance, confirming my own strong hunch that the dying of every living creature, the most natural of all experiences, has to be a peaceful experience. I rely on nature. The long passages on all the strings at the end, as close as music can come to expressing silence itself, I used to hear as Mahler's idea of leave-taking at its best. But always, I have heard this music as a solitary, private listener, thinking about death.

Now I hear it differently. I cannot listen to the last movement of the Mahler Ninth without the door-smashing intrusion of a huge new thought: death everywhere, the dying of everything, the end of humanity.[10]

Three transitional ideas are repeated in the short first sentence of the second paragraph from the last sentence of the first paragraph—the pronoun "I," the verb "hear," and the pronoun "it." But the pronoun "it" seems to carry most of the weight, for it refers to the word "music" and to the general topic of the paragraph that begins with a reference to Mahler's Ninth.

No book can show all the possible transitions in good writing. But the principle is obvious. Transitions work by looking backward and by reaching forward, by repeating words or ideas. The repetition should not be in the spirit of telling readers exactly what you have told them before. It is rather a kind of base from which you spring off to tell them something new.

From what you have learned so far in this chapter, you should be able to analyze the paragraphs in any book or magazine you enjoy. Test your own skill by locating transitions that bind paragraphs together in some enjoyable piece of prose. You will note that good writers seldom use the mechanical transitional words such as *thus, therefore, moreover, furthermore,* and *however.* Well-constructed paragraphs rarely require them; learn to connect your paragraphs without them.

Length of Paragraphs

How long should a paragraph be? Journalists break their paragraphs every two or three sentences. Most newspapers and many magazines are printed in narrow columns; copy editors indent frequently to break up multiple lines of type. In academic writing, paragraphs may run on for a page or more. One rule of thumb based on visual effect holds that the length of a paragraph should not exceed its width. In student papers, I like to see about two indentations on each page of typewritten copy. Experience tells me that when inexperienced writers run on and on without an indentation, their thoughts may be rambling or fuzzy.

No sure rule can guide us. Some long paragraphs are just right; some short ones are incoherent. The flow of one sentence into another makes a better measure of the unity of a paper than does the length of its paragraphs. If you weave your sentences together by the patterns of repetition and extension that I have shown, you may indent almost at will. I sometimes look at a page in my own writing and decide that I want to divide a paragraph that has become too long for my taste. I can always find a place where the flow changes just enough to justify a new indentation.

Whatever the length of your paragraphs, observe the first-sentence rule. Make your first sentence the introduction. Take one of the thoughts from it, and develop that thought in the next sentence. Then choose whether you want to make the third sentence develop a thought from the second sentence or whether you want to leap back over the second sentence and pick up something from the first. Always remember that an essay develops thoughts. Sentences repeat something mentioned earlier and push forward into something new.

Concluding Remarks on Paragraphs

If you have trouble with paragraphs, your first efforts to build paragraph unity may be hard. But as you get the hang of analyzing your own sentences, the going gets easier. Writing can be like dancing: learning the first new steps requires concentration, and you will step on your partner's feet or else—in more modern dancing—collide with somebody on the floor. But suddenly the knack comes, and you keep time to the music with your feet as if you were born to it. When you write, pay attention to the development of your thoughts. Look at the relation of your sentences to one another, and paragraphs will take care of themselves.

Six

Writing Sentences

❖❖❖

Fundamental Principles of Sentences

Sentences make statements or ask questions. We learn to make sentences naturally when we talk because we must if we are to be understood. Some people say that we seldom communicate in complete sentences, but such views are mistaken. In any conversation we speak in complete sentences unless we are answering a question or adding information to something we say or somebody else says. To say that a sentence is complete is only to say that it makes a comprehensible statement, that it makes sense. If we did not use complete sentences, we could not be comprehensible in either our talking or our writing.

Most sentences make sense by naming a subject and by making a statement about it.

My son is asleep upstairs.

Here the writer names a subject, "My son," and makes a statement about it: "is asleep upstairs." The completed statement is called a *predicate* to the subject; a predicate is any affirmation or statement made about something else (the subject) in the sentence.

Once you form a basic statement, clauses, phrases, and other modifiers may amplify it, just as harmonies amplify the theme of a melody. The statement itself is primary. Sentences often go wrong because the writers lose track of the statement they want the sentence to make. To reduce the confusion, name your subject and make a statement about it. Once you have arrived at your basic statement, you can better weave clauses, phrases, and other modifiers around it.

Sentences like this one may turn up in the first drafts of most writers:

Since the Japanese, a people whose artistic care for the common things of daily life has always excited Americans, live crowded together on their small islands, they have been forced to construct social customs to help them endure living so close together, which are the basis for much of their art, including their love of miniaturization.

The sentence loses us. In the second draft the writer should decide on the main statement of the sentence. It would probably be something like this:

The Japanese have made art from the necessity of living close together in their crowded islands.

Once we have arrived at the basic statement, we can do several things with it. We can add some elements:

The Japanese have made art out of the necessity of living close to-gether on their crowded islands—an art that includes social customs and miniaturization.

We can also break our thoughts into several sentences, expanding some of them:

The Japanese have made art out of the necessity of living together on their crowded islands. Part of that art has been their social customs that provide careful ritual forms for daily life. Another has been their fondness for miniaturization. Americans have always been fascinated by Japanese art—probably because its dedication to the small is oppo-site to their own taste for the grandeur of the huge.

Know the main statement in your sentences. In writing each sentence, try to have the core statement in mind before you start. Take a breath, form the main idea in your head, and only then start to write. As you write, you may wish to add elements. That will be no problem if you know what the main statement of the sentence will be. You will not get lost. Too many of my students appear to start sentences in the mood of a motorcycle rider who leaps onto his machine at night and, without turning on the lights, roars off into the dark, hoping that the gods of the road will help him get somewhere. Some of my students appear to start sentences without having any idea where they will end up.

Think for a moment what you want to say. What is happening? Who is acting? Who or what receives the action? Don't confuse read-ers by packing too many important details in a single sentence. But don't condense things so much that you leave out information re-quired to complete your thought.

English sentences make three kinds of statements. A sentence may tell us that the subject does (or did or will do) something:

Thick clouds passed over the sun.

In this sentence the subject of the sentence is the word *clouds*. The clouds did what? They acted. They passed over the sun.

A sentence may describe a condition. It may tell the state of the subject's existence.

> The mountains were dark and mysterious.

In what condition did the mountains exist? They existed in a condition that was "dark and mysterious." Sentences describing conditions use a *linking verb* to tell what that condition is. The most common linking verb is some form of the verb *to be*. If we say, "She is tall," we describe her condition or some quality of her existence, and we link the subject *she* with the adjective *tall* by using the linking verb *is*, a form of the verb *to be*.

A sentence may describe an action done to the subject.

> We were suddenly soaked by the rain.

Here the subject is *we*, and the action of being soaked is done to that subject. When action is done to the subject, we say that the verb in the sentence is in the *passive voice*. To be passive is to be still or accepting while someone else acts. In thinking of the passive voice, it may be helpful to imagine the subject as being still or at least not responsible for whatever is done to it. The subject does not act through the verb; the subject is acted upon.

With these fundamental principles in mind, let's turn to some more general principles of sentence style. The balance of this chapter focuses on guidelines for writing good sentences.

Writing Good Sentences

1. Use the active voice.

The strongest sentences are those in which the subject does something. The verb tells what the subject does. Although the passive voice is a good and necessary part of the English language, it will deaden your style if you use it too much.

We seldom use the passive voice when we speak. We don't say, "Jack's car was driven into the reservoir Saturday night"; we say, "Jack drove his car into the reservoir Saturday night." We want to know agents. Who did it? The passive voice does not answer that question.

Bureaucratic publications often use passive constructions to evade responsibility.

> An oversupply of ten thousand blackboard erasers was ordered for the city school system.

This sentence tells us that the city schools now have enough erasers to last a hundred years. But who ordered them? The passive voice permits the writer to avoid saying that the brother of the school superintendent was in the school supply business and nearly bankrupt and that the superintendent helped him out by placing a big order. Use of the passive form of the verb—*was ordered*—assigns no responsibility; it makes the affair sound like a misprint on somebody's computer.

Inexperienced writers may use the passive voice because they think it sounds impressive. But the passive often sounds impersonal, voiceless.

> Minor characters in Shakespeare's plays have often been studied.
> The book was recommended as a good one.
> A good time was enjoyed.

Who studied the minor characters? Who recommended the book? Who enjoyed the good time? We want to know. Yes, you can add a prepositional phrase to provide the agent—"The book was recommended as a good one by Professor Greasy"—but it is better to be simple and direct: "Professor Greasy recommended the book."

Use the passive voice when the recipient of the action is more important to you than the actor is.

> Hoover was elected in 1928.
> My Uncle Mike was hit by a bicycle as he left the saloon on Saturday night.
> The Mona Lisa was once stolen from the Louvre.

A writer may use the passive voice in paragraphs that make a series of statements about a subject. The writer may wish to keep attention fixed on one spot. To do so, he may use the passive voice, as Robert Caro does in this paragraph from his biography of Lyndon Johnson. Caro describes Johnson's first congressional campaign in Texas:

> The speeches *were* generally *delivered* on Saturday: traditionally, rural campaigning in Texas *was* largely *restricted* to Saturdays, the day on which farmers and their wives came into town to shop, and *could be addressed* in groups. On Saturdays two automobiles, Johnson's brown Pontiac and Bill Deason's wired-for-sound gray Chevy, would head out of Austin for a swing through several large towns. On the outskirts of each town, Johnson would get out of the Pontiac ("He thought it looked a little too elaborate for a man running for Congress," Keach says) and walk into the town, while the Chevy would pull into the square, and Deason or some other aide would use the loudspeaker to urge voters to "Come see Lyndon Johnson, your next Congressman," and to "Come

hear Lyndon Johnson speak at the square"; to drum up enthusiasm, records *would be played* over the loudspeaker.[1]

The passive verb phrases—italicized in this paragraph—allow Caro to keep his focus. Now and then, as in the first sentence, he might have changed to the active voice—"Johnson generally delivered these speeches on Saturdays"—but Caro probably supposed he was repeating Johnson's name too often in his large book and shifted here to the passive form of the verbs to give readers some relief.

Use the active form of a verb whenever you can. When you do use the passive form, have a reason for doing so.

2. Make most of your verbs assert action rather than tell a condition.
You can say this:

> It would seem that voters in Massachusetts are in favor of capital punishment, at least for convicted murderers, given the results of yesterday's referendum on the subject.

Or you can say this:

> In yesterday's referendum, Massachusetts voters approved capital punishment for convicted murderers by almost two to one.

Stating the action gives you a more vivid sentence. It also usually helps you make a statement in fewer words.

Don't use too many *to be* verbs. Change them to more active verbs instead. You can say this:

> Most Americans *are* believers in capital punishment.

But it is more vivid to say this:

> Most Americans believe in capital punishment.

You can say this:

> Many Americans *are* of the opinion that foreign cars *are* more durable than American cars.

But it is more vivid to say this:

> Many Americans *think* foreign cars *last* longer than American cars.

Occasionally check your use of *to be* verbs—*is, am, are, was, were*—by circling them on a page. If you have many of them, you will see a lot of circles, and you can revise. Don't be a fanatic about changing them; *to be* verbs are part of the language, and you must use them sometimes. But too many of them will dull your prose.

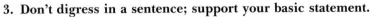

3. Don't digress in a sentence; support your basic statement.

Everything in your sentence should support your basic statement. Sometimes inexperienced writers throw needless information into a sentence to show how much they know or because the information is interesting.

> Napoleon Bonaparte, who some people now think may have been poisoned when he was in exile on St. Helena Island, invaded Russia on June 21, 1812.

The basic statement is this: "Napoleon Bonaparte invaded Russia on June 21, 1812." What does a story about his death much later on have to do with the invasion? Nothing. So we must cut it out.

4. Combine thoughts to eliminate choppy sentences.

We usually apply the criticism *choppy* to a string of short sentences, but choppiness does not reside in the shortness alone. Choppiness refers to the inability of a writer to subordinate minor thoughts to major thoughts and to a needless and monotonous repetition of the same sentence forms. Choppiness may also result from a seeming lack of connection between the sentences. We read a paragraph like this with increasing annoyance:

> We biked steadily up hill. We biked along the river. We were silent now. We were too tired to talk. The ridges above us were covered with trees. Most of them were conifers. They were dark green. They gave a tinge of melancholy to the day. A wind blew. It was soft. It whispered in the trees. Below us the river splashed over the rocks. It was in the valley floor. We heard the two sounds distinctly. The wind in the trees. The river splashing over the rocks. And our own breathing. It was ragged and hard. That was a third sound. A fourth sound was the whisper of the bike tires on the road. The road was asphalt. That sound was scarcely audible.

Writing such sentence in a first draft may not be a bad idea. Setting down these impressions in order helps you pull memories together. But in revising, you can combine and subordinate some thoughts to others.

> We biked steadily up hill along the river. We were silent now, too tired to talk. Above us the ridges were covered with conifers, dark green, giving a tinge of melancholy to the day, and a wind blew, whispering in the trees. Below us the river splashed over the rocks in the valley floor, and we heard the two sounds and a third sound—the sound of our own breathing, ragged and hard. A fourth sound, scarcely audible, was the whisper of the bike tires on the asphalt road.

Combining sentences can greatly improve the flow of a paragraph. Study your sentences to see what you can compress and combine.

I have written of the necessary bonding of sentences by a pattern of repetition from one sentence to the next. But you should avoid *unnecessary* repetition that slows the pace of your prose. Don't make readers ask themselves why you are telling them something you have told them before. Repeat only enough to make transitions from your earlier thoughts in the essay.

5. Avoid a proliferation of dependent clauses in a single sentence.

Dependent clauses help us write with a mature style. All good writers use them to amplify thoughts in a sentence.

> *After he had done all his Christmas shopping for the many people who expected presents from him*, he bought a large gift for himself, wrapped it up in gaudy paper with a bright holiday ribbon, put it under the tree, and told visitors *that it was from his best friend*.

The italicized words in this sentence represent three dependent clauses. The first, beginning with *After*, is an adverbial clause modifying the verbs *bought*, *put*, and *told* in the independent clause. That adverbial clause includes an adjectival clause, *who expected presents from him*, modifying the noun *people*. The final dependent clause, *that it was from his best friend*, is a noun clause, the direct object of the verb *told*. This sentence has one example each of the three general classes of dependent clause—adverbial, adjectival, and noun. Every dependent clause serves as an adverb, an adjective, or a noun in another clause. An independent clause can usually stand by itself as a sentence.

Too many dependent clauses clutter your thought, weakening the force of the basic statements. Be aware of them, and avoid the temptation to stuff too many into a single sentence. The lean style now most popular in America keeps dependent clauses to a minimum.

One dependent clause in a sentence rarely makes trouble. But don't put one in every sentence. When you put two dependent clauses in a sentence, a warning flag should go up in your mind. When you have three, the flag should start waving back and forth, and you should reexamine the sentence to try to simplify it. Now and then three dependent clauses will be just right in a sentence. But don't write too many such sentences. The cumulative effect will be devastating.

This sentence gives no trouble:

> Americans eagerly collect pennies, although the value of the penny is sometimes less than the copper that goes into making it.

This one begins to lose its focus:

> Americans, who sometimes show a mania for collecting, eagerly collect pennies, although the value of the penny is sometimes less than the copper that goes into making it.

This one gets out of hand.

> Americans, who sometimes show a mania for collecting, a hobby which may be part of our materialistic culture, eagerly collect pennies, although the value of the penny, which is used largely as an advertising gimmick as in the price $4.99 instead of $5.00, is sometimes less than the copper that goes into it.

In the rush of doing a first draft, you may write many over-crowded sentences. When you revise, pull out distracting dependent clauses. Make them into sentences of their own, or eliminate them altogether.

Like the other principles put forth in this book, this one is observed with wide variations among writers. Weekly news magazines use dependent clauses sparingly, substituting for them modifying phrases. We can analyze this style by looking at a paragraph from a *Time* story about science fiction writer Isaac Asimov. I have inserted numbers before each sentence (or independent clause, if the sentence is compound):

> [1]By performing this alchemy for four decades, Isaac Asimov has become an oracle, particularly in the world of science. [2]These are, after all, the Years When the Earth Talked Back, [3]and long before the politicians, he was listening. [4]Today readers search works like *The Intelligent Man's Guide to Science* and *Today and Tomorrow and . . .* for advice on space programs and the greenhouse effect. [5]Many of them go directly to the source with their questions. [6]If Asimov has respect for the interrogators, he answers thoughtfully, in detail. [7]If not, he has a habit of assuming an abstracted, extraterrestrial manner, as if he had a lunch date on the other side of time.[2]

We find no dependent clause in 1; one in 2; none in 3; none in 4; none in 5; one in 6; one in 7. In seven independent clauses, we have three dependent clauses. In no independent clause is there more than one dependent clause. The most readable writers train themselves to use dependent clauses sparingly. Make your own tests. Calculate the ratio of dependent clauses to independent clauses in publications such as *The Reader's Digest* and *Scientific American*.

Don't be fanatical about cutting out dependent clauses. Some material requires them. But reduce them when you can.

You can often change a dependent clause into a modifying phrase. Clauses beginning with *who, which, that,* and *what* can often be reduced to phrases. Sometimes the desire to revise such constructions will make you change the wording of your original sentence.

Don't write this:

> The island, which had appeared as a spot on the horizon earlier, now broadened into a large land mass which had palm trees waving over a long, white beach.

Write this instead:

> The island, only a spot on the horizon earlier, now broadened into a large land mass with palm trees waving over a long, white beach.

Don't write this:

> Our captain, who was an arrogant young man who spoke to us as if he had been an old sea dog and we had been ignorant children, pointed at the shadowy blue rocks which lay beneath the surface of the sea.

Write this instead:

> Our captain, an arrogant young man, spoke to use like an old sea dog instructing ignorant children, and pointed out the shadowy blue rocks lying beneath the surface of the sea.

Don't write this:

> What is important about the test is its measurement of how quickly students can respond to the questions it asks.

Write this instead:

> The importance of the test is its measurement of the quickness of student response.

6. Begin most sentences with the subject.

The normal pattern for sentences is *subject* + *predicate*. Experienced writers follow this pattern. Look through a copy of almost any book or magazine, and you will discover that two-thirds to four-fifths of the sentences begin with the subject. Here is a paragraph from Stephen Jay Gould's "The Criminal as Nature's Mistake." Every sentence begins with a subject.

> Biological theories of criminality were scarcely new, but Lombroso gave the argument a novel, evolutionary twist. Born criminals are not simply deranged or diseased; they are, literally, throwbacks to a previous evolutionary stage. The hereditary characters of our primitive and apish ancestors remain in our genetic repertoire. Some unfortunate men are born with an unusually large number of these ancestral characters. Their

behavior may have been appropriate in savage societies of the past; today, we brand it as criminal. We may pity the born criminal, for he cannot help himself; but we cannot tolerate his actions. (Lombroso believed that about 40 percent of criminals fell into this category of innate biology—born criminals. Others committed misdeeds from greed, jealousy, extreme anger, and so on—criminals of occasion.)[3]

Here is a paragraph from Barbara Tuchman recalling how she wrote her book *The Guns of August* about the first month of World War I in 1914:

> I do not invent anything, even the weather. One of my readers told me he particularly liked a passage in *The Guns* which tells how the British Army landed in France and how on that afternoon there was a sound of summer thunder in the air and the sun went down in a blood-red glow. He thought it an artistic touch of doom, but the fact was it was true. I found it in the memoirs of a British officer who landed on that day and heard the thunder and saw the blood-red sunset. The art, if any, consisted only in selecting it and ultimately using it in the right place.[4]

Again you will note that every sentence begins with the subject. That is the most natural way to write. As we shall see, a writer does not begin *every* sentence with the subject. But if not the subject, what?

7. When you do not begin with the subject, usually begin with some form of adverb—a word, a phrase, or a clause.

About a fourth of published sentences begin with some form of adverb—a single word, a phrase, or a clause. Sentence-opening adverbs almost always modify the verb in the main clause. Adverbs answer the questions *where* and *when* and sometimes *how, how often*, and *how much*.

> *There* is a spider, too, in the bathroom, with whom I keep a sort of company.[5]
>
> *In the beginning* it did not rise very quickly.[6]
>
> *When I was eighteen or thereabouts*, my mother told me that when out with a young man I should always leave a half-hour before I wanted to.[7]

8. Usually avoid participial sentence openers.

A participial opener uses a participle as an adjective to modify the subject of the sentence. Professional writers sometimes use participial openers to compress information:

> *Peeping through my keyhole* I see within the range of only about thirty percent of the light that comes from the sun.[8]

A participial opener may let a writer invert a sentence, putting the subject after the verb, to obtain a pleasing variety.

Standing uninvolved for the moment but nevertheless carefully observing these practices was the young Providence pitcher Monte Ward, who, before his time was out, would do much to revolutionize the whole player-owner relationship.[9]

Even though these uses are valid, any study of professional writing will reveal that participial openers are rare. Such openers violate the general rule that a readable written sentence follows the common patterns of speech. We rarely use participial openers in spoken sentences. We don't say, "Having been out in the cold wind all day, I'm nearly dead." We say something like this: "I've been out in the cold wind all day, and I'm nearly dead."

Participial openers must modify the grammatical subject; otherwise we get confusing sentences like this one:

> Buried under a pile of dust for forty years, he found all the records intact.

(Was *he* buried under a pile of dust for forty years? Or were the records?)

This sentence with a confusing participial opener was immortalized in a collection of newspaper gaffes collected from the nation's press by the *Columbia Journalism Review*:

> Bound, gagged and trussed up nude in a denim bag, with plugs in her ears and tape over her eyes, Cleveland teacher Linda L. Sharpe told yesterday how she was kidnapped to Florida, not knowing where she was going or why.

(Was she in this miserable condition while she told of how she was kidnapped to Florida?)

A participle may dangle, seeming to modify nothing, as in this sentence:

> Flying every week between Boston and New York, it was hard for her to maintain her fear of airplanes.

(Was a mysterious *it* flying between Boston and New York every week?)

The rule is this: Use participial openings sparingly. If you do use them, be sure they modify a concrete grammatical subject.

9. In general, avoid beginning sentences with *there.*

Now and then all of us begin a sentence with *there is, there are, there were,* or *there was.* We should not do so without second thoughts. *There* can sometimes make us substitute vague description for action. Don't say this:

> There were several reasons he refused to smoke.

Say rather this:

> He refused to smoke because he feared cancer, his wife and children hated the smell, and he once set fire to his bed with a cigar.

Avoid the indefinite *it is* for the same reason that you avoid *there*. We can say this:

> It is common for people who tan every summer to get skin cancer.

But this is stronger:

> Skin cancer is common among people who tan every summer.

Now and then we all use *it is*, just as we all use *there*, but try to minimize such usage so that your prose will be more vigorous.

10. Be economical with adjectives.

Adjectives add qualities to nouns and pronouns. Don't try to do without them, but use them only when they are necessary. Too many adjectives clog prose and weaken sentences.

Here are paragraphs from two writers. See how few adjectives they use. See how the basic statements stand out sharp and clear:

> The color of an orange has no *absolute* correlation with the maturity of the flesh and juice *inside*. An orange can be as *sweet* and *ripe* as it will ever be and still glisten like an emerald in the tree. Cold—coldness, rather—is what makes an orange *orange*. In *some* parts of the world, the weather never gets *cold* enough to change the color; in Thailand, for example, an orange is a *green* fruit, and *traveling* Thais often blink with wonder at the sight of oranges the color of flame. The *ideal nighttime* temperature in an *orange* grove is *forty* degrees. Some of the most *beautiful* oranges in the world are grown in Bermuda, where the temperature, night after night, falls consistently to that level.[10]

The author of this passage, John McPhee, uses fourteen adjectives in this paragraph of 127 words—about one adjective in every nine words. By my count that is high compared to most writers. Even so, the adjectives do not intrude.

Here is Philip Caputo, writing about the Vietnam War:

> They had been together for years and assumed they would remain together until the end of their enlistments. Sergeant Sullivan's death shattered that assumption. It upset the sense of unity and stability that had pervaded life in the battalion. One-Three was a corps in the *old* sense of the word, a body, and Sullivan's death represented the amputation of a *small* part of it. The corps would go on living and functioning without him, but it was *aware* of having lost something *irreplaceable*. Later in the war, that sort of feeling became *rarer* in *infantry* battalions. Men were killed, evacuated with wounds, or rotated home at a *constant* rate, then

replaced by *other* men who were killed, evacuated, or rotated in their turn. By that time, a loss only meant a gap in the line that needed filling.[11]

In this passage of 140 words, we count only eight adjectives or a proportion of about one adjective to every 17.5 words. If any single quality marks the style of those counted as good writers in America today, it is probably stinginess in the use of adjectives.

11. Don't use nouns as adjectives.

Much official language from bureaucracies groans under the tyranny of nouns pretending to be adjectives. Proper nouns can sometimes serve as adjectives. You can talk about the *Gettysburg* Address, the *Marshall* Plan, or the *Bowery* Bank. Some words have the same form whether they are nouns or adjectives—*volunteer, deputy, savage, poor*, and many others. But most common nouns, especially those ending in *tion, sion, ism*, and *ness*, seldom work well as adjectives.

A careful writer will avoid constructions like the following:

They worked hard in skills acquisitions.

She was expert in writing improvement practices.

He was a jaded secretary retraining expert.

The reporters learned scrutiny thoroughness.

A careful writer would revise:

They worked hard to acquire skills.

She was an expert at improving writing.

He helped retrain secretaries who had become jaded at their work.

The reporters learned to be thorough.

Writers may use nouns as adjectives in a mistaken effort to make their writing seem more important. Instead such usage makes prose stiff and ugly. Here again normal speech patterns offer a standard. We don't say, "We want to implement these quality control procedures in automobile manufacturing." That's a mouthful. We say something like this: "We want to set up some procedures to control quality in making cars." As writers we should follow the natural inclinations of the spoken language.

12. For sentence variety, occasionally use free modifiers and absolutes.

A free modifier is a participial phrase placed at the end of a sentence but modifying the subject. Free modifiers may replace dependent clauses. I have placed the free modifiers in these sentences in italics:

She sprinted up the street, *racing for the bus*.

The house collapsed, *shattered by the earthquake*.

"Here is man as microcosm, *representing in all his parts the earth, perhaps the universe*."[12]

Sometimes you can place several free modifiers at the end of a sentence, all of them modifying the subject, providing a sense of vigorous action. Here is a paragraph from Bruce Catton's book *The Coming Fury*. I have italicized the free modifiers. Catton describes the preparations to defend Fort Sumter in Charleston harbor at the start of the Civil War:

> The soldiers had not yet been called into action, but they were busy, and the materials to force a decision were piling up—in Fort Sumter, and on the mud flats that surrounded it in Charleston harbor. Major Anderson was doing what he could to perfect his defenses, *mounting additional guns on the barbette, making his walls more solid by bricking up embrasures that could not be manned, removing stone flagging from the parade ground so that shells that might be thrown into the fort would bury themselves in the sand before exploding*.[13]

The participles "mounting," making," and "removing" introduce free modifiers, all modifying the subject "Major Anderson." The three phrases —a couple containing clauses embedded within them—provide a sense of simultaneous action, showing a busy commander protecting his post.

Free modifiers may also carry a sense of progression, showing one thing happening after another, leading to a climax:

> Slowly she inched her way up the face of the cliff, *feeling* for holds in the rock, *moving* with infinite care, *balancing* herself delicately step after step, not *daring* to look down, *breathing* hard, *fearing* exhaustion, *going* on, *wallowing* at last onto a shelf of rock and safety at the top.

You can extend a series of free modifiers almost indefinitely because each modifies the same thing—in the preceding example, the pronoun *she*. Memorize the form—participle followed by a phrase, all modifying the subject.

Some free modifying phrases imply the participle *being*:

> He looked around, uncertain, frightened, and lonely.

You understand in this sentence that *he* was uncertain, frightened, and lonely and your mind fills in a participle:

> He looked around, [being] uncertain, frightened, and lonely.

Absolutes share many qualities and stylistic advantages of free modifiers. Whereas a free modifier is a participle introducing a phrase modifying the subject, an absolute is a noun followed by a phrase that modifies the whole clause in which the absolute appears.

> Robinson made a miracle stop behind third, *his throw beating Mays to first by a step.*

The absolute compresses action. Another writer might have done this:

> Robinson made a miracle stop behind third. His throw beat Mays to first by a step.

The use of the absolute turns two choppy sentences into a vigorous one. Absolutes express action well, making them useful in both non-fiction and fiction.

> Then she fled beneath his fist, and he too fled backward as the others fell upon him, swarming, grappling, fumbling, *he striking back, his breath hissing with rage and despair.*[14]

In this example William Faulkner uses both absolutes and free modifiers, providing a sense of swift, violent action.

13. Use compound verb phrases for variety.

Compound verbs compress action and quicken the pace of prose. The triple compound verb setup—a single subject controlling three verbs—has become common in the modern English and American style:

> From 1600 on, when modern warfare developed in Europe, the German states (even with the rise of Prussia) *spent* fewer years at war than any other nations except Denmark and Sweden, *engaged* in fewer battles, and *suffered* fewer casualties.[15]

> To signify his right to punish, the Prince twice rejected a good price offered by towns to buy immunity from sack. His letters express only a sense of satisfied accomplishment. His raid *had enriched* his company, *reduced* French revenues, and *proved* to any wavering Gascons that service under his banner was rewarding.[16]

> The attack on the Fascist redoubt which had been called off on the previous occasion was to be carried out tonight. I *oiled* my ten Mexican cartridges, *dirtied* my bayonet (the things give your position away if they flash too much), and *packed* up a hunk of bread, three inches of red sausage, and a cigar which my wife had sent from Barcelona and which I had been hoarding for a long time.[17]

The third example, from English writer George Orwell, points to another quality in modern English style—the fondness for triads, or groups of threes. Note that he not only uses a triple compound verb but also a triple direct object at the end—*hunk of bread, three inches of red sausage, and a cigar.*

Triads are everywhere in modern style.

> I assume that a diet high in *calories, cholesterol and cognac* would eventually do me in.[18]

> So Allen Ginsberg was speaking now to them. The police looking through the plexiglass face shields they had flipped down from their helmets were then obliged to watch the poet with *his bald head, soft eyes* magnified by horn-rimmed eyeglasses, *and massive dark beard,* utter his words in a croaking speech.[19]

Our fondness for triads is so great that sometimes we make them when they are not there. When Winston Churchill became Prime Minister of Great Britain in May, 1940, when Germany seemed about to win World War II, he told his people, "I have nothing to offer but blood, toil, tears and sweat." But in popular memory his noble phrase has been transformed into "blood, sweat, and tears."

Triads are a vital part of our style now; you should use them to enliven your prose, and, like Churchill, you should sometimes surprise by using four elements instead of three. Tom Wolfe, writing here about Las Vegas, pulls off a foursome in a compound verb:

> But most of these old babes are part of the permanent landscape of Las Vegas. In they go to the Golden Nugget or the Mint, with their Social Security check or their pension check from the Ohio telephone company, *cash* it at the casino cashier's, *pull* out the Dixie Cup and the Iron Boy work glove, *disappear* down a row of slots and *get* on with it.[20]

14. Use appositives to speed the pace of your sentences.

An appositive is a word or phrase written after a noun to rename or otherwise define the noun. The simplest appositives are single nouns:

> His car, a *Chevy*, was not as fast as mine, a *Buick*.

Sometimes an appositive may be a long phrase:

> An age of faith is almost certain to become an age of quarrels among the faithful. They divided into bitterly hostile sects, *each with his own leader and each hoping for support from one group or another among the infidels.*[21]

The appositive may be a phrase or several phrases set off by dashes:

> Everything—the operating room, the morgue, the emergency room, the patients, professors, even the nurses—was terrifying.[22]

Or it may be a clause set off by dashes:

> Napoleon said, "The best troops—*those in whom you can have the most confidence*—are the Swiss.[23]

You can often revise dependent clauses into appositives and so speed up the pace of your prose. Look carefully at clauses that begin with *who, that,* or *which*.

> Abraham Lincoln, *who was born in 1809*, moved around as a boy and never developed a great attachment to any one state.

Revised to an appositive:

> Abraham Lincoln, *born in 1809*, moved around as a boy and never developed a great attachment to any one state.

15. When you must write long sentences, balance them with short sentences to give readers some relief.

Readers search for the basic statement every sentence should make. The longer the sentence, the more difficult it is to find the basic statement. We can all understand this sentence, although it is fairly long:

> Although the rain fell hard enough to strip the leaves from the trees, leaving the air thick with the smell of shattered foliage, the drought had been so severe that we still needed water after the storm had passed on up the valley and the rain had stopped.

Several sentences of such length running together on a page would make us slow down to absorb them. Since readers read at a constant pace, they will likely keep their eyes moving whether they understand the sentences or not. They tend to skip over what they don't understand. When you write one long sentence after another, you do not communicate well. After a long sentence such as the one above, a short one is in order:

> An inch below the surface, the ground was dry.

No one can make an ironclad rule about the length of sentences. For obvious reasons, short sentences are more readable than long ones, but no one wants to write like the old Dick-and-Jane readers. Our language is an almost infinitely complex pattern of different sounds that make sense because we give meanings to the differences. A cat is not the same as a bat or a hat or a gnat. For reasons beyond the power of a mere writer to explain, we take pleasure in the differences between words, finding satisfaction in creating or hearing variety in language. This quality seems to be built into the human mind. Not only do we seek variety in our words, but we look for it in sentences, both in their structure and their length. We don't want all sentences to be alike. We do not want them all to be the same length; we do not want them all to have the same structure. Good writers aim at clarity but at more than clarity: they try to give pleasure. Part of that pleasure is to construct sentences of different lengths that fit together *naturally.* At least we think such sentences are natural when we read or hear them; we absorb them with ease and sometimes with delight.

All this is to say that a steady progression of short, clear sentences might convey the writer's meaning but crush readers with boredom because such sentences do not satisfy the craving of the mind for variety in language. Somehow as writers we must find the golden mean between a clarity that sounds childish and a complexity that is beyond comprehension.

Concluding Remarks on Sentences

You can teach yourself to write good sentences by paying attention to how professional writers make them. When you read something you enjoy, study the sentences. Look at structure. Try to incorporate into your own writing some of the stylistic devices you see in things you like to read. Remember that the main job of the sentence is to make a comprehensible statement. You can write foggy sentences in your first draft, but let the light shine in your later drafts. Ask yourself this question: "What is the most important thing I have to say in this sentence?" Be sure you answer that question clearly in one statement. That statement should form the core of the sentence.

Seven

Avoiding Wordiness

Writing should be efficient. That is, you should use only enough words to express the meaning you wish to convey. Readers do not have time for wordiness; besides, wordiness confuses them and blunts the effect of your writing.

Brevity does not mean mindless simplicity. You must use enough words to express your meaning. Otherwise, your brevity will be confusing. Give readers enough information to let them understand you. Don't assume they know more than they do.

Being brief does not mean cutting the drama out of your prose. It does mean that you eliminate words that do not convey the effect you want to convey. As you write and revise, you rethink your purposes. Make your style conform to those purposes. Achieve them as efficiently as possible.

Identifying and Revising Wordiness

Revise everything you write. See your sentences as puzzles; the object of writing is to make every sentence as efficient as possible. When you have developed the habit of revision, you will habitually revise sentences like this one, typical of a first draft:

> It may be concluded from his many angry interviews with representatives with the media that Red Sox pitching ace young Roger Clemens showed himself to be an unhappy millionaire.

You can turn the sentence into something like this:

> In angry interviews Red Sox pitcher Roger Clemens showed he was an unhappy millionaire.

We can conclude without announcing that we are concluding. We don't have to say that the angry interviews were with representatives of the media. Most baseball pitchers are young; we don't have to state the obvious. Think through your sentences. Avoid the temptation to provide needless information ("young") or to use clumsy phrases ("It may be concluded that. . . . "). Simplify.

Turn clauses into phrases when you can, especially clauses beginning with *who, whom, which*, and *that*. You don't have to say, "Ralph, who was my best friend, advised me to submit the book to a publisher." Say this instead, "Ralph, my best friend, advised me to submit the book to a publisher." Sometimes you can reorganize sentences to turn a clause into an adjective. Don't say this: "The Pharaoh who ruled Egypt at the time of the Exodus was almost certainly Rameses II." Say this instead: "The Egyptian Pharaoh at the time of the Exodus was almost certainly Rameses II."

The passive voice creates wordiness. Don't say, "It must be recognized." Say instead, "We must recognize." Don't say, "It is not to be thought." Say, "We should not think." Don't say, "The car was repaired by my neighbor." Say, "My neighbor repaired the car." Don't say, "You will be reminded by this letter that your bill is three months overdue." Say, "Your bill is three months overdue."

Be natural. People who strain for effects may become wordy. We find an unnatural style in many institutional publications. Professor Richard Lanham of U.C.L.A. calls this wordy jargon "the official style." It seems to be everywhere. The main problem of the official style is that its authors have two motives that may contradict each other. On the one hand they want to communicate; on the other they want to seem impressive while they are doing it. The desire to be impressive may get in the way of the communication. Here is an example taken from a university job listing:

> Network Engineer. Office for Information Technology. Responsible for the planning, design, and implementation of communications networks carrying data, video and voice signals throughout the University. Evaluates the relative technical merits of alternative technologies and design approaches. Prepares initial system specifications and designs for proposed networks or subnetworks.

The author of this document intended to avoid ambiguity about the job but fell hard into the official style. Note the use of "impressive" words like *implementation* and *alternative*, and also note the use of nouns like *information* and *design* as adjectives. Professional writers don't *implement* things; they *do* them. They don't talk about *alternative* technologies; they speak of *various* technologies or of technologies.

And they don't use *relative* unless they are talking about kin. Could the listing be translated into something like this?

> Network engineer wanted to design and install communications lines throughout the University. Should know modern technology and design.

But suppose we keep all the elaborate qualifications of the original. We could still write a simpler, less wordy announcement.

> Network engineer. Responsible for designing and installing communications networks for data, video, and voice signals throughout the University. Evaluates the merits of various technologies and designs. Prepares specifications for systems and designs for networks.

The official style arises from fear. Writers are afraid someone may blame them for something. They try to be careful, extra careful—and so they become like trapeze artists afraid of falling and thinking only of their feet. Users of the official style try to explain everything, to qualify every statement, to leave no possible room for misunderstanding, but in the effort to avoid every ambiguity, they create almost unreadable prose. They are moved by fear that readers will not take them seriously if they write naturally; they may also fear that what they have to say is not worth saying but that if they put it in complicated language, others may think it is profound.

Here are a few sentences from a carefully researched article in a recent issue of *American Sociological Review,* a professional journal aimed at sociologists. The authors investigated the craze of streaking that beset many college campuses in the early 1970s. (Students ran naked through the streets and sometimes across football fields during games.) Why did people streak? The question could be of general interest, and the article is an intelligent work by two intelligent men. But it is hard to imagine that many people understand prose written like this:

> The greater the complexity and heterogeneity of previous streaking events, the greater the probability that schools will adopt the fad. The innovation is more likely to be adopted when the complexity of the previous incidents of the fad in neighboring schools is greater. The complexity of streaking incidents is a stimulus for potential adopters. For example, if many males and females, students and non-students, streaked repeatedly day and night, on and off campus, then many categories of persons in other nearby schools could identify with the faddish behavior. As a result, the events are no longer performed by the rowdy but become acceptable to many potential adopters.[1]

I don't think an ordinary person can grasp the meaning of this text without wrestling with it; perhaps a reader must work through the whole article, as I have done, before any of it becomes comprehensible. I think the passage means something like this:

> The more people streaked, the more others were likely to streak—especially if streaking incidents were elaborate and highly publicized. If multitudes of students and non-students streaked day and night in a given school, the behavior would not be limited to the rowdy, but many different kinds of students would streak in a neighboring school.

Why do the authors of articles in the *American Sociological Review* write like this? The question deserves some thoughtful reflection. The *New England Journal of Medicine* treats complicated medical issues in readable and widely read prose; so does *Scientific American*. Why must the *American Sociological Review* be unreadable? A major reason is that the journal itself (like streaking) feeds on habits that it has created. Several graduate students in sociology have told me they must write in this overblown style to be respected in the field. One can pick up any copy of the journal and riffle the pages and find articles written in this well-nigh incomprehensible prose. Any budding sociologist may be forgiven if she supposes that she must make her writing as turgid as possible to make it acceptable to the editors of the review.

But then we must ask why any writers should choose this unnatural style. They appear to try to avoid any ambiguity—an almost impossible burden for prose to bear. No writing except the densest kind of legal prose can be entirely without ambiguity. Take this sentence as an example: "The greater the complexity and heterogeneity of previous streaking events, the greater the probability that schools will adopt the fad." Why both "complexity" and "heterogeneity"? Evidently the authors feared that we might suppose that complex events were not heterogeneous events. Some process like this must have gone on in their minds: "If we say, 'the more people streak, the more others are likely to streak,' we might not convey our feeling that the more *diverse* people streak, the more others are likely to follow their example." Taking this fear of misunderstanding into account, they spell out some of the diversity—males and females, students and non-students, streaking on and off campus. Later they speak of "many categories of persons" because they seem to think that if they said "many people," we might not understand that they meant many *different* people. The authorial mind at work here is like a lawyer's, resolved to write a will that no one can break. The authors do not trust their readers. In seeking to avoid every ambiguity, they write in unreadable prose.

Perhaps, too, they feel insecure with their own discipline. Sociologists long to be considered as "scientific" as physicists and mathematicians, and they suppose that no true scientist writes clearly. They surmise that pedantic language indicates profound thought. One consequence is that they limit their articles to members of a closed circle of sociologists who write to one another without trying to reach a more general audience. The discipline of sociology might seem to betray in such prose a gnawing lack of self-confidence, and that is a loss to all of us who might find such scholarship interesting and influential—as, for example, the great sociological work of David Riesman, Nathan Glazer, and Ruel Denney proved to be in *The Lonely Crowd* and the work of Norbert Elias proved to be in *Power and Civility*.

Always remember that good writing arises out of confidence. If you are confident that you have something to say, you can say it simply. Or at least you can say it as simply as possible given your purposes. If you have studied an issue and had thoughts of your own about it, and resolve to make sense of those thoughts by writing about them, you can be confident in yourself and your readers. Confidence helps build a sound style—one that uses no more words than necessary and that uses the simplest words possible to express the meaning you intend.

No one idea about brevity can suit everyone, and there are no easy shortcuts to a brief style. You can pick up the habit of brevity only if you go over your drafts again and again. Read everything you write two or three times before you let it go. I have mentioned that my style of revising used to be to type the same page again and again until it came out right. Typing it all over again made every word come through my fingers and my brain in a satisfying way. It made me see everything anew. Now I read the computer screen again and again, inserting and deleting as I go. Most writers read a typed or printed manuscript, pencil in hand, making corrections as they read.

Whatever you do, reread your work. Read slowly but steadily. Give yourself time enough to think through every sentence, every word. Cut out the unnecessarily fancy words, the verbose phrases, the unnecessary modifiers. Combine sentences when you can unless the combination makes a long and clumsy sentence. Examine stock phrases to see if you can shorten them.

Stock phrases can often be eliminated. In a first draft you may write this:

> In the final analysis, the Japanese victory at Pearl Harbor may be regarded as a disaster for Japan.

Here we find the stock phrases "In the final analysis" and "may be regarded as." Revision can eliminate both:

> The Japanese victory at Pearl Harbor was a disaster for Japan.

You may write this in a first draft:

What was most important was Hamlet's decision to agree to fate.

But write this in a revision:

Most important was Hamlet's decision to agree to fate.

Don't be afraid to be wordy in your first draft when you are forming your thoughts. But afterward slash and burn. Cut out the unnecessary.

Common Problems of Wordiness

No chapter in a small book can solve all the problems of wordiness. But here I address a few common problems. As you study them, you may become sensitive to similar problems in your own style. Cutting the fat out of prose is a habit—like exercise for the body. Cultivate the habit; let it take control of your writing. Nobody is going to hang you if you use one of the expressions I have listed below, and many of them spring to the fingers of most of us sometimes when we are writing. Now and then you can indulge yourself in a "perfectly good word" or a "final analysis." But prose stuffed with redundancies and general wordiness becomes difficult or at least vaguely unpleasant for readers. The writer's job is to make readers as comfortable as possible in the act of reading. (The writer's job may also be to make them as uncomfortable as possible in *thinking* about an issue, but that's another matter.) Eliminating the following phrases will ease your reader's task.

When you eliminate or abbreviate writing, you must sometimes rearrange whole sentences. You cannot always be content merely to cut out an unnecessary word or two. Study the following examples.

Area/Region
Don't say, "The weather in the area of the Southwest is hot and dry." Say this instead: "The weather in the Southwest is hot and dry."

Aspect
Don't say, "Another aspect of the problem that should be considered is the feasibility of the project." Say this instead: "We should consider whether the project can be done."

At the present time/At this point in time/At that point in time
Eliminate these expressions. Use *now* or *then*, or let the present or past tense give the time you want.

Case/Cases

You can often eliminate these words. Don't say, "In this case we see Faulkner's use of an old woman as oracle." Say this instead: "Faulkner here uses an old woman as oracle." Don't say, "In some cases exercise can kill." Say this instead, "Sometimes exercise kills."

Certainly/Assuredly/Surely/Obviously

You can often eliminate these words. Paradoxically enough, we tend to use them when we realize that a statement may not be obvious or certain to someone else. If we draw an inference that we know may not be certain, we tag it with one of these words. Someone may write this: "He refused to let the police enter his house without a search warrant; obviously he had something to hide." The writer cannot prove that the person had something to hide; the writer tags an inference with the word *obviously*. But it is not obvious at all.

Character/Manner/Nature/Color/Stature

You can often eliminate these words. Don't say, "Their love affair was of a complex nature." Say instead, "Their love affair was complex." Don't say, "Mr. Dawson had an ingratiating manner." Say this instead: "Mr. Dawson was ingratiating."

Close proximity

Use *near* instead. Don't say, "The barn was in close proximity to the house." Say, "The barn was near the house."

Completely destroyed/Totally demolished

If something is destroyed, it is destroyed. If it is not completely destroyed, it is damaged. *Demolish* has an even stronger connotation than *destroyed*; so to say something is totally demolished is linguistic overkill.

Consensus of opinion

The word *consensus* implies opinion. Don't say, "The consensus of opinion in the group was that boxing is barbaric." Say this instead: "The consensus in the group was that boxing is barbaric."

Considering the fact that

Use *although* or *because* instead. Don't say, "Considering the fact that she had been sick, she ran the marathon in good time." Say this instead: "Although she had been sick, she ran the marathon in good time."

Different

Often used unnecessarily. Don't write, "He had taught in seven different states and knew five different languages with two different methods." No one could imagine that the states, the languages, and the methods could not be different, so you do not need to use the word.

Doubled phrases

English has a special liking for doubled phrases such as "null and void," "cease and desist," and "advise and consent." They come from our legal tradition, and they sound like judges stating stern but unremarkable opinions. In ordinary writing such doubling is usually unnecessary. Don't write the phrase "pick and choose." Use the word *choose* instead. Don't write "each and every one." Use *each* instead. Don't write "first and foremost." Use either *first* or *foremost*. Don't say, "For all intents and purposes the Red Sox were out of the pennant race by May 1." Say, "The Red Sox folded in April this year."

Due to the fact that

Replace with *because*.

Each individual

Don't use these two words as adjectives to modify a noun. Don't say, "Each individual member of the team has her own talents." Say, "Each member of the team has her own talents."

End result

Use *result* instead.

Final outcome

Eliminate *final*.

Free gift

Eliminate *free*. If we pay for a gift, it is not a gift.

Full and complete

A doubled phrase. Use *full* or *complete*, but not both.

Future plans

Plans are always for the future. Don't say, "If your future plans call for travel to Knoxville, we hope you'll choose Delta Airlines." Say, "If you fly to Knoxville again, we hope you'll choose Delta Airlines."

If and when
A doubled phrase. Use either *if* or *when*, but not both.

In a sense
Often unnecessary. "In a sense you could say he died of alcoholism." In what sense? Spell out your meaning. "He died of a heart attack brought on by heavy drinking."

Incumbent
In the "official style," many people will write this: "It is incumbent upon us to write more readable memos." Most of the time I don't think they know exactly what the word *incumbent* means. It's much better to say this: "We must write more readable memos."

In effect
Usually omit. Again, be direct. Don't say, "In effect the editor refuses to allow any criticism of More to appear in the journal." Say, "No criticism of More's life ever appears in the journal."

In other words
A stutter in writing. Omit it.

Instrumental
Often wordy. Don't say, "She was instrumental in establishing the poetry group." Say instead, "She helped form the poetry group."

Intensifiers
In informal speech we often try to intensify the effect of some adjectives by tacking on an intensifying adverb, usually spoken emphatically. "She was *really* intelligent." These intensifiers clog up writing, and you should usually omit them, though now and then you may find a use for them—but only now and then. Your prose will be leaner if you shun *absolutely, basically, certainly, definitely, fabulously, incredibly, immensely, intensely, perfectly, positively, utterly, really, quite, rather, simply,* and *very.*

In terms of
Almost always needlessly wordy. Don't say, "Antigua, in terms of weather, was dry." Say instead, "Antigua is arid."

In the event that
Replace with *if.*

In the final analysis

Either use the word *finally* or make your final point without an-nouncing that it is final. (Your readers can see that for themselves.)

In the realm of

Omit or use a shorter word. Don't say, "It is in the realm of pos-sibility that he may come." Say instead, "He may come."

In a position to

Use *can* instead. Don't say, "She is in a position to help him." Say, "She can help him."

It is possible that

Use *can* or *may* instead. Don't say, "It is possible that some cho-lesterol is good for us." Say, "Some cholesterol may be good for us."

Located

A common word in journalese—the language of unthinking re-porters. Don't say, "The house was located at 35 Oak Street." Say, "The house was at 35 Oak Street."

Observable fact

Usually omit. People who use this locution want to impress us with their perception. They know that we can observe some facts and that we can't observe others. But we all know that, and we know, too, that people who speak of observable facts are trying to impress us. They would impress us more if they got straight to the point. Don't say, "It is an observable fact that people read magazines more quickly than their income tax returns." Say, "People read magazines more quickly than their income tax returns."

One of the things that

Usually omit. Don't say, "One of the things that you need to do is practice revision." Say this: "Revise your work."

On the occasion of

Usually cumbersome. Don't say this: "On the occasion of her coming, we shall all proceed into the open to offer our greetings." Say this instead: "We will all go out to meet her when she comes."

Period of time

Don't use both *period* and *time* in the phrase. Say, "At that time" or "In that period."

Positive effects

Usually pompous and vague. Don't say, "The rehabilitation program has had some positive effects." Say this: "The rehabilitation program has done some good."

Prior to

Replace with *before*. Don't say, "Prior to the game we had a picnic." Say, "Before the game we had a picnic."

Prove conclusively

Something is either proved or not proved. Omit *conclusively*. (See *different*, above. The principle is similar.) Do not use words to express supposedly subtle distinctions that no person of ordinary intelligence can confuse.

Situation

A good word that often leads to wordiness and confusion. A former Boston sportswriter produced this almost incomprehensible sentence:

> Fisk and Lynn have been allowed to leave Boston in the last few years, and the Red Sox management is on the edge of the players' perception as becoming another Calvin Griffith situation.

He meant something like this:

> The Red Sox lost catcher Carlton Fisk and outfielder Fred Lynn because the owners would not pay them enough. The remaining players are on the verge of seeing the Red Sox as the Boston version of the Minnesota Twins, whose owner Calvin Griffith gladly sold off good players rather than pay them high salaries.

I have lengthened this version for readers who are not baseball fans. For fans the writer could have said this:

> The Red Sox lost Fisk and Lynn, and the remaining players are beginning to think Boston's management is as stingy and unconcerned with winning as Calvin Griffith.

The killer word is *situation*. It is so vague that both writers and readers lose track of what it means.

Take into account

Use *consider* instead. Don't say, "We must take the weather into account when we make our plans." Say this instead: "We must consider the weather in our plans."

The question of whether

A common padding phrase. You can trim it. Don't say, "We must consider the question of whether subways are efficient means of mass transport." Say this instead: "We must ask if subways are efficient means of mass transport."

To some extent

Often redundant. Don't say, "To some extent living in the suburbs has some advantages." Say, "Living in the suburbs has some advantages."

Veritable

Almost always unnecessary and a little pompous. Don't say, "Charles was a veritable wonder." Say, "Charles was a wonder."

Voiced the opinion
Use *said*.

What was/what is

Usually a wordy construction when it is used as the start of a dependent clause:

What was essential for Russia was peace.
What he wanted in life was not clear.

You can shorten such sentences by revising away the *what*:

Peace was essential for Russia.
His purpose in life was not clear.

With a view toward

Revise to eliminate. Don't say, "She bought the boat with a view toward fishing." Say, "She bought the boat so she could fish."

With regard to

Revise to eliminate. Don't say, "With regard to letter writing, she was slow." Say this instead: "She was slow to write letters."

Eight

Good Diction

*D*iction is our choice of words when we write or speak. Good diction helps intelligent readers understand us, respect us, and believe us. Words are mysterious, puzzling, beautiful things, and although we use them every day, we never quite master them. They have histories, connotations, shades of meaning, associations with a long tradition of writing and speaking. If we call somebody an opponent, we mean one thing; if we call her an enemy, we mean another. If we say a man is charming, we usually mean to compliment him; if we say he is smooth, we imply a slight insult; if we call him oily, we mean a stronger insult, and perhaps we mean to warn people who may meet him.

Finding the right word is one of the joys of language, defining our experience to ourselves, helping to convey it to others. What word best describes the sun? Hot? Incandescent? Vengeful? Mild? Weak? Benign? Pale? White? Red? Every one of those words conveys a slightly different impression of the sun, useful under different circumstances. English may be the most marvelously varied language. People sometimes ask me what one book I would take with me to a desert island. I always respond, "A good dictionary." No other book I know offers so many outlets to human sensibility or makes us better aware of the seemingly infinite shadings of experience the human mind is capable of. Finding the right word may help us to be specific and to discover a quality of meaning that is new to us, one that the word will make vivid to our readers. We look at a face; it inspires feeling within us; but how do we express it? When we find the right word, we understand that feeling better; the word may help us define our own attitude.

The Principles of Good Diction

Words are always used with other words; they take meaning from one another. Because English is as gloriously flexible as it is, diction has no rules, only principles. These principles are firm enough to enumerate; careful writers observe them and use them to interpret specific choices in language. As you review the following list, you will see that the various items overlap.

1. Use language efficiently.

We should not pad our thought or inflate our utterances in an effort to be impressive. Some speak of *preplanning* supposing that word to be more impressive than mere *planning*. Almost every bureaucrat nowadays speaks of *preconditions* for agreement when the word *conditions* does at least as well. The use of *prior to* instead of *before* seems to have become a linguistic virus, calling forth awkward sentences such as the following: "Prior to the implementation of the recently recommended policies by your office, certain preconditions require to be satisfied." Such writers find it almost insulting if someone suggests that this highfalutin language be reduced to this: "Before we do what you ask, we [or you] need to meet certain conditions."

Many writers seem almost to struggle to make their sentences verbose and incomprehensible. Here is a medical example sent to me by a reader who is a doctor.

> The cancer burden and its financial ramifications have escalated to enormous proportions on the community level. Early diagnosis with open communication to the patient and cost containment are dominant in the perspective of community medicine.

By deciphering the article in which these sentences appear, I think they mean this:

> The personal and financial burden of cancer represents a crisis to community hospitals. They must contain costs while they seek early diagnosis of the disease and try to communicate frankly with patients.

The most efficient language is always simple and natural. It creates its effects by the information it conveys and by the grace of the writing rather than by a pretense of erudition.

2. Use words in keeping with the written traditions of English.

Avoid words that might lead educated readers to suppose that you are ignorant of the traditions of the written language. Writing once maintained a supreme authority that carried over easily from handwritten copies of books to the revolution of printing. What could be printed was severely restricted in all countries until very recently. Even in the United States, with its constitutional freedoms, editors and censors regulated what might appear in print, giving an aura of almost holiness to the written language, reining it up before the limits of the unprintable.

Just about anything is printable now; "acceptable usage" is much broader than it once was because we hear words on radio and television and in the movies that once would have been considered inappropriate in polite society, and many writers use those words freely in their work. The speech patterns of talk-show hosts and television commentators of various sorts have insinuated themselves into the written language. At times a result has been a loss of clarity. The television commentator can use tone of voice and even body language to convey meanings not conveyed by an atrocious vocabulary or garbled syntax. Students exposed to such language from youth naturally fail to see that the written language must stand by itself, without a commentator to whisper the true meaning of a text into the ear of the reader. These days the written language of formal prose seems to borrow more and more from the spoken language of daily conversation.

Some words and usages remain so questionable that you should not use them. "Irregardless" is one. *Regardless* is the accepted word. "Irregardless" is a double negative in a single word, for both the prefix *ir* and the suffix *less* convey a negation. You will never find the word in a published essay unless it occurs in a direct quotation. Despite its popularity with high school and college students, *funner* is still not an acceptable synonym for *more fun*. And although many people now say, "Myself and Cleo are giving a party Saturday night," writers who wish to be taken seriously must say, "Cleo and I are giving a party."

Nor will you find the word *ain't* in normal literate discourse, although it occurs frequently in quotations because all sorts of people use it in speech. For some reason *ain't*—a Cockney English word that originated in the eighteenth century—has never caught on. Educated people consider it a sign of illiteracy, perhaps because of its social origins. The Cockneys were lower class. Perhaps it should have made the grade, for we do not have a contraction for *I am not* or *am I not*. It would seem efficient to write "I ain't" or "ain't I?"—but we do not.

3. Avoid fads in usage that impoverish the language.

Fads in language come and go with mysterious speed, almost like epidemics. Someone calls a financial consequence "the bottom line," and suddenly millions are using the phrase "bottom line" as a synonym for the most important consequence in any action or condition. "The bottom line of our love affair is trust."

At the Watergate hearings, televised for the world in 1973, one witness after another stalled for time by saying—usually with great deliberation—"At that point in time," and suddenly time ceased to stand by itself. It had to have a point attached.

Commentator Edwin Newman has pointed out the sudden proliferation of nouns with *-ize* tacked on the end to make them verbs. He says, "The ize have it," and so they do. People now "verbalize" rather than talk; they "concertize" rather than give concerts. A newspaper I saw some time ago urged, "Accessorize your garden." When the radiators went dead in my office a few winters ago, dropping the temperature to just above freezing, a workman came in, felt the chill, knocked on some pipes, and left, telling me his crew would certainly "priortize" my office. I wanted him instead to thermalize it before the cold finalized my health and traumatized my fingers and face.

We have some perfectly acceptable *ize* words in English. I think it's fine to *summarize*, and I don't complain when people *utilize* things, although I have never thought that *utilize* says much that *use* does not. *Victimize* seems to be solidly lodged in our vocabulary now, and it's all right to be *scandalized* or to *theorize* or *fraternize*. Still we need to curb the promiscuous *-ize* lest we turn English into some species of pig Latin in which every word ends with the same sound. To use faddish new forms where perfectly acceptable forms already exist in the language betokens a poverty of mind. Experienced readers recognize that poverty when they see it and can seldom be persuaded to spend their time on writing that exhibits it. For example, there is a community hospital just down the street from my home, and the article I quoted earlier on community medicine might tell me something interesting about the problems of an institution I know at least slightly. But having sampled the first few paragraphs, I might be persuaded to continue reading it only if the penalty for not reading it were a good beating.

4. Use language idiomatically.

Idiom is an unfamiliar word to most students, yet it is as important as any word applied to English usage. It refers to habitual usages in a particular language that have no clear logic to them; we "take in a movie" or we "hang out at the mall." No language is entirely rational, and English seems more irrational than most. Its irrationality is perhaps a sign of the vitality of the people who use it, people who refuse to be squeezed into the bondage of excessive rules. Idioms are the usages that are most irrational for any language. Foreign speakers learning English have trouble with idioms—and English speakers have similar troubles when they learn foreign languages. When someone learning English asks why a certain expression is wrong, often our only answer is, "That's not the way we speak English."

For example, to speak and write idiomatically, we have to know how prepositions are used. We recognize that if we make *up* with someone, we become reconciled. But to make *out* with that person implies something else, and to make *off* with something indicates some sort of dishonest flight. To pass *out* means one thing, to pass *off* means another, and to pass *on* means something else still.

We are more likely to encounter ill-used idioms with common words. For some reason we do not guess *on* the answer; we guess *at* the answer, though logic tells us that we might merely *guess* the answer. Habit makes us speculate *on* the outcome of next week's game rather than to speculate *in* it, though bankers speculate *in* stocks and bonds. We may say that the game is *up* and mean that someone has been found out, but when we say the game is *over* we mean only that the contest has ended.

Not all idioms involve prepositions. When we say that a carpenter *cut corners* on the job, we mean that his work was shoddy rather than that he used a saw on the wood corners of a project. When we say that a speaker *took the floor*, we do not mean that she ran off with it and used it in her house. And I know that I can *twist your arm* to get you to eat dinner with me and yet never touch you. We both may be *up in arms* on account of the poor food without ever having drawn our swords on the waiters. And even a bald executive can *let down his hair* at the office party.

Idioms change. In nineteenth-century prose, the idiom "to make love" meant to propose marriage, and Anthony Trollope in his hilarious novel *Barchester Towers* has the odious and slightly intoxicated Obadiah Slope "make love" to beautiful Eleanor Bold in a carriage. Both the gentle Trollope and his Victorian peers in England would have been outraged by the modern confusions among students reading his work.

Always idiom involves a subtle feel for language, a sense of what is appropriate to the context and the purpose. A student of mine writing a few years ago on the battles of Lexington and Concord in 1775 announced that the patriots gathered on hilltops and *affronted* the British as they came by. I had a vision of lines of patriots mooning the British troops and of puritanical British officers saying, "Don't pay any attention to them, men! What can you expect from these Americans!"

5. Accept change conservatively.

From what I have said so far and from your own experience, you know that language is always changing. Now it seems to be changing more rapidly than ever before.

New words come into English with amazing frequency. Some innovations show vitality. One of my favorite books, entitled *9,000 Words: A Supplement to Webster's Third New International Dictionary*, is a collection of words new to English within the past fifteen years. In it I find modern coinages such as *software, dunk shot, monokini, printout*, and *life-support system*, all of them signs of the nearly miraculous talent human beings have of finding names to help them describe and control their experiences. (Only a few years ago the ancestor to that book was called *6,000 Words*.) I like many new words when they are used in appropriate contexts. When a baseball writer tells me that a shortstop is *showboating*, I find the word stronger than the older term *showing off*. *Ditsy* describes some of my students who seem too happy with the world to pay much attention to their work or much of anything else that requires prolonged concentration. I don't think I would like to read that John Paul Jones was one of the great hot dogs of the American Revolution or that Mussolini was one of the most ditsy politicians of the twentieth century, but I don't mind reading a lighthearted sports story that tells me that a former pitcher for the St. Louis Cardinals was a hot dog or that an outfielder for the Boston Red Sox was ditsy. Some new words fit into formal contexts, but some do not.

Not only do new words continually flow into the language, but old words change their meaning. In Shakespeare's day the word *shrewd* meant "wicked," not "clever" as it means today. Back then *courage* could mean "male sexual prowess," and a *queen* could be a prostitute. In my own boyhood on a farm in mountainous East Tennessee, people still used *prevent* to mean "go before" or "announce," just as the word is used in the King James Version of the Bible by the Psalmist who says, "I prevented the dawning of the morning."

Some good words mysteriously pass out of the language altogether. When sixteenth-century Englishmen spoke of whispering, they used the word *rouning*. I like the word. It catches the low murmuring of some whispering, especially the kind that occurs in a crowd of people who do not so much whisper as grumble. But the word is gone. Our parents or grandparents talked about *swells* who put on a great show of wealth. From it they derived the adjective *swell* and spoke of having a swell time at a party, meaning "a time befitting the rich." The word is all but gone now. Other words, like *spiffy, zany, snazzy*, and *gosh* are similarly fading away.

Today the language is changing so swiftly that moderate conservatives like me want to slow it down a little. Our language is a currency of meaning; currencies work best when their values remain fairly constant. If too many words mean one thing today and another tomorrow, the possibility of communicating between generations is called into question. It is a great gift that an adolescent can read and enjoy Jonathan Swift's *Gulliver's Travels*, written over two centuries ago, and that the novels of Charles Dickens still live for readers more than a hundred years after Dickens died. The American democracy rests on a constitution written generations ago, and it still makes sense to us.

In the novel *1984* George Orwell invented the word *newspeak* to stand for the terrifying loss of the common meanings of words. When words lose precise meanings, thought becomes confused. Now we have the reprehensible use of the words *people's democracy* to describe harshly totalitarian states in which the people dare not dissent from government edicts and where no election is honest and no voice represents the general will. In the United States something called *national security* has enabled our own government to invade the privacy of its citizens, burgle their houses and offices, tap their telephones, limit their freedom of speech, and threaten them for having unpopular opinions.

Yet the conservative critics of language often express themselves foolishly. In my introduction to this book I referred to the critic John Simon. Simon has uttered these sentiments, apparently with a straight face:

> Why does language keep changing? Because it is a living thing, people will tell you. Something that you cannot press forever, like a dead flower, between the pages of a dictionary. Rather, it is a living organism that, like a live plant, sprouts new leaves and flowers. Alas, this lovely albeit trite image is—as I have said before and wish now to say with even greater emphasis—largely nonsense. Language, for the most part, changes out of ignorance.[1]

Simon is a priest in the self-constituted church of linguistic puritans who live in terror lest anyone appear to be enjoying language without obeying all the rules. In reality, usage is finally king; English is finally what people speaking and writing it understand to be English. The language is no more in decay now than it was in Shakespeare's time or even in the time of *Beowulf*. It is only changing. Ambrose Bierce early in this century defined *laundry* as "a place where clothing is washed." He added, "This word cannot mean, also, clothing sent there to be washed."[2] Richard Grant White, the Edwin Newman of his day, published *Words and Their Uses* in 1870 in the general conviction that English was going to the dogs. He disliked the word *editorial* for the essay editors write expressing their opinions in newspapers.

He condemned the use of *execute* as a verb meaning "to put to death." He thought *ice water* and *ice cream* should be *iced water* and *iced cream*.[3] (I once had a friend who corrected me for ordering *ice tea* in a restaurant. "It's *iced* tea," he said.) Not long ago the only definition standard college dictionaries gave for the word *sweater* was "one who sweats."

Many purists become angry at usages of which they disapprove. With respect to the word *hopefully* used as a synonym for "I hope" or "It is hoped," poet Phyllis McGinley is quoted as saying, "'Hopefully' so used is an abomination and its adherents should be lynched."[4] The linguistic puritans see language as the property of the educated, and a territorial imperative impels them to fight off invaders. Language to them is a measure of status, and it is hard to escape the feeling that they assault the common language of others as a means to exalt themselves.

Yet while I deplore the bad temper and nonsense of these puritans, I sympathize with some of their intuitions. The language should not be sterile, but it should be stable—not only because a stable language allows us to communicate across space in the present but also for the reason that I have mentioned already: a reasonably stable language allows us to communicate across generations and provides a tradition that, in a fine phrase by Saul Bellow, allows the living to break bread with the dead.

I find it also cogent to measure usage by the practice of good writers. Ah, but who are the good writers? That, of course, is a matter of taste. I have my own canon, and I think most of its members accept innovations with some caution.

Some Lively Problems in Usage

On the following pages I express some opinions about lively problems in usage. When readers looked at the first draft of this book, several commented with dismay that I was far too conservative and that the strictness of some of my definitions might make writing more difficult for the inexperienced. I am as aware as anyone that mine is the kind of list that a century from now may be ridiculed by as yet unborn readers who will see that many words that make me wince are by then completely accepted in the language. Usage commands, and at a certain point the most rabid purist must step aside. Usually nature herself intervenes, for purists die, and the language goes happily on without them. Even John Simon is mortal, though one would not think so from his divine tone of wrathful judge over the doom of English.

Since the first edition, I have changed my mind about some matters. For example, in the first edition I included a distinction between *ensure*, which means "to make sure," and *insure*, which means "to provide insurance." Since then I have noticed that *The New York Times* has folded the two meanings together into the word *insure*, and its headlines regularly speak of efforts to *insure* peace or lower prices or whatever. Earlier I would have supposed that to insure peace meant to take out a policy so that if peace should be damaged or killed, someone might receive some sort of financial payment. But no, the *Times* always means that someone is trying to make sure of peace. Who am I to stand against the august authority of *The New York Times*? I have dropped the distinction.

Yet my suggestions remain on the conservative side. Of course many people will disagree with some of my readings. I freely admit that my commentary on usage—like all commentaries—reflects my own reading, experience, taste, and simple prejudice. I serve on the usage panel for the third edition of *The American Heritage Dictionary*— a task I have much enjoyed despite its long questionnaires and its demands for extended notes about my choices. I hope that I have read enough and thought enough about language to make my comments have some authority, but no informed reader will agree with all of them. *The American Heritage Dictionary* provides percentages of the members of its panel who vote on controversial usages, and these votes are never unanimous. Even so I believe that the majority of professional writers and editors share my views. Whether they will for long is another question.

Perhaps the greatest value of my list will be to make you check my views against what you read and against your own views. Look carefully at the prose in good magazines and popular nonfiction books to see how many times my rules are broken. This exercise will make you more conscious of language and more conscious of your own usage. To be aware that usage offers problems and requires choices is to start making the distinctions that make for good writing. It is also fun to study words closely, to see their origins, and to observe the connotations that hover about them. Every good writer I know loves to study words, to play with them, to compare their definitions in various dictionaries, and to see how other writers use them. If you are going to write well, you have to love words and take care of them. Perhaps the fallible list that follows will help you love words and their puzzles more.

All together/Altogether

If you say, "They gathered *all together* in one place," you mean that they all were present. If you say, "They were *altogether* mad," you mean they were completely mad. The adverb *together* always refers to some kind of collection; the adverb *altogether* always refers to some kind of completeness.

Alot/A lot

To me this is a mysterious but common error. There is no such word as "alot," yet my students write *alot* as one word time and time again as though it were *awhile*. Even the correct form *a lot* is too colloquial and too vague for my taste. It seems dull to say something like this: "Custer discovered that he had stirred up a lot of Indians." It's better to say, "Custer saw thousands of Indians riding down on him and realized he was in trouble."

Alright/All right

The spelling *alright* is not acceptable to most editors, although it turns up in thousands of student papers every year. Use two words: *all right*.

Alternative

Many purists say that we can use *alternative* only when we have but two choices in a matter. They reason that since the Latin word *alter* means "the other," implying only two, the derivative *alternative* can never be used when there are three or more choices. Common usage has long since buried this rigorous etymological logic, and we happily speak of three or four alternatives as we ponder a decision.

Yet *at least* two choices must present themselves if *alternative* is to be sensibly used. If we say, "Our only alternative is to keep going," we say that we have only one choice, and of course that is no choice at all. You can say, "We can die; our only alternative is to keep going." Then you have two choices. You can say, "Our only course is to keep going." That means what it says.

Amount/Number

The distinction is similar to that between *less* and *fewer*, which you will encounter later in this list. You have an *amount* of something you cannot divide into units that you can count. You have a *number* of things you can count.

A large *number* of people applauded her performance.

They left a large *amount* of litter on the floor.

Number as a word has some idiomatic quirks. If we say, "*The* number of something," we use a singular verb:

The number of writers in any society *is* relatively small.

But if we say "*A* number of something," the verb is plural:

A number of his friends *were* arrested.

Anxious/Eager

The debate about this pair of words goes back at least a century. It seems better to use *anxious* to indicate an element of fear or anxiety, *eager* to show pleasure in some expected occurrence.

I am *eager* to attend opening day in Fenway Park each April.

I am *anxious* to see if the Red Sox fold this year in May rather than in August.

Anymore/Any more

The adverb *anymore* means "nowadays" and has traditionally been used only in negative constructions. You can say, "He doesn't smoke anymore," and everyone will understand that he once smoked but stopped and does not smoke now. Sometimes people say, "Anymore I drink tea rather than coffee." The positive construction of the verb confuses readers and hearers. On reflection we can see that the speaker means she once drank coffee but now drinks tea instead. A negation is implied, but the implication confuses most people accustomed to the convention that *anymore* must follow a negative and come *after* the verb phrase. The more customary and clearer statement is this: "I don't drink coffee anymore; I drink tea instead."

Always make a distinction between *anymore* and *any more*.

I never see her *anymore*. [Adverb. I used to see her, but now I don't.]

I don't want to see *any more* friends today. [Adverb *any* + adjective *more*.]

Apt/Liable/Likely

To say that someone is *apt* is to remark on a skill, especially one that seems somewhat casual or general.

She is *apt* at good talk.

He is an *apt* student.

Strictly speaking, *liable* has a legal connotation, always unpleasant.

He was *liable* to be sued.

To say that someone is *likely* to do something is to remark that he or she will probably do something.

Roger Clemens will be interviewed tonight and will *likely* insult Red Sox fans again because they don't pay enough for his autographs.

As/Since

English writers commonly use these words as synonyms. Charles Darwin did so in *The Origin of Species,* and Charles Dickens did the same in his novels. The American practice of differentiating between the two words seems preferable. *As,* used as a conjunction, connotes contemporary time, something happening while something else is happening. *Since* gives the sense of something happening after something else, quite often causing the later event.

These sentences do not confuse:

He waved at me *as* the boat pulled away from the dock.
Since her mother became ill, she seldom goes out of the house.

But a sentence like this one can be confusing:

As I commute to work by bicycle, the cuffs of my pants sometimes get blackened by the oil.

Does the commuting by bicycle *cause* my cuffs to be blackened by oil, or does this blackening happen mysteriously as I bike along? *Since* conveys a stronger impression of causation than *as,* and the conjunction *because* conveys an even stronger impression.

Because I commute to work by bicycle, the cuffs of my pants sometimes get blackened by oil.

So my advice may seem somewhat perverse. If you wish to indicate causation, choose *since* over *as*; but choose *because* over both.

A while/Awhile

Awhile is an adverb used to modify verbs: "He stayed *awhile.*" *While* is a noun expressing an unspecified but usually short period of time. It is often the subject of a preposition: "He stayed for *a while.*"

The sense of the two forms is so close that good writers often confuse them. The meaning given by most dictionaries for the adverb *while* is "for a while." Careful writers should make a distinction—if only to call attention to their care. It is an easy matter. When *while* follows a preposition—usually *in* or *for*—you should make two words: *a while*; when *while* is used with a verb and without an intervening preposition use *awhile.*

Between/Among

The standard rule is that *between* should be used to speak of two things, *among* to speak of more than two:

It was easy to make a distinction *between* the two words.

She moved gracefully *among* the guests in the room.

So far, so good. But the difference between the two words sometimes gets fuzzy. We don't speak of the infield on a baseball diamond as the space *among* the four bases, and we don't say that a treaty banning genocide was signed *among* most of the nations of the world. We say the treaty was made *between* the nations. If I am sitting with four friends at a table and wish to share a bit of gossip, I say, "Just between us, I think his best friends hate him." I somehow don't feel comfortable saying, "Just among us."

The best rule seems to be to let literate people follow their inclinations. We should not fear using *between* with more than two when the intent is to show some kind of active participation of every party following someone's lead—as in signing a treaty. We should not fear using *between* to refer to an enclosed space and its boundaries, no matter how numerous those boundaries are. Even these rules are not sufficient to cover all the ways we can use *between* when we speak of more than two.

There are other concerns in the usage of *between*. You should never write *between you and I* or *between she and I* or *between he and she*. When I hear these constructions I wince. *Between* is a preposition here, and the objects of prepositions should be in the objective case. So you should use the phrases "between you and me" or "between her and me" or "between her and him."

You should also avoid the phrase "between each" as in this construction: "A wall was built between each of the rooms." *Each* is singular; *between* implies more than one. It does not make sense to use "between each" unless you add another parallel noun: "A wall was built between each room and the one adjacent to it."

Co-equals

This is a redundancy like "irregardless." Two captains in an army unit are not co-equal in authority; they are merely equal. But *co-*words are becoming common, probably in imitation of the word *co-pilot*. The problem is that we sometimes don't know whether *co-* signifies "equal to" or "assistant to." A copilot is an assistant to the pilot on an airplane. Some high school football teams have a captain and a *co-captain* who, like a *copilot*, takes over when the captain is unable to function. Other teams have no captain at all and instead have co-captains who are supposedly equal to one another. The *co-* scene is a mess, and I think it is better to abandon *co-* words except when we have to speak of copilots. (Fortunately we don't have to speak of them very often.)

Common/Mutual

Many writers and more speakers have used these words as synonyms since at least the time of Shakespeare. In 1658 the English writer George Starkey wrote of "our mutual friend," and in the nineteenth century Charles Dickens wrote a novel called *Our Mutual Friend*, for which he has incurred the scorn of purists ever since. Yet people commonly speak of "mutual friends" today, although they may be silently condemned for doing so by many who hear them.

Strictly speaking, we should use *mutual* to describe some reciprocal action, something going back and forth between two things or two persons. In *Measure for Measure* Claudio comments wryly on "The stealth of our most mutual entertainment" which has made his lover Julietta pregnant. Sexual intercourse is indeed an example of the reciprocity implied in the more "correct" use of the word *mutual*. People can also have a mutual affection or a mutual dislike of each other. If they share something like an interest in photography, we should say, "They had a common interest in photography," or, "They shared an interest in photography."

The term *mutual friend* seems so established in the American and English habits of speech that it seems unfriendly to fight it, and no one will hang you if you say, "You and I have a mutual friend in Arkansas." Even so I still prefer to say, "You and I are both friends of Dee Post."

Comprise/Compose/Include

These three words often get mixed up. *Comprise* means "to embrace." So we say, "The Senate comprises 100 members." The 100 members do not *comprise* the Senate; they *compose* the Senate. They *include* lawyers, judges, farmers, businesspeople, and a fair number of people who will someday to go prison. You could not say the 100 members *embrace* the Senate. *Comprise* calls attention to all the parts. When you wish to call attention to only a few of the parts, use *include*.

Conditions

The high frequency with which this word is used may originate with TV meterologists. They talk about "snowy conditions prevailing in Minnesota" or "stormy conditions over New England." They cannot bear to say, "Snow is falling in Minnesota tonight," or "Thunderstorms are flooding Arizona." Now we have traffic conditions, economic conditions, and housing conditions. When an Air-Florida jet crashed taking off from Washington National Airport in 1982, one official was reported as saying, "Weather conditions are such that they are not conducive to rapid recovery." He apparently meant that it was too cold to recover the bodies swiftly from the icy Potomac River.

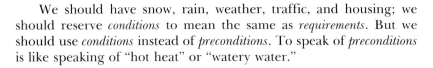

We should have snow, rain, weather, traffic, and housing; we should reserve *conditions* to mean the same as *requirements*. But we should use *conditions* instead of *preconditions*. To speak of *preconditions* is like speaking of "hot heat" or "watery water."

Contact

Many writers object to the use of *contact* as a verb. Strunk and White, in their classic little book *The Elements of Style*, advise readers to telephone, to write, or to get in touch with someone, but never to contact him or her. The objection sounds oddly genteel to me, a bit like the prohibition of the word *legs* in polite Victorian society, even when one spoke of the legs of a table. *Contact* means "touch," and to use *contact* as a verb probably seemed vulgar to some because it is more direct than "to get in touch with." But thoroughly respectable professional writers have been contacting people for decades, and few of us object if someone contacts us about next week's meeting—though we may object to the meeting itself. *Contact* means that some of us may be telephoned, others written to, and still others hailed on the street and invited to come.

Continuous/Continual

Something *continuous* goes on without interruption; something *continual* goes on at intervals.

> The movement of blood through our bodies is *continuous* until death.
>
> Rich Gedman's career with the Red Sox was marked by his *continual* complaint that he was not appreciated enough.

Don't tell someone that you expect to be with him continuously unless you intend never to let him out of your sight.

Cope

People often use this word to give the impression that they are saying much more than they really are. If you must use the word, write *cope with* and follow the two words with some reasonable object:

> Tammy Bakker looked as if she could not *cope with* age without layers of cosmetics to defend her.

Some of us would prefer a revised sentence: "Tammy looked as if layers of cosmetics painted over her face might defend her from the indecencies of age." *Cope* carries with it a vagueness that I don't like. If you must use it, try to be as specific as you can. To say, "I can't cope," is to admit some general debility, a frustration of some sort, but it does not locate the source of the frustration. It leaves readers and listeners and perhaps the person using the word in a general confusion. Usually the expression is so mild that the confusion is unimportant, especially in casual speech. But in writing, unimportant and confusing locutions are like mud on a bicycle chain; they provide an unnecessary drag on the motion of prose. Neither you nor your readers have the time or the energy for them.

Couldn't care less/Could care less

The original idiom, which had a certain force in my adolescence, was "I *couldn't* care less." It seemed straightforward and emphatic. It meant that someone cared so little for a person or thing that he could not possibly feel less concerned. "I couldn't care less about Jackson" meant that Jackson was so insignificant that the speaker could not have less feeling about him, no matter what he did.

Now the idiom has become convoluted into the nonsensical "I could care less." It seems to be everywhere, like the virus of the common cold. "I could care less about Jackson." If we take language seriously, this idiom means that the speaker does care something about Jackson. Perhaps she adores Jackson. Perhaps she hates him. Whatever her emotion, for some unspecified reason she *could* care less about him. We wonder what Jackson would have to do to provoke such a lowering of her esteem. With an idiom like "I could care less," language has become not communication but incantation.

The problem can be avoided by a simple, less hackneyed expression, direct and to the point: "I don't like Jackson." At best, even when used sensibly, "I couldn't care less" has become a cliché, and we may as well bury it. Even so, the cliché that makes sense is better than the nonsensical phrase "I could care less."

Crafted/Handcrafted

These are advertising words with almost no meaning, part of the general dilution of language advertising has brought about. They are, alas, in the language to stay, but careful writers among us should realize how empty they are since that recognition may clean up our language a bit. Supposedly the words *crafted* and *handcrafted* mean the same thing—that something has been made by hand by a combination of strength and skill and that the handwork guarantees a special quality. Often we say that writing is a craft, meaning that writing is a manual activity—something we do skillfully with our hands, something we can improve by spending more time on it.

In fact, many crafted items these days are made by machine, and a great many crafted or handcrafted items have to be made by hand, and things made by hand can be good or bad. If you buy a handcrafted shirt, for example, you may be sure that the stitching has been done by a sewing machine—probably by some sweatshop in Hong Kong. Even if the pieces of shirt were cut out by a machine, somebody had to operate the machine. So advertising copywriters can still speak of crafting. We could speak of the crafting of automobiles, since so much of their manufacture is done by hand. But we may get much higher quality if robots build our cars. Robots don't have hangovers on Monday morning or rush to quit early on Friday afternoons.

Different from/Different than

Most writers use *different from* and consider *different than* to be bad diction, but the distinction seems to be fading. Most writers I know prefer to say, "His tastes in literature are *different from* mine." *Different than* is often used before a clause: "His tastes in literature are different *than* they used to be." I prefer *different from*, and most editors are still more comfortable with this form. "His tastes in literature are different *from* what they used to be."

Dilemma

Properly speaking, a *dilemma* is a vexing problem that presents us with two equally unattractive choices and requires us to make one. Confirmed cigarette smokers face a dilemma: they can give up a habit that provides them much pleasure and suffer discomfort, prolonged nervousness, irritability, and perhaps a failure of concentration; or they can keep on smoking and die horribly of lung cancer if heart disease and emphysema do not kill them first.

Careless writers often use *dilemma* to indicate any serious problem, and the language is poorer in consequence. To ensure clarity, use *dilemma* only when speaking of a necessary choice between painful alternatives; then tell what the contrary choices are. Don't use the word dilemma unless you tell us what the dilemma is—or was.

The Germans in 1914 faced a dilemma. They could refuse to support the Austro-Hungarian Empire in the Balkans and see their only ally in Europe progressively weakened by Russia and the South Slav peoples who hated the Austrians. Or they could support the Empire and risk a catastrophic war.

Disinterested/Uninterested

Disinterested may be one of those words we should retire from the language for a time, substituting the word *impartial*. Much confusion might thereby be averted.

Most of us take the *disinterested* person to have nothing to gain or lose no matter who wins an argument or a contest. Juries, umpires, referees, judges, and teachers should be *disinterested*. Jonathan Edwards, the great American Puritan preacher of the eighteenth century, defined love as "disinterested benevolence," the kind of benign feeling toward others that does not demand anything from them in return. But a judge should not go to sleep with a murder trial going on under his nose; he should be *interested* and *disinterested* at the same time. To be *uninterested* is to have a lack of interest. I happen to be *uninterested* in chess, professional football, and books by Joyce Carol Oates.

The confusion of these words has been around for a long time, and it is not likely to disappear soon. So it may be time to send *disinterested* into honorable retirement.

Dubious/Doubtful

Things are *dubious* when they cause doubt; people are *doubtful* about dubious things.

> Many people wanted to believe the *dubious* story that Adolf Hitler had kept a diary throughout his dictatorship of Nazi Germany. But many became *doubtful* when chemical analysis showed that the paper on which the diaries were written was manufactured long after Hitler's death.

The distinction between these words has long been generally recognized in English, though since the seventeenth century some have seen them as synonyms, and more do so now. I think the distinction is worth preserving, and careful editors and writers still maintain it.

Due to/Because

A journalism professor of mine years ago use to say that the only safe use of *due to* was in a sentence like this: "The train was *due to* arrive at two o'clock." He thereby neatly avoided the annoying complexity of the debate over this apparently simple little phrase when it is used with nouns. Purists hold that the phrase should be used only as an adjective, as in the sentence, "Her victory was due to her stamina," or, "Bryan had a heart attack due to overeating." In such "correct" sentences, *due to* is a synonym for *caused by*, and nearly everyone will accept it as grammatically correct. Purists object to using *due to* as a preposition, synonymous with *owing to*, as in the sentence, "He won *due to* bribery," or, "The mayor felt handicapped due to his jail sentence."

I object to the use of *due to* even when it is formally correct. For one thing, it leads to clumsy constructions, especially when it is used as a synonym for *because* at the opening of clauses: "She was late due to the fact that her car broke down." It is much simpler to say, "She was late because her car broke down."

For another, the use of *due to* often makes the statement of a sentence vague. "He was convicted *due to* the pistol." What pistol? Why? Perhaps the context will spell out these details. But it seems better to state the situation more specifically by writing another sentence entirely. "The jury found him guilty because ballistics proved that the murder weapon was the pistol that police found in his belt when they arrested him." Here is another example of the clarity you may add to a sentence by using enough words to state your meaning fully.

Even if *due to* is used as the purists demand, only as an adjective, it can be vague. "He suffered a demotion due to incompetence." Whose incompetence? We want to know. Even the "correct" use of *due to* does not tell us. *Due to* often makes writers think they have said much more than they have in a sentence. Try to avoid the phrase.

Effect/Affect

A perennial problem! The word *effect* is usually a noun, as in the phrase "cause and effect." "The *effect* of her decision was to create a boom in the computer business."

Affect is usually a verb: "My attitude always *affects* my performance."

Occasionally *effect* is used as a verb meaning "to cause." "Luther's revolt against the Catholic Church *effected* a revolution in Western thought." *Effect* used as a verb carries with it the connotation of completeness, of having done something to the full.

Either/Both/Each

Either indicates one or the other. "You may read *either* the speeches of George Bush or Ronald Reagan to help put yourself to sleep at night." Either may be unclear if it is used to mean *both* or *each*. The flight attendant who announces that emergency exits are on *either* side of the aisle is not as helpful as the one who says that the exits are on *both* sides or on *each* side. If *either* is permitted to have both meanings, passengers who are told to sit on *either* side of the aisle will be confused.

Enthuse/Enthusiastic

It is still not widely acceptable among professional writers and editors to use the word *enthuse* as a verb, as in the sentence, "I am *enthused* at the prospect of teaching writing." It is much more acceptable to use the adjective *enthusiastic*: "I am *enthusiastic* about the prospect of living without television."

Factor

A much overused word, *factor* sends a verbal signal that a paper using it will be dull. Like other such words, its chief fault is not that it is wrong but that it prevents us from making a more specific statement. It lets us shilly-shally. "His character was a factor in the breakup of our friendship." It's much better to say, "He was a liar and a cheat, and so I ended our friendship." Or: "He was much more successful than I was; so I decided I disliked him."

Factor is one of those words that substitute easy writing for the hard work of finding words to express our thoughts exactly. Though it is a different kind of word, it fails in the same way that *intensifiers* fail (discussed later in this listing). It's better by far to ask yourself exactly what you want to say, say it, and forget about *factor*.

Feedback

This word, like *input*, has come into the language from electronics. It originally denoted a circuit by which part of the output of a radio source was brought back to its origin. Sometimes this feedback was unintentional, and the result was a high electronic shriek in the loudspeaker when a speaker got too close to a microphone. To some of us that sound is as reminiscent of high school as the smell of fetid clothes in the dressing rooms of the gym. Now *feedback* is commonly used as a synonym for *response* when people talk about other human beings. *Feedback* is becoming increasingly common in all sorts of bureaucratic writing, but it seldom appears in well-edited books and magazines. I strongly object to mechanistic metaphors to describe things human beings should do with their brains. *Feedback* makes us sound like robots.

Feel bad/Feel badly

We *feel bad* when something makes us sorry; we *feel badly* if we have burned our fingers or otherwise damaged our skin so that we have reduced our sense of touch. If I say, "Loretta *feels badly* because Leo lost their cat in a poker game," I mean that Leo's rash bet numbed her fingers. If I say she *feels bad* about the loss of her pet, I mean she is sorry.

The verbs of sense used with several common linking verbs cause trouble because some writers and speakers mistake a predicate adjective for an adverb. A predicate adjective modifies the subject of a clause. We do not have any trouble with sentences like this one: "He looked healthy and happy." We understand that the meaning of the sentence is this: "He looked to be healthy and happy." No one would write, "He looked healthily and happily." We also say, "Mary sat *still* in the house." We do not say, "She sat stilly in the house." We say, "He felt *damp* after being caught in the rain." No one would say, "He felt damply after the shower." We write easily, "He walked into the room *resolute* and *angry*," knowing that his walking is not resolute and angry but that *he* is resolute and angry. We should close a door *tight* because we mean it to be tight in its frame. If we close the door tightly, we imply that we are drunk—or at least *tight*—as we shut the door. We have our steak cooked *rare* because to have it cooked rarely implies that most of the time we eat raw steak but that once in a great while we put it on the stove and cook it.

So we feel *bad* when something displeases us or when we do something foolish or thoughtless that we regret—just as we smell *bad* when we have not taken a bath in a while and smell *good* when we have just bathed with nice soap. We feel *good* when our team wins, *bad* when it loses.

Flaunt/Flout

To *flaunt* something means to wave it proudly, even arrogantly, for everyone to see. The implication is that some people will be displeased for all that waving, but the flaunter does not care.

> Hurst *flaunted* his dislike for his drunken Red Sox teammates.

Flout means to disobey, to scorn, or to run in the face of some convention, and to do so flagrantly, openly, arrogantly.

> Boggs *flouted* his marriage vows by taking another woman with him on road trips.

Both *flout* and *flaunt* imply pride or even arrogance. This pride, combined with the similar beginnings of both words, accounts for their confusion. Careful writers and nearly all editors preserve the distinction.

For free

Many advertising writers and journalists on small newspapers have recently begun using this form.

> Senior citizens have been given their fishing licences *for free*.

It's much better to use the simple and conventional *free*.

> Senior citizens have been given *free* fishing licenses.

Former/Latter

Avoid using these words to refer to two preceding persons or things. In doing so, you require the reader to look back to see which is which.

> David Halberstam and Neil Sheehan both became celebrated for books they wrote about the Vietnam War, the former for *The Best and the Brightest* and the latter for *A Bright Shining Lie*.

A reader cruising through prose that contains this sentence has to stop, go back, and see that Halberstam is the former and therefore author of *The Best and the Brightest* and that Sheehan is the latter and therefore author of *A Bright Shining Lie*. The writer should have said this:

> David Halberstam and Neil Sheehan both became celebrated for books they wrote about the Vietnam War, Halberstam for *The Best and the Brightest* and Sheehan for *A Bright Shining Lie*.

If you do use *former* and *latter*, they should never refer to more than two. For more than two things you must use *first* and *last*, although these terms cause the same hesitancy and confusion as do *former* and *latter*. This is not a good sentence, although it is correct:

> McLain, Martin, and Steinbrenner were all embarrassments to baseball, the first because he had no personal discipline, the last because he quarreled so often and so openly with his team.

Fortuitous/Fortunate

Something that happens *fortuitously* happens by chance or by accident and may be good or bad:

> It was *fortuitous* that when the police raided the drug dealer's hotel room they found the mayor there, and he ordered them to leave without making an arrest.

We can hardly argue that this event was *fortunate* for anybody except perhaps for the mayor's enemies. *Fortuitous* suggests randomness, something happening entirely by chance.

> Some scientists think life on earth may have begun by the chemical reaction of a *fortuitous* burst of lightning in the soil.

Yet *fortuitous*, like *disinterested*, seems to have lost so much strength that you should consider using another word to avoid causing misunderstanding. I would not now write this sentence: "He happened to be home sick that day, and so his presence in the house at the moment of the burglary was entirely *fortuitous*." I would say, "He happened to be home sick that day, and so it was entirely by chance that he was in the house when the burglars broke in."

Fulsome

Here is another word so often misused that its proper meaning has perhaps been irretrievably buried. Until recently the common meaning of "fulsome praise" was praise so flattering that it could not possibly be sincere. *Fulsome* meant "disgusting" or "obsequious" or even "nauseating," and anyone who received fulsome praise without protest was taken to be blindly arrogant. Anyone who gave fulsome praise was a bootlicking sycophant. But now *fulsome* often means "great" or "enthusiastic."

It is a shame to lose the distinction, for our language will be impoverished by the loss of such an ironic and useful term. *Insincere* praise carries none of the scornful force of *fulsome* praise, but now the cult of exaggeration makes the simple offering of praise or even *lavish* praise or *high* praise seem inadequate. All our expressions must be inflated until they are sound and fury, signifying nothing very much, depending on the exuberance with which they are delivered rather than on the plain meaning of words. Writers and speakers who exaggerate everything are responsible for turning *fulsome* into yet another inflated adjective, and in their eagerness for emphatic utterance, they have failed to see that the traditional and useful meaning stands opposite to their intention.

Head up

People now seldom *head* or *direct* or *lead* things. Instead they *head up* committees, bands, groups, classes, and clinics on posture. I don't know what *up* adds to *head* except perhaps a specious bureaucratic importance.

Healthy/Healthful

Something is *healthy* if it enjoys good health, if it is strong, vigorous, and alive.

Jack kept himself *healthy* by eating well and biking every day.
Marge had a *healthy* arrogance.

Something is *healthful* if it contributes to the health of something else.

Oat bran is a *healthful* food.
Nuclear weapons are not *healthful* to society.

Hopefully/Hope

Few words provoke more antagonism and debate these days than *hopefully* used as a hanging adverb meaning "I hope" or "it is hoped." Writers and speakers have used the adverb for centuries to mean "in a hopeful spirit" when it, like other adverbs, modifies a verb, an adjective, or another adverb. But since about 1932 it has developed this new and more general and objectionable sense. *Webster's Ninth New Collegiate Dictionary* (Merriam-Webster) delivers a scornful note against the "irrationally large amount of critical fire" drawn from the word when it is used as a synonym for *I hope* or *it is hoped*, and it offers analogies with *interestingly, presumably*, and *fortunately*, which are often used as "sentence modifiers," that is, modifiers of entire sentences.

While willing to admit that usage is king and that probably no great good is accomplished by opposing *hopefully* as a hanging adverb, I must nevertheless record some reservations that to me are compelling. For one thing, 76 percent of a usage panel assembled by Wright Morris, editor in chief of *The American Heritage Dictionary*, and Mary Morris, a distinguished authority on usage, said they would not use *hopefully* in the sense of "I hope" or "it is hoped." That such a lopsided majority should oppose the word should make us hesitate to use it.

The words *interestingly, presumably*, and *fortunately*, cited by the editors of the Merriam-Webster dictionary, offer little of the ambiguity of *hopefully*. If we say, "Presumably Ted joined the army," we know that the adverb does not modify the entire sentence but that it modifies the verb *joined*, and there is no ambiguity. It is presumed that Ted joined the army; we do not know if he did or not. But if we say, "*Hopefully* Ted joined the army," we are left in confusion. Thanks to today's usage, we do not know if Ted joined the army with hope in his heart—the grammatical meaning of the sentence—or if the writer of the sentence hoped Ted joined the army. It is just this ambiguity that makes foes of *hopefully*—including me—find the word unattractive.

Other adverbs are equally ambiguous. "*Briefly*, the battle of Verdun lasted for ten months." People may use *briefly* in such a way to mean that they are going to be brief in their statements. But the statements would be far clearer if the authors of such sentences left the word *briefly* out. "*Unhappily*, the dog ate all the hors d'oeuvres before the guests arrived." Unhappily? Probably the hosts were unhappy, but I suspect the dog enjoyed himself immensely. "*Thankfully*, the terrorist died in a hail of bullets before he could injure anyone." The terrorist probably was not so thankful.

So it is with *hopefully*, as in the sentence, "Hopefully the faculty will get a raise this year." Does the sentence mean that the faculty is certain to get a raise and that it will do so with hope in its collective heart? Or does it mean that the writer of the sentence hopes that the faculty will get a raise? The latter meaning is more in accord with current informal usage, although the administration may hope with all *its* collective heart that the faculty not get a raise. Is it too much to ask writers to tell where the hope originates? "The faculty hopes it will get a raise this year." "I hope the faculty will get a raise this year."

To use *hopefully* or any of its random children among hanging adverbs in the peculiar sense it has now assumed creates another disadvantage. Adverbs cannot be inflected; they have only one form for present, past, and future. Nobody can say, "Hopefully when I was young, I would be rich." We must say, "When I was young, I hoped to be rich." The verb *to hope* can be inflected to show when the hope goes on. If you want to use the past tense, you must say, "I hoped." Why not use the verb in the present tense as well and say, "I hope"?

But the main objection to *hopefully* is that it makes something abstract that is personal. Hope does not float around in the air like nitrogen; hope is an emotion we feel as persons, and we ought to locate its source and identify the people who have it. I hope readers will take seriously these comments on a common usage.

Illusion/Allusion

We make an *allusion* by referring to something without mentioning it specifically. We create an *illusion* by making an image that is not reality:

> When he told me that he wanted nothing but to lie down in green pastures, he was making an *allusion* to the Twenty-third Psalm.
>
> In our society, movies create *illusions* that take our minds off our troubles.

An *allusion* is always indirect. It is not the same as a mention or a citation or a quotation. Literary allusions often enliven writing by making us recall other things we have read. When we read, "All his ambitions were only sound and fury," we recall Shakespeare's Macbeth and the hopelessness into which Macbeth's ambitions led him, for Macbeth declares that life is a "tale, told by an idiot, full of sound and fury, but signifying nothing." A writer does not have to mention Macbeth by name; we might think him insulting if he did so. The allusion is sufficient.

Impact/Impacted

For centuries *impact* was used only as a noun and *impacted* as an adjective. Our forebears spoke easily of the impact of hooves on cobblestones or the impact of a new revelation about the government. They never said, "Victoria impacted her Parliaments but did not control them." *The Oxford English Dictionary* (*O.E.D.*) shows that John Wesley in a sermon of 1791 used the word as an imperative. "Impact fire into iron by hammering it when red hot." Wesley was old then and probably in less control of his language than he had been earlier in his career. Every other use that the *O.E.D.* gives under *impact* as a verb has the past participial form, which in English may serve as an adjective. For centuries the person who said, "I am impacted," was saying, "I am constipated."

But of late *impact* has become a universal synonym for *influence*. Polls impact elections. Reform movements impact welfare programs.

Such usage is only another corruption of language, spread by bureaucrats so uncertain of their own places in the world that they must devise strong-sounding language to convey the impression that they are doing far more important tasks than in fact they are. Shun *impact* as a verb. It is a neologism of the worst and most pretentious sort.

Imply/Infer

Here is another confusion that has lasted for centuries, and concerning it I can express only a majority opinion, not a unanimous verdict. We *imply* something by conveying a meaning in some way other than a direct statement; we *infer* a conclusion by reasoning out the evidence although that evidence may not deliver the solid proof we may wish. The writer or the speaker *implies*; the reader or the hearer *infers*.

> By not mentioning South Korea as an area the United States would defend, President Truman *implied* that he would not oppose militarily a North Korean invasion.
>
> The North Koreans *inferred* as much and invaded—only to discover that they had been wrong.

Cognates of *imply* and *infer* are *implication* and *inference*, with which we seldom find confusion. "There was an implication in his words that I did not understand." That is, he *implied* something I could not grasp. "The inference I drew was that she did not want to tell me everything." That is, I *inferred* that she did not wish to tell me everything she knew.

Incredible/Incredulous

Something is *incredible* if we cannot believe it. We are *incredulous* if we cannot believe something incredible:

> His belief that taxes could be cut, military spending increased, and the budget balanced was *incredible*.
>
> Her remark that she had read all the works of Tolstoy in a week left me *incredulous*.

Indicate/Say

To indicate is much the same as *to imply*, though the connotation of *to indicate* is usually a little stronger. That is, something *indicated* is nearly always true, but something *implied* may be true or false. Even this distinction between the two words is not always observed. *Indicate* is often used to show that something happens without any special intention on the part of the actor. *Imply* is customarily used when the actor of the verb wishes to convey some significance beyond the plain meaning of the words.

Smoke *indicates* fire. The smoke is impersonal; it has no intention. It is a sign that a fire burns even if we cannot see the fire. A woman laughing *indicates* that she is happy. She may be laughing spontaneously without meaning to show that she is happy, but she shows happiness whether she intends to or not.

Do not use *indicate* as a synonym for *say*.

> "Tuition will go up by 14 percent next year," the president *said*.

The president did not *indicate* that tuition was rising; she made a plain statement of fact that should not be softened by the weaker word *indicate*. But you can say this:

> When she was asked if tuition would rise next year, the president said, "No comment," *indicating* that it may.

Individual

A much overused word. Use *individual* only when you make a deliberate comparison between a single person or object and a group:

> One of the great philosophical problems has always been to define the rights of the *individual* against the rights of society as a whole.

It is stiff and pretentious to write, "Three individuals came to collect their bribes."

Sometimes the word *individual* is used for no good reason with the pronoun *each*: "Each individual house on the block has a porch and a garage." A little thought shows that *each individual* is redundant. You get the same meaning by saying, "Each house on the block has a porch and a garage."

Intensifiers

These words are intensifiers: *very, absolutely, definitely, incredibly, basically, certainly, positively, fantastic, terrific, wonderful, marvelous, dreadful, horrible, fabulous*, and so on.

As I have mentioned frequently already, we live among exaggerations and ruthless claims for our attention, a kind of Las Vegas mentality where flaming electric signs whose spurting jets of gaudy color dull us to insensitivity—calling forth from their makers even more flamboyant displays. Few advertisers subtly bid for our attention; they scream at us. The habit has carried over into the language of daily discourse like some sickness infecting multitudes.

Intensifiers deaden prose. They sound like shouting, and if you use them over and over, people shut you off. Resist the trend.

Lay/Lie

One of the most commonly violated distinctions. Both the verbs are irregular in the past and in the past participle, which is a major reason for the confusion they cause writers and speakers. To complicate things still more, the past tense of *lie* is *lay*. No wonder even educated people mess them up! In the present tense:

I *lie* on the floor to take a nap in the afternoon.
I *lay* a paperback book under my head as a pillow.

The past tense is more troublesome:

Yesterday I *lay* on the floor and took a nap.
I *laid* a paperback book under my head as a pillow.

The past participle can also give trouble:

I have often *lain* on the floor to take a nap.
I have *laid* a paperback book under my head for a pillow.

The *lay/lie* affair gets more complicated when we consider some folk usages that come down to us from the time when English reflexive verbs were more common than they are now: "Now I lay me down to sleep; I pray the Lord my soul to keep." In modern idiom we might say, "Now I lie down to sleep."

To add still further to the confusion, *lay* and *lie* are both used as nouns to indicate how something is lying. The choice is entirely idiomatic; that is, it has no rules. We speak of the *lay* of the land but the *lie* of a golfball. A friend tells me of playing golf with a new acquaintance who became nervous when he discovered that my friend was a high school English teacher. The acquaintance hit a ball off into the woods, was gone for a long time, and when he emerged after hitting the ball out, apologized for taking so long. "I had a bad lay in there," the acquaintance said, conveying a different impression from the one he intended.

Despite the confusions, be careful with this one. The distinction is important, and people with an ear for language notice when others confuse the words.

Less/Fewer

Some authorities think this distinction has been lost, and it has indeed often been blurred, but most careful writers and editors preserve it. The distinction resembles that of *amount* and *number* commented on early in this list. *Less* is used for quantities not customarily counted by unit; *fewer* is used for quantities that can be counted.

"There was *less* litter on the floor because *fewer* people used the room."

Some idioms call for *less* when we might at first suppose that *fewer* would be preferred.

> She gave me *less* than ten dollars.
>
> Today's highest temperature was ten degrees *less* than yesterday's.

In these idioms we sense a unity of quanity in the money and in the temperature, and we use *less* to indicate our sense of the wholeness of what we describe.

Like/As

This distinction is changing before our eyes. The supposed rule, followed by most editors and writers, is that *like* should never be used as a conjunction to join two clauses. But in speech and informal writing, many educated people have been using *like* as a conjunction for years. Charles Darwin wrote, "Unfortunately, few have observed *like* you have done."[5] Not long ago N. R. Kleinfield wrote in the business pages of *The New York Times* about the decline of an audience for televised professional football games:

> One result is that disgruntled advertisers, complaining that they are not getting the audience for commercials that they expected have been banging on the networks' doors, looking for restitution. And it looks like they will be successful.[6]

Many authorities want *like* to govern only nouns, pronouns, or a noun substitute such as a gerund. No one could object to this sentence: "I felt like coming in the summer." *Coming* is a gerund, a noun substitute, and can be governed by *like*. But many will object if you write, "I felt like I might come in the summer." Like now becomes a conjunction, and to many this usage seems improper. Purists will prefer that you write, "I felt *as if* I would come in the summer."

You will be safe from attack if you use *as if* instead of *like* to introduce a clause. But to many ears *like* is a more simple and even more pleasing choice. This is a place in the grammatical rule book where you should make up your own mind—knowing that if you do use *like* as a conjunction, many people will be annoyed.

The confusion between *like* and *as if* is not nearly so obnoxious as the ill-considered efforts of some dislikers of *like* to purge *like* from our vocabulary as if it were some vagabond bringing shame on the club. It is correct to say, "The party included some distinguished guests *like* the dean of the college and the president of the university." The fastidious substitute *such as* for *like*. There is nothing wrong with *such as.* But there is nothing wrong with *like* either. The rule that some writers follow in using *such as* is aptly phrased by one textbook, which gives this advice: "When you are using an example of something, use *such as* to indicate that the example is a representative of the thing mentioned, and use *like* to compare the example to the thing mentioned." This rule would give us these sentences: "The party included distinguished guests *such as* the dean of the college," and, "He aspired to be distinguished *like* the dean of the college." The rule is harmless, but it also not binding.

A somewhat more troublesome use of *like* is in comparisons like these: "She sings like a bird"; "He walks like an elephant." The fastidious say that these sentences imply a verb following the final noun: "She sings like a bird sings"; "He walks like an elephant walks." So if the verb were written, the sentences would be formally incorrect. In fact the verb is *not* written, and we can let her sing *like* a bird if she can and let him walk *like* an elephant if he must. It would be a false note to have her sing *as* a bird and heavy-handed at least to make him walk *as* an elephant.

Literally

This word gives notice to your readers that you are not using metaphor or hyperbole. When you say, "My papers were *literally* scattered to the winds," you mean that a storm blew your papers in confusion down the street. When you say, "He *literally* did not have a dime to his name," you mean he could go through all his assets and not fine ten cents.

Avoid using *literally* merely to be emphatic when you don't mean what you are saying. Don't say, "My blood literally boiled" unless your temperature rose to 212 degrees Fahrenheit and you started giving off red steam. Most of the time you can avoid the word. Instead of saying "Literally thousands gathered to hear her speak," you can say, "Thousands gathered to hear her speak."

Masterful/Masterly

This distinction has been all but lost, and I regret its passing. *Masterful* once meant "domineering" or "overbearing"—acting like a master ruling his slaves or apprentices. *Masterly* meant "with the skill of a master." If we say, "Coach Dixie did a *masterful* job preparing his team for the game with Alabama," we mean that he treated his team like a chain gang. If we say he did a *masterly* job arranging his schedule so his team would remain undefeated, we mean that he did supremely well what publicity-conscious coaches do nowadays to ensure their teams national ranking. Confusion of the words has eliminated a fine distinction.

Me/I

We have already considered the phrase "between you and me" in the rubric dealing with *between*. The phrase should always be "between you and me." *I* should never be a direct object or the object of a preposition in a sentence. Don't say, "He told Rocky and I that he would not fight the challenger," or, "She sent Jill and I to the library for the book."

Oddly enough, just as *I* has become misued in the objective case, *me* is now often misused in the nominative, or subjective, case. Many young people say and write, "Me and Paul went to the movies Friday night."

The same failures in proper case often turn up in other ways. *Myself* is a reflexive pronoun; that is, it calls attention to a special emphasis on the subject *I* or indicates action by the subject on itself. So we can say:

I myself have often made that mistake.

I shot myself in the foot.

But don't say "He invited Jean and myself to the party." Say, "He invited Jean and me to the party." And don't say, "Myself and Abigail invite you all to our party."

Medium/Media

The word *medium* is a singular noun that signifies anything that enables something else to work or appear. Until recently its most common use was in the phrase "medium of exchange," which means money or anything else that allows people to carry on trade. In recent times the plural form *media* has come to mean all the instruments of mass communication that serve society. The *media* include radio, television, newspapers, and magazines. A connotation of the word seems to be something ephemeral, something that does not remain important for long. Books are a medium of communication, but somehow they are usually excluded when we speak of the *media*.

Two objections may be raised against the word *media*: it is less specific and therefore less vivid than the words it replaces, and it is often misused by appearing with the singular form of a verb or pronoun. You should not say, "The media *is* responsible for the shallowness of American politics." If you use the term, it should be in the plural; however, it seems far better to say something specific: "The effort of candidates to shape their pronouncements to fit the four-minute sound bite on the television news has contributed to the shallowness of American politics. Few people can be profound, complex, or subtle in four minutes."

Militate against/Mitigate

Mitigate means "to lessen," often for good reason. If your neighbor sues you for driving your power lawn mower through her flower garden, your lawyer may claim the *mitigating* circumstance that you are allergic to petunias and that you could not sit in your yard when your neighbor's petunias bloomed without breaking out into hives. The judge may then *mitigate* the rigor of the law that applies to your case.

Militate is related to *military*, and anything that *militates against* a position offers a strong reason not to accept it:

> Her declaration that she would rather go to the party with a cabbage than to go with him *militated against* his hope that she would change her mind and accept his invitation.

The common confusion of the expressions arises because people want a hard *g* sound to go with both words in the phrase "militate against." So they use "mitigate against" when in fact the phrase makes no sense. Here is a rare instance in English where spoken rhythms, otherwise so desirable, may lead the unwary writer astray.

Model/Replica

A *model* duplicates the appearance of something else but on a larger or smaller scale—usually so different a scale that there can be no confusion between the model and the real thing. A model railroad duplicates the appearance of a railroad but will fit on a table. A model of the DNA molecule is millions of times larger than the real thing to allow students to study it.

A *replica* must be like the original in every detail, including size. The *replica* of the *Mayflower* in the harbor at Plymouth, Massachusetts, is exactly like the original ship. (At least it is exactly what we know of the original.)

Note that the term *exact replica* is redundant. A replica is exact by definition.

More important/More importantly

It is incorrect to say, "The Yankees lost the pennant, but more importantly, they lost money." In constructions like this one, the clause *what is more important* is implied. This elliptical clause (we call it *elliptical* because often some of its words are ommitted when it is used in a sentence) works as a noun rather than an adverb. In this sentence a *Time* writer uses the expression correctly:

> *More important,* he sat at Stengel's side, learning the game from one of its managerial geniuses.

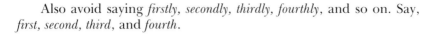

Also avoid saying *firstly, secondly, thirdly, fourthly,* and so on. Say, *first, second, third,* and *fourth*.

Nauseous/Nauseated

When you are sick at your stomach and ready to vomit, you are *nauseated*. If you come on a dead horse and get sick at the sight and the smell, the horse is *nauseous*. Something *nauseous* will make you feel *nauseated*. So don't say, "I'm nauseous" unless people habitually throw their hands over their mouths, make gasping noises, and run for the bathroom whenever you walk into a crowd.

Ongoing

A bureaucratic synonym for *continuing*. *Ongoing* is another of those flat, dull words that usually signal bad prose to come.

Oriented/Orientation

We live in a *wealth-oriented* society.

He was *success-oriented* as a youth but *leisure-oriented* as an adult.

The suffix *-oriented* and the noun *orientation* turn up all over the place now. They are vague and colorless, keeping us and our readers from concrete thought. It is much better to say that we live in a society that seeks wealth and admires it too much in people. It's more concrete and enlightening to say, "As a young man, MacDougal aspired to work hard and earn a hundred thousand dollars a year, but when he grew older he wanted only to drink beer, play golf, watch television, and read trashy novels."

Parameters

This word has become a synonym for *limits*, which is a good, strong word that says everything most people mean by *parameters* and says it without pretense.

The original meaning of *parameter* is "a constant in mathematics that may be applied to variable situations." This strict use of the word is most common in speaking of numerical quantities. For example, you can set the parameters of a computer to give you sixty-six characters on a line and twenty-nine lines to a page, and the computer will paginate for you according to that setting, no matter how many pages you write or what file you choose to work on. If you figure compound interest at 18.5 percent per annum, your parameter is the figure 18.5, no matter what transaction you are considering.

Parameters may well be used on occasion in nonmathematical discourse. I can imagine saying, "Grace and courtesy have always been parameters of social success," or, "Creativity is the intellectual parameter for all the great disciplines." However, it is only pretension that makes some people say, "We want to carry out this construction project within certain parameters."

Posture

This has become a word much like *conditions* and *case* and the intensifiers *definitely, absolutely*, and *incredible*. It is popular—and says almost nothing that cannot be said more simply and more vigorously by other words. Instead of saying, "They adopted a defensive posture," why not say, "They became defensive," or, "They went on the defensive"?

Preplanning/Advanced planning

Both these terms are tautological; that is, they say the same thing twice. *Preplanning* must take place before the thing that is planned. Since planning comes before the act that is planned, it is an unnecessary inflation to add the prefix *pre-* or the modifier *advanced* as if some kinds of planning could go on after the occasion being planned for.

Presently/Currently/Now

The adverb *presently* most properly denotes something about to happen: "The actors will appear *presently*."

Recently the word *presently* has become a synonym for *now* or *currently* so that pilots come on the intercom to tell us, "We are presently flying over Tuscaloosa, Alabama." It seems better to hold to the older meaning of *presently* and to use either *now* or *currently* or, better still, let the present tense stand by itself to express something happening now. "We are flying over Tuscaloosa, Alabama."

Yet *presently* as an inflated synonym for "now" may be here to stay. In the first edition of this work, somebody in production wrote of me in the note "About the Author" that I was "presently working on another novel." I groaned within and without.

Principal/Principle

Principal has always had the connotation of *first*. It is most often an adjective, meaning the first or the most important.

> The *principal* reason for her irritation with me was that I had run over her cat.

It is sometimes used as a noun to designate a person of primary authority:

Our high school *principal* told us that fair play was fine as long as it did not keep us from winning games.

The *principals* in the final drama of the Civil War were Ulyssees S. Grant and Robert E. Lee.

Principle is always a noun meaning an ideal standard of conduct or an underlying system that helps explain some things we may see only in a superficial way until we think about them.

One man's *principle* is another's poison.

The *principle* of the mercury thermometer is that mercury expands with heat and contracts with cold.

Quotation/Quote

Quotation is a noun; *quote* is a verb, although lately it has become more and more common to see *quote* used as a noun. Even so, I still think it bad form to write a sentence like this: "His quotes from the Bible prove that Faulkner knew it well." I prefer this: "His *quotations* from the Bible prove that Faulkner knew it well."

Respective/Respectively

Use these words only when some large confusion might result without them.

The winners of first and second prizes were Jack Rowdy and Meg Loader *respectively*.

Without *respectively* in the sentence, someone might suppose that Jack and Meg had somehow shared the two prizes. It is probably better to write, "Jack Rowdy won first prize, and Meg Loader took second."

Simple/Simplistic

Something *simple* is uncomplicated. People, machines, novels, poems, and plans can be simple. Only ideas or utterances can be *simplistic*. The connotation of *simplistic* is always bad, implying that the person with, say, a simplistic idea has not thought out all the consequences.

A *simple* way to raise enough money to repair the American highway system might be to impose an additional tax of fifty cents a gallon on gasoline and diesel fuel. A *simplistic* idea might be to turn all the highways into toll roads. This idea would be *simplistic* because the person advancing it would not have thought of how much money it would cost to build and operate the toll booths, how many accidents they would cause, and how much they would increase fuel consumption by making cars stop and start again.

That

This excellent and useful word has lately been pressed into service as a synonym for the adverb *very*. *Very* is a weak adverb; *that* seems to be stronger. So we get sentences like this one: "The game wasn't that close." The usage seems always to be in the negative, and the logical question is to ask what the referent of *that* might be. We can readily understand the word if it occurs in a sentence like this: "I have been sunburned through a shirt, but my son's skin is not that sensitive."

The preceding statement about my sunburn gives some context to the statement that my son's skin is not *that* sensitive. But what of this sentence standing without a referent? "His skin was not *that* sensitive." How sensitive? As sensitive as a baby's? As the skin of a rhinoceros? We have no context to tell us.

Perhaps the original idiom was *all that good* or *all that bad*. By ellipses we have shortened it to merely *that*. It was not a good idiom in the first place, and shortening it has made it worse.

This

Now and then you can get away with a vague *this* in your prose if your context is clear:

> Frederick Bazille and Claude Monet started painting in the open air; *this* was the real beginning of French Impressionist art.

The *this* in the sentence above refers to the act of painting in the open air, described in the first independent clause. We have no trouble understanding the reference. But the vague *this* often leads to confusion.

> In their war plans of 1914, the Germans assumed that they would have to fight a hard war against the Russians but that they would have an easy time with the French, especially if they could send an overpowering army crashing through Belgium to capture Paris within weeks after the outbreak of hostilities. With France quickly defeated, the Germans could turn all their force against the Russians. This was why a local conflict so quickly became a European war.

In a text this complicated, the vague *this* causes all sorts of trouble to the reader who does not already know the story. For clarity, always try to have *this* refer to a noun or pronoun.

> This German military thinking explains why a local conflict so quickly became a European war.

Thrust

Another lazy word like *factor*, used by writers who wobble and weasel. We hear of "the thrust of an article" or "the thrust of an argument." Writers telling us of the *thrust* are usually trying to tell us that they are so clever that they see many different issues but that by their superior wisdom they have picked out the main line of discourse. They protect themselves from the accusation that they have missed the point, and they provide room for themselves to whirl around and run the other way should anyone challenge them. Don't weasel and wobble. Don't use *thrust*.

Tragedy/Calamity

Strictly speaking, a *tragedy* is a drama played out in life or on the stage in which a great human being is brought down to defeat by forces beyond his control either within himself or in the world around him. Macbeth is tragic; so is Othello. Macbeth cannot control his ambition, and Othello cannot control his jealousy. Tragedy has been part of the human experience for centuries, for it reveals the glory and depravity of the greatest of human beings and comforts us with the assurance that we are not alone in feeling both glory and depravity within ourselves.

But the rise of modern sensational journalism has confused *tragedy* with *calamity*, *misfortune*, and *accident*. In consequence, the tragic sense, having nearly vanished from our language, may be in danger of vanishing from our sensibilities. Now an airplane crash is a *tragedy*, as is the wreck of a truck that kills somebody. *Tragedy* should be restored to its original high use, and other words should be used to describe accidents that do not involve high human characters as much as they originate in carelessness or mechanical failure. But the word may have been already diluted beyond the power of restoration.

Transpire/Occur

Transpire originally meant "to sweat," a meaning the French word *transpirer* keeps. From this meaning *transpire* took on the sense of "passing from the hidden to the open," a useful concept in sentences like these:

It *transpired* that high officials in the United States government realized by 1967 that Americans could not win the Vietnam War.

It *transpired* after they had talked for a little while that they had both been in college at the same time thirty years before.

To use the word *transpire* as a synonym for *happen* or *occur* is portentous discourse, as in this sentence: "The game transpired on a golden autumn afternoon before 94,000 screaming fans in Knoxville."

Try and/Try to

The proper idiom is *try to*, although in speaking many people say *try and*. Proper: "I will *try to* attend the concert tonight." Try takes an infinitive when it is used with another verb.

Unique

Unique means "one of a kind," and it can be modified only by words like *nearly* or *almost*. You cannot logically describe something as being very unique or rather unique or the most unique or somewhat unique. Something is either unique or it is not. If something is not unique, you can describe it as rare, uncommon, or unusual, or you can say that it is *almost* or *nearly* unique.

Varying/Various

The distinction between these words gives unusual trouble. If we are discussing changes in the same thing from one time or place to another, the appropriate word is *varying*. If we are discussing different things with attention to the differences between them, the appropriate word is *various*. *Varying* is used before a singular noun, *various* before a plural noun. These sentences uses *varying* correctly:

> Her love was *varying*, depending on whether she saw the mess I made around the house or the devotion I felt for her.
>
> The *varying* weather made the day interesting though not especially pleasant.

The following sentences use *various* correctly—with a plural noun:

> *Various* friends told her she was correct.
>
> The responses to my proposal were *various*.
>
> *Various* black musicians created jazz.

Viable options/Viable alternatives

Both phrases occur as inflated discourse designed to deceive readers into believing that something important is being said. Are *nonviable* options really options at all? If not, why should we bother to speak of *viable* options? The word *viable* should be reserved for its proper meaning, as in the phrase "viable seeds," meaning seeds that will germinate if planted.

Violent/Vehement

If you hit somebody with your fists or with a club, you are *violent*; if you attack only with words, you are *vehement*. If you *violently* protest an umpire's call in a baseball game, you run out onto the field and hit him; if you *vehemently* protest, you may scream at him, suggest an oculist, or profanely discuss his Mafia connections.

While/Although

Some writers use *while* as a synonym for *although*, with confusing results: "While MacDougal was an athlete in college, he became as fat as a keg when he stopped taking exercise." What does this sentence mean? It could mean that although MacDougal was an athlete in college, he stopped taking exercise after graduation and became as fat as a keg. Some might suppose from the sentence that during the time MacDougal was an athlete in college, he stopped taking exercise and became as fat as a keg—but still remained an athlete. The example may be extreme, although if MacDougal was a baseball pitcher, it is plausible. *While* conveys a momentary confusion any time it is used as a synonym for *although*, and good writers should protect readers from momentary confusions.

Which

In my chapter on false rules (Chapter Ten) I reject the *that/which* rule, and readers interested in that oft-inflated subject may seek enlightenment there. *Which* itself causes another difficulty, similar to that of the vague *this* discussed earlier in this list. When *which* does not refer to a clear antecedent, the reader often feels an absence that may create bafflement.

> In many universities, writing teachers love teaching but often work only part-time, without adequate benefits and at low salaries and without much contact with the rest of the teaching faculty, *which* accounts for the low morale many of them feel.

The *which* clause here has no clear antecedent. We can grasp the meaning only if we assume that the *which* clause does not apply to the statement that writing teachers love teaching. Morale may be low because of the other facts mentioned in the sentence. The sentence could be fixed by saying this at the end: "*disadvantages which account for the low morale many of them feel.*"

Which should always have a clear antecedent expressed as a noun or a pronoun. Such clarity will save readers the trouble of backing up to read again to see if they have missed anything.

Who/Whom

This distinction provokes much acrimonious debate among writers and grammarians. Some want to get rid of *whom* altogether or use it only immediately after a preposition. Then we would have sentences like these:

We did not care who he chose to represent us.

She did not know to whom she spoke.

Whom may be withering away. My friend Richard A. Lanham, U.C.L.A.'s distinguished authority on grammar, titled one chapter of a good book he wrote "Who's Kicking Who?" He says that "who's kicking whom" sounds stilted to him. It does not sound stilted to me, and other conservative grammarians agree. You must make up your own mind. Many people will object if you fail to use *whom* in its traditional place; no one will object if you use it in the traditional way.

If *whom* sounds stilted to your ear, revise your sentence to get rid of it. *Who* and *whom* clauses are not frequent in some styles. You can read page after page of *Sports Illustrated, Time, Smithsonian,* or *National Geographic* without encountering a clause introduced by *who* or *whom*. Many serious books use such clauses rarely. Richard Ellmann's *James Joyce* can go for many pages without using a *who* or *whom* clause. It may be that good writers sense that such clauses introduce distracting elements in sentences. Everybody uses them now and then, but when you write one in a first draft, consider changing it.

As in the great debate over *like* and *as*, some people want to preserve the distinction between *who* and *whom* but unfortunately do not know what the distinction is. They use *whom* when *who* is proper. The rule is this: Use *who* or *whom* according to how the pronoun is used in the clause where it appears. If it is used as the subject of the clause, use *who*; if it is used as the object of the clause, use *whom*.

This rule sounds more complicated than it is. The following sentence is incorrect:

The university wanted a football coach *whom* the president said would be able to break NCAA rules without being caught.

The writer of this sentence saw that *coach* was a direct object and assumed that the clause modifying *coach* should begin with *whom*, in the objective case. But the sentence should read like this:

The university wanted a football coach *who* the president said would be able to break NCAA rules without being caught.

In the dependent clause modifying *coach, who* is the subject of the verb *would be able*. Therefore *who* must be in the subjective case. The short clause *the president said* is parenthetical, inserted in the *who* clause but not governing the subject *who*. You can check such clauses by trying to replace the *who* or *whom* with *he* or *him* in a sentence constructed from the clause. You can say, "*He* would be able to break NCAA rules without being caught." You cannot properly say, "*Him* would be able to break NCAA rules without being caught."

In the illustrative sentence we used above, *whom* is correct, not *who*. "We did not care *whom* he chose to represent us." Here *whom* is a direct object. "He chose *whom*." We could say correctly, "He chose *him*." We could not say, "He chose he."

It's important to remember that parenthetical elements such as *he said* within a *who* or *whom* clause do not govern the pronoun. These sentences are correct:

> The candidate *who* they thought would be the best librarian was rejected by the chancellor for being too outspoken.
>
> The assistant coach *whom* they believed Coach Dixie would choose lost his chance when he was arrested.
>
> The trustees fired the president, who had been beloved by the faculty, because he had insisted that student football players attend classes.
>
> The man whom they chose to replace him promised to be guided in all his academic decisions by Coach Dixie.

It is also important to recall that *who* and *whom* should not be confused in writing questions. In speaking, many people say things like this:

> Who do you expect to be Coach Dixie's assistant now?

But it is better to say and to write this: "Whom do you expect to be Coach Dixie's assistant now?" *Whom* in the sentence is the direct object of the verb *expect*, and it should be in the objective case.

Whom is always used if it is the object of an infinitive, that is, the recipient of the action described by the infinitive.

> They wondered *whom* to send as their representative.

The greatest problem with *whom* seems to come in the use of its associated pronoun *whomever*. Here is a sentence that appeared recently in a book published by Yale University Press:

> Haskell sold land to whomever would buy.

The author and the editors at Yale Press both must have seen the preposition *to* and remembered the rule that the object of a preposition should be in the objective case. They forgot that the entire clause following *to* serves as the object of the preposition and that within that clause the pronoun is governed by how it is used in relation to the verb. The sentence should have read, "Haskell sold land to whoever would buy." *Whoever* governs the verb *would buy* and must be in the subjective case.

Who or *whom* should be used to refer to persons. You should not say, "The German generals that planned the war later blamed it all on Hitler." You should instead say, "The German generals *who* planned the war later blamed it all on Hitler."

These rules may seem so complex that you may be tempted to accept Richard Lanham's advice and throw *whom* onto the garbage dump of language along with other obsolete words. I would say only that *whom* is not obsolete yet, and if you want your work to be respected by the educated, you're better off with *whom* than without it. The *whom*less writer may find it difficult to gain attention.

Whose/Of which

Some authorities insist that the possessive *whose* be used only when the antecedent is a person or a group of persons. They object to any use of *whose* in connection with an impersonal antecedent. Even H. W. Fowler, a conservative authority, ridicules this notion. It would require us to write sentences like this: "The aircraft, the tail of which fell off on the approach to the runway, landed safely." Most of us would write, "The aircraft, whose tail fell off on the approach to the runway, landed safely." We may rewrite the sentence to avoid the problem altogether: "The aircraft lost its tail on the approach to the runway but landed safely." Often such rewriting is neither feasible nor important, and we must use *whose* or *of which*. Whenever we do have a choice between *of which* and *whose* we should let the rhythm of the sentence dictate our solution. That solution will usually be to use *whose*.

-wise

I'm in no hurry *time-framewise*.

Pricewise, German cars failed to compete with Japanese cars, and *saleswise* the Japanese began taking over the American import market.

Sticking *-wise* onto the ends of nouns to turn them into adverbs has become a virus of the variety of tacking *-ize* onto nouns to make them verbs. The practice represents a lazy mind, and you should avoid it.

With

With should not be used loosely in the sense of *and* or *in addition*. Don't write this: "Chip took first place with Yoke coming in second." Write this: "Chip took first place, and Yoke was second."

Nine

Figurative Language

❖❖❖

*F*igurative language is the use of words in any but their literal sense. If I say, "She floated easily on her back in the pool," I use the verb *floated* in its literal sense. If I say, "She floated gracefully from person to person at the party, making everyone feel like one of her intimate friends," I use the verb *floated* in a figurative sense. If I say, "The water boiled for tea," I mean that the water was heated to 212 degrees Fahrenheit, that it bubbled violently, and that it passed into the air as steam. If someone says, "His condescending attitude made my blood boil," *boil* becomes figurative. This particular device we call *hyperbole*—exaggerated speech used to make a point emphatically.

Figurative language must do three things: (1) it must draw on some common experience that binds a writer to her audience, (2) it must be fresh and engaging—often surprising, and (3) it must be appropriate to the context the writer is developing.

Similes and Metaphors

Similes and metaphors, which take one form of experience and apply it to another, rank among the most common figurative devices. In the writing program I direct, we have a metaphor for a certain kind of research paper that comes to us filled with quotations, demonstrating hours of hard work but lacking any ideas from the student writer herself. We call this the model ship paper. You can buy such a model at a hobby shop and spend hours or even weeks putting it together until you have an impressive object on your dining room table. But you will have contributed nothing of your own to the model except your labor and dexterity.

❖

We want papers that show careful labor, but we also want some original thinking. We want our student writers to do more than paste sources together; we want them to bring the design of their paper out of their own experience, their own struggle with the ideas and information they find in the sources. We want them to produce a paper that cannot be entirely predicted before they begin. Our use of the model ship metaphor helps students understand the difference between writing a paper that is formally correct and producing a paper that shows some creativity by the writer.

Grammarians often make an unnecessarily sharp distinction between *metaphor* and *simile*. Simile and metaphor differ in their construction. A simile is a kind of metaphor. A metaphor speaks of something as if it were something else: "Johnson was a bulldog in argument." A simile tells us that something is *like* something else. We could say, "Johnson is like a bulldog in argument," or, "Johnson is as tenacious as a bulldog in argument." In both cases we isolate a quality in bulldogs—their legendary tenacity—and apply it to Johnson. We don't apply every quality in bulldogs to Johnson. He does not, for example, walk on all fours and bark and eat dog food. He is tenacious; that is the only point we want to make in the metaphor or simile.

Both metaphors and similes depend on some shared experience between writer and reader. When I say, "Johnson is a bulldog in argument," I assume that my readers know something about bulldogs or at least that they *think* they know something about bulldogs. (Bulldogs are in fact gentle creatures.) Their knowledge of bulldogs helps me tell them something about Johnson. If my readers were Siberian fishers who had never seen or heard of a bulldog, my metaphor would make no sense.

The balance between the reader's knowledge and the writer's intent is delicate. Suppose I said, "Johnson is a salmon in argument." Most readers cannot think of anything about salmon that would apply to arguments, so the metaphor fails. I might say this: "Johnson is a salmon in argument; he starts in one place and goes all around the world and comes back to where he began, no matter what contrary views we put in his way." Now the metaphor works a little better, but it is still clumsy. Good metaphors work a little like jokes: They make a sudden and vivid impression. Jokes and metaphors that have to be explained are usually awkward. Like good jokes, good metaphors depend on a common experience. Most of us have at some time failed to get a joke that convulses everyone else in a group. We don't get the joke because we have not shared the common experience that makes it funny to others. Unless we make metaphors out of the common experience of our readers, they will not get the point.

THREE KINDS OF METAPHOR

Most metaphors may be classified under three general headings. The first, the descriptive metaphor, helps us understand one concrete object by reference to another. The second, the abstract metaphor, helps us understand an abstraction by reference to a concrete object. The third, the embedded metaphor, makes language more vivid by substituting metaphorical terms for literal reporting. Metaphors that help us see one concrete entity by reference to another help us describe things; metaphors that use a concrete reference to illuminate an abstraction help us explain ideas; and embedded metaphors brighten our language in more subtle ways.

The descriptive metaphor   Descriptive metaphors help us imagine scenes. Loren Eiseley describes a flight of birds like this:

> It was then that I saw the flight coming on. It was moving like a little close-knit body of black specks that danced and darted and closed again. It was pouring from the north and heading toward me with the undeviating relentlessness of a compass needle.[1]

One concrete metaphor in this passage speaks of "a little close-knit body of black specks." The other speaks of the "undeviating relentlessness of a compass needle." Each refers to something we commonly know—specks and a compass needle—and applies it to the flight of birds to help us see better what Eiseley saw.

Here is a metaphor-rich passage by Tom Wolfe writing about women relentlessly playing the slot machines in Las Vegas:

> They have a Dixie Cup full of nickels or dimes in the left hand and an Iron Boy work glove on the right hand to keep the callouses from getting sore. Every time they pull the handle, the machine makes a sound much like the sound a cash register makes before the bell rings, then the slot pictures start clattering up from left to right, the oranges, lemons, plums, cherries, bells, bars, buckaroos—the figure of a cowboy riding a bucking bronco. The whole sound keeps churning up over and over again in eccentric series all over the place, like one of those random-sound radio symphonies by John Cage.[2]

Here is a passage by John McPhee:

> This, after all, was Switzerland, where everything works; Switzerland, where trains run like clocks, and clocks run like watches, and watches are synchronous with the pulse of the universe.[3]

Always the descriptive metaphor uses something readers know to help them see better something they do not know. Eiseley assumes that we have seen enough black specks to understand what a distant but undefined group of them might be, and he thinks we know that a compass needle always points north. Wolfe makes a bolder assumption, that his readers know the bizarre music of composer John Cage. (That assumption helps us define the audience he is addressing—a fairly urbane, well-educated, perhaps sophisticated group of readers.) He is on firmer ground when he assumes that we know the sound a cash register makes just before the bell rings. (With the advent of computerized cash registers, however, this sound may soon become unfamiliar.) John McPhee, using hyperbole, assumes that we know the reputation of Swiss clocks and watches for accuracy, and with his metaphor he tells us that Swiss trains run with the same exactitude.

The descriptive metaphor has often made personal writing more powerful. Philip Caputo, writing about his days as a Marine in the Vietnam War, describes the heat:

> It was noon, without a breath of wind, and the sky seemed like a blazing aluminum lid clamped over the world.[4]

The abstract metaphor   A different kind of metaphor helps us explain ideas by attributing a concrete reality to an abstraction, making the abstraction more manageable to readers. Such metaphors have been used for centuries. In Psalms we read, "My cup runneth over." In this statement the writer, feeling the blessings of God, uses the cup as a metaphor for the life that can receive God's goodness. In the book of Proverbs we read, "The candle of the wicked shall be put out." The "wicked" walk by a man-made light that will be extinguished, leaving them in darkness. Some people speak of "bearing a cross," meaning a suffering they endure through no fault of their own. Sometimes we speak of death as a person, recalling both the apostle Paul's personification of death in his epistles and the figure of the Grim Reaper with his scythe that has been with us since the Renaissance. A famous metaphor in economics was Adam Smith's "invisible hand," a term he used to explain how supply and demand work in the marketplace.

This kind of metaphor—the abstract metaphor—easily translates into political cartoons. Hunger becomes an emaciated skeleton devouring the world. War becomes a cruel warrior in classical Roman armor with a leering expression on his face. Such metaphors have a long history in our political past. When Southerners claimed, before the Civil War, that every state had the right to "nullify" or disregard laws made by the United States Congress, Daniel Webster replied that if Southerners were correct, the federal union was no more than a "rope of sand." Abraham Lincoln, some years later, used a biblical metaphor when he spoke ominously of a country part slave and part free, declaring that "a house divided against itself cannot stand." In our own century, when Franklin D. Roosevelt proclaimed that his administration would give a "new deal" to the American people, the slogan *New Deal* became one of the most powerful metaphors in American history. Millions felt they had been dealt an unlucky hand by the Great Depression through no fault of their own. The image of a "new deal" made them think they might now have another chance, another deal of the cards of life. The metaphor suffered the fate of many good metaphors: it became a cliché. Now the term *New Deal* calls up the Roosevelt administration, and in hearing it, few think of the deal of a card game.

A good metaphor may help us think. As aids to thinking, metaphors are important—perhaps necessary—to modern science. Some might argue that without metaphor some current scientific thinking could scarcely go on. Albert Einstein's theory of relativity deals with phenomena so removed from commonsense experience that most people can scarcely begin to understand it. Indeed, the *London Times* once called Einstein's theory "an affront of common sense." Metaphors have helped explain it.

Einstein himself tried to imagine how the universe would look to someone traveling at the speed of light: he made a pictorial leap in his mind similar to the kind of leap we make when we read a good metaphor. He began with the notion that the speed of light is constant, seen from any vantage point in the universe, whether the light is moving toward us or away from us. Einstein taught that nothing in the universe could move faster than the speed of light and that anything in motion at that speed has a set of relations with other objects that is radically different from those of anything in motion at a lesser speed. This idea, so alien to common sense, called forth from English philosopher Bertrand Russell this metaphorical utterance:

> Everybody knows that if you are on an escalator you reach the top sooner if you walk up than if you stand still. But if the escalator moved with the velocity of light, you would reach the top at exactly the same moment whether you walked up or stood still.[5]

Since we ourselves sense motion at much lesser speeds than the speed of light, scientists and science writers after Einstein have had to use figurative language to enable the rest of us to understand what they are talking about.

Metaphors are common in explanations of other kinds of complicated data. You may make your ideas memorable by finding a good metaphor to illustrate them.

The embedded metaphor   The embedded metaphor is perhaps the most common metaphor—so common, in fact, that we do not recognize it as a metaphor. The embedded metaphor uses a verb or a noun in something other than its literal meaning.

Suppose I write, "The fire devoured the house." I might say, "The fire burned the house down," or, "The fire destroyed the house." When I use the word *devoured*, I employ an embedded metaphor to suggest that the fire is like a ravenous animal eating something up. The metaphor *devoured* treats the fire as a living thing.

Richard Selzer, writing of the scalpel with which he does surgery, calls it "this terrible steel-bellied thing,"[6] referring to the fat part of the instrument with which the surgeon grips it with his fingers. Norman Mailer, writing of the police riot in Chicago during the 1968 Democratic Convention, writes a passage rich with metaphor:

> The police cut through the crowd one way, then cut through them another. They chased people into the park, ran them down, beat them up; they cut through the intersection at Michigan and Balbo like a razor cutting a channel through a head of hair, and then drove columns of new police into the channel who in turn pushed out, clubs flailing, on each side, to cut new channels, and new ones again.[7]

Selzer gives his inanimate scalpel a living, animal quality, speaking of it as a "steel-bellied thing." Mailer gives human beings the quality of an inanimate cutting instrument, and eventually he extends the metaphor into a full-fledged simile so that the police cut "like a razor cutting a channel through a head of hair."

This interplay of metaphor takes place in much writing. At times living things are likened to inanimate objects; at other times inanimate objects are given the qualities of living things. The object of the metaphor is always to make us bring two parts of our experience together so that the immediate object of our attention becomes much more vivid. (The pleasures of a good metaphor are probably as great to the writer who creates the metaphor as they are to the reader. Metaphors provide another example of how writing sharpens thoughts that might otherwise be dull and commonplace.)

METAPHORS AND ATMOSPHERE

Atmosphere, tone, and *voice* all refer to the complex and sometimes only partly conscious emotional response a piece of writing sets out to create in readers. How do we feel when we read something? Metaphors may have a lot to do with our response. Suppose you want to call attention to how thin someone is. One metaphor can create an impression of unhealthiness:

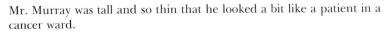
> Mr. Murray was tall and so thin that he looked a bit like a patient in a cancer ward.

Another can create a more positive impression:

> Mr. Murray was tall and so thin that he looked like a long distance runner ready to run a marathon.

Some writers create atmosphere with a stunning metaphorical power. Study the metaphors (I have italicized them for emphasis) in the following passage by Joseph Conrad, a master of the metaphorical art. Conrad's metaphors here create a mood of awe and foreboding:

> You know how these squalls come up there about this time of year. First you see a darkening of the horizon—no more; then a cloud rises *opaque like a wall*. A *straight edge* of vapour lined with *sickly* whitish gleams *flies up* from the southwest, *swallowing* the stars in whole constellations; its shadow *flies over* the waters and *confounds* sea and sky into one *abyss* of obscurity.[8]

Few writers today would dare to duplicate this rich and subtle use of metaphor. The first image is of a cloud rising "opaque like a wall," then of a "straight edge"—a ruler—of vapor lined with "sickly whitish gleams," as if the stormy sky were a person sick with some tumultuous disease. Next the passage tells of the vapor flying up, and we easily imagine some monstrous bird "swallowing the stars in whole constellations." Then its "shadow flies over the waters," giving us another image of a bird of prey swooping over the sea after something—perhaps a ship—that it may find floating there. Afterward a swell or two of the sea runs "like undulations of the very darkness." Those familiar with the first chapter of the book of Genesis, as most literate people were in Conrad's day, remember the chaotic darkness at the beginning, when "the earth was without form and void, and darkness was on the face of the deep"—an image we are prepared for with the words "confounds" and "abyss," which recall the primordial universe before God created light.

Conrad in effect gives us two worlds, the world of the storm on the sea and the eerie world of imaginary association called up in his mind by the storm—a world he transmits to us with his metaphors. The association includes in it not only what we may have experienced of violent tempests but also what we have read and thought of the biblical story of creation, where God struggles against the chaos at the dawn of time. Conrad creates in us something of the primitive fear, probably lurking in the subconscious of most of us, a legacy of the terror felt by our remote ancestors in the face of the forces of nature. Without this string of metaphors, Conrad's prose would not accomplish these effects. The metaphors are numerous, but we accept them because they are consistent, and they work together to create an atmosphere of awe and gloom. It is a different view of a storm from that which we might see on the evening television news in our own time, with the brightly made-up meterologist gesturing and grinning and happily telling us that a hurricane is coming.

In his inaugural address of January 20, 1961, President John F. Kennedy delivered a series of metaphors that gave his speech an aura of vigorous energy and, by extension, conveyed a like feeling to the administration he was about to lead and to his ideal of America. He said:

> Let the word go forth from this time and place, to friend and foe alike, that the torch has been passed to a new generation of Americans, born in this century, tempered by war, disciplined by a hard and bitter peace, proud of our ancient heritage, and unwilling to witness or permit the slow undoing of those human rights to which this nation has always been committed and to which we are committed today at home and around the world.

Reading or hearing Kennedy's image of a torch passed, we think of the Olympic runners carrying the flame from one to another across a country until they arrive at the place where the games are held. The new generation of Americans is described as "tempered," which refers to the process of making steel stronger by first heating it and then plunging it into cool water. We are told that these Americans have been "disciplined by a hard and bitter peace," and we think of soldiers trained by hardship to do their duty. We are told that Americans will not allow "the slow undoing of . . . human rights," and we think of a carefully knitted garment being unraveled before our eyes by some perverse child or some malicious adult.

So it goes through the speech, one vigorous metaphor after another conveying a total image of strength, vitality, endurance, and courage. Presidents always convey some sense of what they think of their administration when they use metaphors. You can read their speeches and see what they believe about their own leadership and the people they are trying to lead. In your writing, the metaphors you use will tell readers much about yourself and what you think of them.

CAUTIONS ABOUT METAPHORS

Metaphors should make one point sharply. Extended metaphors seldom interest readers. You may think it clever to create an extended metaphor that likens getting a college education to climbing a mountain: Admission is like arriving at the base; enrolling in your first classes is like putting on your helmet and climbing tentatively over the first rocks; social life is like rain on the side of the mountain because a little of it is refreshing but too much may wash you off the cliffs. You can go on and on with such metaphors, but to most readers they are contrived and tedious, and by the time you have climbed to the top, they will have long since abandoned your work. When an author employs a poor and overextended metaphor the British say he is "making a metaphor walk on all fours." This is a scornful expression, mocking metaphors that try to do too much.

Arguments based on metaphors are usually inappropriate and may be dangerous. The so-called organic metaphor has long been popular in the study of history. Plants and other organisms are born; they enjoy youth; they pass into maturity and then into old age; finally they die. Edward Gibbon's eighteenth-century *Decline and Fall of the Roman Empire* accustomed several generations of literate readers to thinking of the final centuries of the Roman Empire in the West as a decline, a sickness, much like the aging and death of a human being.

There was no special harm in Gibbon's metaphor. But more recent historians such as Oswald Spengler and Arnold Toynbee made the organic metaphor into an argument. Metaphors may illustrate arguments, but they should not *become* arguments. From the organic metaphor, Spengler and Toynbee constructed elaborate patterns that human history was supposed to have followed. Both of them frequently twisted the historical evidence to make events conform to the design they had imposed on the past. Spengler in particular wrenched history into a plantlike shape whereby all civilizations were seen as passing through the same stages, every stage likened to a similar stage in the development of an organism. He provided a design for history in which no individual striving could make much difference and no collective effort could change the implacable pattern of rise and fall. History in his view repeated itself just as the life cycle of a plant repeats itself again and again in the members of a species. Because Spengler believed that the twentieth century represented the last stage in the organic life of western civilization, he provided no hope for the future. Toynbee, though more moderate in his judgments, fell into much the same trap.

Metaphors are helpful to thought and expression, but they should not take over our minds or our writing. In a fundamental way, metaphors are not *real*. Describing Cleopatra's barge in *Anthony and Cleopatra*, Shakespeare wrote:

> The barge she sat in, like a burnish'd throne
> Burn'd on the water.

We are supposed to imagine that Cleopatra's state barge was so polished that it *seemed* to burn like fire on the water of the Nile. As one scholar has remarked, if we supposed that Cleopatra's barge were literally on fire with she and her sailors jumping into the river to escape the flames, we would have no metaphor.[9] When we make metaphors, we use our imaginations. We play with words. We take part of one thing and make it intensify our sense of another. But a metaphor takes *only* a part; it does not take the whole. Human history is not like a plant in all its particulars; to make the metaphor of growth, maturity, and decline an ironclad rule for how human societies develop is to confuse a metaphor with an argument. A metaphor may illustrate an argument, but it cannot provide the substance of the case.

Avoid packing your prose with so many metaphors that they become confusing or ridiculous. *The New Yorker* frequently runs a little feature called "Block That Metaphor." This feature presents a passage from some writer who has solemnly jumbled metaphors together without thinking of their total effect—like this passage from a book review of James Michener's *Alaska*:

> Perhaps the problem is Michener has grown "formula" in preparing such all-encompassing works. But here at least, the fluffy snowdrifts thaw, exposing a permafrost of substance.
>
> To survive the long polar night of prose, readers must dig in and await spring when the narrative thaws and the verbal tundra becomes hospitable. It takes a gold miner's stamina, though, to pan away, discard the trivial tailings, and be rewarded—not by a mother lode of meaning but by precious flecks of literary gold.[10]

What can this passage mean? It would be difficult or impossible to say. Many writers think this sort of metaphorical profusion indicates verbal brilliance. It fact it indicates only confused pomposity.

Your metaphors should make sense. To make them do so, it is a good idea to slow down and think about them.

CULTIVATING METAPHORS

How do we cultivate metaphors in our own prose? The first step is to to believe that we can use metaphor effectively. That takes a little daring, a willingness to make some mistakes (even some howlers), to laugh about them, and to try again. You can begin to cultivate metaphors by doing some exercises. Jot down some qualities in things and people you observe, and make metaphors from those qualities. You will make some ridiculous combinations, but be dauntless. Keep at it. Here are some exercises to show what I mean:

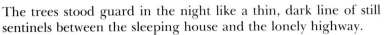

The trees stood guard in the night like a thin, dark line of still sentinels between the sleeping house and the lonely highway.

The trees stood like a congregation of bereaved faithful after the death of summer, their naked branches lifted skyward in prayer for spring after the long winter.

The trees in the cold early dusk looked like a party of other-worldly creatures gathered to discuss the best plan of attack before advancing through the gloom against the house.

The trees stood like a group of giant friends idly holding hands at the bottom of the field and whispering secrets to each other in the tireless way of gossips who love the talk as much as the tale.

The singer squeezed out the lyrics like a bleating sheep whose leg had been caught in a steel trap, while behind him the guitar players whanged on with expressionless faces like spectators who refused to acknowledge that a crime was going on before their eyes.

The generals, like children having a tantrum in front of a candy store, kept crying, "More! More!"

You can make a pleasant and diverting game of making metaphors in the privacy of your notebook. Make some howlers, give yourself some prizes, and the little game will help you develop a habit that will enliven your writing.

APPROPRIATE METAPHORS

Metaphors should be appropriate to the topic at hand. This is a matter of taste. Some writers may feel comfortable using certain metaphors and similes that would annoy some other writers. I would not want to read that General Robert E. Lee's theory of battle was to crash into his foes as if he were trying to drive a bulldozer through a brick wall. General Lee never saw a bulldozer in his life, and a careful reader, considering the incongruity of such a simile, might be annoyed by it.

In making similes and metaphors fit your subject, use your wit. Here is an instructive simile from an article in *Time* about computer software:

> A computer without software is like a car without gasoline, a camera without film, a stereo without records.[11]

You can get into trouble by mixing metaphors. A university memo I saw a few years ago urged the faculty "to grapple with the burning issues." I rather hoped we would be issued insulated gloves before we had to do that grappling. I once heard a speaker say that the young people in his audience could "climb the ladder of success only by keeping their noses to the grindstone." I thought of how painful it would be for the young people to lug that heavy grindstone up the ladder while keeping their noses pressed to it. Another item picked up by *The New Yorker* includes a hilarious string of mixed metaphors—uttered in solemn seriousness by a speaker:

> But a fellow user pushing for stricter security counters: "Perhaps I am flogging a straw herring in midstream, but in light of what is known about the ubiquity of security vulnerabilities, it seems vastly too dangerous for university folks to run with their heads in the sand."[12]

You *can* use a series of metaphors effectively, as long as they do not clash with each other. Here is Irving Howe describing the Jewish immigrant housewife in turn-of-the-century New York:

> It was from her place in the kitchen that the Jewish housewife became the looming figure who would inspire, haunt, and devastate generations of sons. She realized intuitively that insofar as the outer world tyrannized and wore down her men, reducing them to postures of docility, she alone could create an oasis of order. It was she who would cling to received values and resist the pressures of dispersion; she who would sustain the morale of all around her, mediating quarrels, soothing hurts, drawing a circle of safety in which her children could breathe, and sometimes, as time went on, crushing her loved ones under the weight of her affection.[13]

Howe's metaphors come so naturally that we may not at first recognize them as metaphors. But then we identify "oasis of order," "circle of safety," and the metaphorical phrase "crushing her loved ones under the weight of her affection."

Match your metaphors and similes to the tone and content of your essay. These examples drawn from Howe nicely fit his subject, the development of the Jewish mother. It is a serious subject but not a somber one. His metaphors fit into that tone. Here is Norman Mailer describing his safe and elevated view of the police riot in Chicago in 1968. Metaphors pour together:

> Let us escape to the street. The reporter, watching in safety from the nineteenth floor, could understand now how Mussolini's son-in-law had once been able to find the bombs he dropped from his airplane beautiful as they burst. Yes, children, and youths, and middle-aged men and women were being pounded and clubbed and gassed and beaten, hunted and driven, sent scattering in all directions by teams of policemen who had exploded out of their restraints like the bursting of a boil, and nonetheless he felt a sense of calm and beauty, void even of the desire to be down there, as if in years to come there would be beatings enough, some chosen, some from nowhere, but it was as if the war had finally begun, and this was therefore a great and solemn moment, as if indeed the gods

of history had come together from each side to choose the very front of the Hilton Hotel before the television cameras of the world and the eyes of the campaign workers and the delegates' wives, yes, there before the eyes of half the principals at the convention was this drama played, as if the military spine of a great liberal party had finally separated itself from the skin, as if, no metaphor large enough to suffice, the Democratic Party had here broken in two before the eyes of a nation like Melville's whale charging right out of the sea.[14]

This passage from Mailer illustrates some of the glories and dangers of metaphors. It is cast in the wild, bare style typical of Mailer now for many years. Parts of it are confused. He assumes that all the delegates to the Democratic Convention of 1968 were men because he speaks of the "delegates' wives" rather than their "spouses." In Melville's *Moby Dick*, the whale did not break in two; rather the whale broke Ahab's ship in two. Even so, the paragraph conveys something of the tumult of the streets and Mailer's tumultuous thoughts as he watched from the safety of a hotel room.

You should be more circumspect. Don't force your metaphors. Don't make them overwrought and unnatural. Don't use them in every paragraph. But do use them.

Other Forms of Figurative Language

Metaphors make up the broadest class of figurative language, but there are other forms of figurative language that you should be familiar with and sometimes use. The classical rhetoricians called these forms *tropes*, from the Greek word for "manner" as in "manner of speaking." Now and then they can help you enliven your work, but all of them have their dangers, and you should use them with brave caution. Many tropes in the following list overlap.

HYPERBOLE

Hyperbole is an exaggeration so great that no one can take it literally. We have already mentioned that the cliché "made my blood boil" is hyperbole. No one expects the person who says such a thing to be emitting red steam. Mailer's paragraph on watching the riot from his hotel room is filled with hyperbole. Note especially his comment on "the gods of history." Hyperbole can be witty. Here is John Kenneth Galbraith on American railroads:

> Railway passenger travel in the United States was at first left to private management—the only important country to try this experiment. It didn't work. There is now a system of rail passenger service called

Amtrak, but it operates on the principle that, being partly public and thus a form of socialism and thus wicked, it should be bad enough to discourage people from using it. Except to passengers with deep ideological convictions, the whole idea seems unfortunate.[15]

UNDERSTATEMENT

Understatement is the opposite of hyperbole. Understatement is especially effective in writing about subjects that might be expected to create passion and exaggeration, and because it seems slightly out of place, it may be humorous. In writing of Adam Smith, whose *Wealth of Nations* gave the theoretical justification for modern competitive capitalism, Galbraith says:

> After the local school Adam Smith went on to the University of Glasgow and then to Balliol College, Oxford, an experience that he celebrates in *Wealth of Nations* with a stern rebuke for the public professors, as they then were called, those whose salary was independent of the size of their classes or the enthusiasm of their students. Thus relieved of incentive, these professors, he alleged, put forth little effort, did little work. Much better, he thought, that they be paid, as he himself would be later at Glasgow, in accordance with the number of students they attracted. Smith's views on this matter would not be well received in a modern American university.[16]

Galbraith's last sentence provides an understatement intended to call attention to the difference between Smith's views and modern university practice. It does so quickly, sharply, and without any passionate declamation that might annoy readers.

IRONY

Irony involves contradiction. We are being ironic if we say something that we intend to be taken in an opposite sense. The person who has a flat tire on her way to the airport and knows that she will miss her plane and an important meeting may say, "This is a fine state of affairs." Her statement is a simple irony, meaning the opposite of what she feels. If I say, "The President bravely condemned burning the flag," the statement is ironic because it takes little bravery to condemn flag burning in the United States. I may actually mean that the President was trying to look brave by making brave-sounding comments that carried no risk at all.

We speak also of the irony of events. Romeo and Juliet die because of a scheme intended to help them escape their families and marry each other. The secret tape recordings of conversations in his office that Richard Nixon intended to preserve as a record of his presidency led to his being forced to resign the presidency. Writers can call attention to ironic events, but the irony of figurative language is the rhetorical device that concerns us here.

Ironic statements have been with us at least since biblical times. Jesus, speaking of those who pray loudly in public to impress others with their show of piety, said, "Truly I say to you, they have their reward," meaning that their reward was that people saw them and not that God heard them.

Irony can be a simple statement, or it can be an extended work of prose or poetry. Probably the best-known ironic work in English is Jonathan Swift's essay "A Modest Proposal for Preventing the Children of Poor People in Ireland from Being a Burden to Their Parents or Country, and for Making Them Beneficial to the Public." Swift, writing in the eighteenth century and appalled by the desperate poverty of rural people in Ireland where he lived, proposed that poor Irish children be raised as food for the wealthy. "I have been assured by a very knowing American of my acquaintance in London, that a young healthy child well nursed is at a year old a most delicious, nourishing and wholesome food, whether stewed, roasted, baked, or boiled, and I make no doubt that it will equally serve in a fricassee, or a ragout."[17]

Occasionally an ironic statement may make a good introduction to an essay.

> I've got to call my state rep right away. I want him to file a bill requiring that everybody in Massachusetts who makes more than I do should reach deep into his or her pockets and hand me enough heavy change so that I can provide my offspring with the lifestyle to which they think they should be accustomed.[18]

The newspaper columnist who wrote this ironic opening paragraph was mocking a state legislator who had introduced a foolish bill only because a constituent asked him to do so. The columnist attacked the legislator for not having the courage to tell the constituent that the bill was foolish, that it would waste the time of the legislature, and that the legislator would refuse to have anything to do with it.

The difficulty of irony is that it must have the *form* of serious, literal statement, but readers must know that the author is playing with them, saying the opposite of what she means. Readers must see the art. Some inexperienced writers in my classes have produced essays that they intended to be ironic, but I took them literally because the irony was not sharp enough to make me see it. If you mean the opposite of what you say, but your audience does not see your meaning, you speak against your purpose. That is the difficulty the nineteenth-century English writer Thomas Carlyle meant when he wrote to his friend John Stuart Mill, "Irony is a sharp instrument; but ill to handle without cutting *yourself.*" When intelligent readers take your irony literally, you have failed. Yet despite its dangers, irony is one of the great uses of language, and a paper that uses it successfully can be memorable.

Irony often points to an outrageous reality. When Swift wrote that poor Irish children should be raised as food for the wealthy, he called attention to rich English landlords in Ireland who worked their Irish tenant farmers into misery and starvation. In a metaphorical sense, these wealthy Englishmen were devouring Ireland. When Swift proposed a literal devouring—cannibalism—he hoped to make readers think of the devastating economic devouring going on under the color of Christian morality.

The ironic statement can provide a dash of wit to an argument. *Time* writer Michael Kinsley wrote ironically in an essay on the 1989 Supreme Court decision that opened the way for state legislators to debate what kind of abortion laws they would have:

> The disaster facing America's state legislators, and potentially its national legislators, is that they may have to address an issue of public policy on which many of their constituents have strong and irreconcilable opinions. This they hate to do and are skilled at avoiding, even though it is what they are paid for. They would far rather pass laws against burning the flag.[19]

Ironies abound in this short passage. As the essay develops, it becomes clear that Kinsley thinks the national debate about abortion will be a good thing. He does not mean that it is a disaster at all. But it is a disaster in the minds of legislators who, he implies, would much rather come out strong about popular issues such as protecting the flag rather than about serious matters such as abortion. The notion that our representatives are "skilled at avoiding . . . what they are paid for" is an ironic comment on politics. Congress members like to pretend that they are brave; Kinsley implies that they are cowardly. They do not like to do what their jobs require.

Irony can be subtle, so subtle that some readers or hearers may not grasp it while those who understand laugh both at the irony and at the misunderstanding by others. In that respect irony is often treated by ethical philosophers as a moral problem. Should one mock others with ironies they do not understand? The only answer a writer can give to such a question is that irony has often served that purpose. This sort of irony is common in some literary works in which the writer intends to appeal to an audience that understands while at the same time he deceives or confuses a less knowing audience that he may wish to mock.

OTHER FIGURES OF SPEECH

There are other figures of speech. In *synecdoche* we make a part stand for the whole. For example, we speak of thirty *head* of cattle (and for some reason we use the singular form *head* when speaking of plural livestock). The book of Deuteronomy in the Bible tells us that we do not live "by bread alone," making bread stand for food in general.

In *metonymy* we use some attribute to indicate the whole. We speak of the "top brass" when we mean the highest military officers, who used to wear brass emblems on their lapels to indicate their rank. We may write of the "Blue" to indicate the Union Army and the "Gray" to indicate the Confederate Army during the Civil War. We speak of the "Orange" to indicate the University of Tennessee football team because its dominant color is orange.

An *oxymoron* joins two terms that seem at first view to be unlikely partners. Earlier I spoke of using tropes with "brave caution," which is an oxymoron because we do not normally think of bravery and caution as belonging together.

Be on the lookout for figures of speech in your reading. Try to make figures on your own. Don't be extravagant, but don't be so fearful that you fail to try to use some of the rich figurative devices we have in our language.

Clichés

Figurative language should make your language vigorous; the opposite of vigorous writing is prose filled with clichés, expressions as predictable as a funeral sermon. A good metaphor surprises us. But when we hear the first word or two of a cliché, we know the whole expression. The plan was as dead as a _____ before it came to a vote. We hear *as dead as* and we know the plan was "as dead as a doornail."

But what is a doornail? Most people would need a dictionary to answer that one. Why should a doornail be dead? We do not know. When we say "dead as a doornail," we repeat a strong consonant *d* sound, and English is fond of such repetitions. In speaking we might get some emphasis into it. But it does not mean anything, and it creates no pictures in our mind.

"The author waxed eloquent on the economic benefits of deficits." Why do people "wax eloquent"? No one seems to know. They do wax eloquent more often than they wax anything else, except possibly their new cars. *Wax* in "to wax eloquent" means to increase, to augment, and so we know that people waxing eloquent are becoming *more* eloquent. People in the sixteenth century used to "wax old." The moon still waxes and wanes. But now people only wax eloquent.

"The *cold, hard facts* are these; *it will be a cold day in July* before you see me *pull his chestnuts out of the fire*." Why must disagreeable facts always be cold and hard? The expression must have had some power once. Facts must have seemed like cold pieces of steel—perhaps the kind of steel with which people made daggers. Unpleasant facts must have made someone think up this expression. Now everybody trying to sound tough and worldly wise uses the expression "cold, hard facts."

So it is with "a cold day in July." The expression might have seemed funny to someone living in a Tennessee valley when suffocating heat gathered every July. It long ago ceased to be either amusing or interesting.

And who has ever pulled chestnuts out of a fire, risking burned hands or a burned face, for someone else to eat? Chestnuts are still around, and a few people may roast them in fireplaces. But does the expression call up an image to most readers? I doubt it.

Writers use clichés out of weariness or uncertainty or hesitancy. A writer sits at a desk, struggling to put something on paper (or on the screen), realizing, as we all do, that writing is hard work. A cliché pops up. The writer grabs it because it is easy. We are all timid when we write. Clichés give timid writers a feeling of security. They are familiar. They make a point. They take up space. They seem like writing. But they are dull, dull, dull.

A young reporter covers a congressional hearing and listens to the president of a coal company explain the economic value of opening a strip mine in Yellowstone National Park. The reporter writes that the coal company executive "had his own ax to grind." Neither the reporter nor the reader will think of the company president, bringing his ax to the community grindstone, forgetting all the other tools in the village, concentrating only on his own interest. No reader of this story has ever ground an ax; the reporter may never have held an ax in his hands. But the phrase pops into his mind, and it feels comfortable. He knows that it refers to those motivated by greed to advocate high causes.

Most clichés convey meaning but not images. They are dead metaphors—dead because they create no pictures in our minds. The cliché makes readers suppose that the writer either would not or could not imagine any original way to express a thought. Clichés open no windows, provide no revelations, give us nothing to remember. And they are quickly forgotten.

Good writing gives an impression of a bright mind, of someone thinking seriously about a topic, saying something worth reading. We heed such writing because we enjoy it. Clichés wear us down after a while. They erode our respect for the writer. He has not worked hard for us—why should we bother to read what he has said?

Clichés come in two packages. Some are dead metaphors, vainly trying to call up an image; some are common phrases, including fad words, that sound like formulas. Dead metaphors include *tight as a drum, fit as a fiddle, sound as a dollar, white as snow, blue as the sky, sharp as a tack, neat as a pin*, and legions more. Common clichéd phrases include such expressions as *to add insult to injury; pick and choose; tried and true; poor but honest; a deep, dark secret; an undercurrent of excitement; the agony of suspense; a bustling city; a brutal murder; a tragic death*—and row on row of others stacked up like fool's gold in the vaults of our minds.

Fad words come and go through our society like pockets of unpredictable clear-air turbulence. Suddenly people start using them to show that they know what's going on. *Parameter* pops up on the page instead of *limit* or *perimeter*. People suddenly start talking about "the bottom line," and they get *feedback* when they submit their *input* to a group discussing a problem. Football coaches tell us that "the name of the game" is defense, although we supposed all along that the name of the game was "football." They tell us that "when the going gets tough, the tough get going," and that they "came to play" (when we thought they might have come to visit the zoo). A good linebacker always "gives 110 percent." Why not 130 percent? I don't know. Since we are now a computer-driven society, we hear that scholars in the English department must *interface* with people who teach writing. We also hear that some people are *programmed* for success or defeat. Ever since the Watergate scandal and the congressional investigation of the early 1970s we have heard not "at that time" but "at that point in time."

Our literary life is almost suffocated with clichés. They pour through newspaper columns, academic essays, student papers, and memos that pass from office to office. They gush out of TV talk shows. They litter conversation. They pollute political campaigns. "Read my lips!" George Bush cried in the 1988 presidential campaign, promising not to raise taxes. What on earth does the expression mean?

Yet you will seldom find clichés in the slick-paper magazines you buy for their essays at newsstands. You do not find many clichés in *The New Yorker, Time, Atlantic, Newsweek, Smithsonian, Popular Mechanics, National Geographic*, or a host of others. You do not find them often in *Sports Illustrated* except as reporters quote the coaches and athletes. These magazines must be carefully edited if they are to survive. Editors know that clichés kill prose and that dead prose does not sell. Here again we may look to good journalists and essayists as models for our own writing. Such writers write to seduce people into reading their work. Intelligent people are not seduced by worn-out old lines.

How do we know when we are writing clichés? They are so pervasive that we cannot always avoid them. Some inexperienced writers cannot even recognize them. I have already given one clue: many clichés give themselves away because they are so familiar that the first word or two will give the rest away. When you start to use such a phrase, try to think of something else.

Be sure you clearly understand every expression you use. Think of what you are writing. We read in the morning paper that a thug shot someone down in the street, and we are told that it was a "brutal murder." The reporter wishes to convey her sense of horror and perhaps outrage. But do we need the worn-out adjective *brutal*? Can we imagine a *gentle* murder? Perhaps a gentle murder is committed by putting rat poison in somebody's hot milk, but even that does not seem gentle to most of us. Murder is murder. "Brutal murder" is a phrase not far removed from "flowering flowers" or "criminal crimes" or "hot heat."

What of those letters of recommendation that tell us that someone is a "personal friend"? Are there *impersonal* friends? When flight attendants tell us on landing to look around and collect all our "personal belongings," do they mean that we should leave our *impersonal* belongings on board? What of those historians of the Renaissance who tell us again and again of "bustling cities" in Italy? The term is used so frequently in history texts that we may imagine cart drivers, merchants, bankers, lawyers, priests, courtiers, prostitutes, and princes hurrying about shouting, "Bustle, bustle, bustle, bustle, bustle."

Couples living together without being married tell us they have "a meaningful relationship," and when they break up they tell us that their love affair was "a learning experience." Young people who learn their profession by apprenticeship are said to have *hands-on* experience. We hear that personal computers are "selling like hotcakes," and we do not stop to think that most of the cakes we know today are cold when we buy them.

All this is to say that writing requires concentration. We must examine every word, measure every sentence, and tailor our expressions to fit our thoughts as exactly as possible. We may write clichés in our first drafts, especially if we write rapidly to get a piece of prose into being in order to have something to tinker with. When we revise, we should pull our clichés out of our text as we might weed a flower garden.

The simplest way to deal with a cliché is to turn it into ordinary language. Cities don't have to *bustle*; they can thrive. We don't have to say that a murder was *brutal*; we can give readers enough details to let them see for themselves how brutal it was. We don't have to "look at the bottom line." We can examine the consequences or decide what the most important issue might be.

The tedious commonplace phrases of modern casual speech, especially on television, have moved into our written language, and we find them difficult to resist. Because of radio, television, and the movies, the spoken language—always more casual and more cliché-ridden than the written language—now dominates. Yet the precision and elegance of the older written language are not values to be despised.

No book like this one can settle the question of dead language. I do say that to be a good writer you must try to make your words stir a response in the minds of readers. Good figurative language can create images, both for you and your readers. Dead language cannot create those images or the resultant desired responses. Now and then we may all use a cliché without being guilty of a capital crime. But too many clichés will smother your prose, and your readers will conduct your literary funeral by refusing to read your work.

Appendix Two of this book provides a short listing of clichés. You will not find every cliché there, but you can open the book to these pages when you are tempted to use a phrase and do not know whether it is a cliché or not. If you find the phrase in my list, try to find a different expression.

Conclusion

Use figurative language when it seems appropriate. Try to make it come out of your own experience; do not put an expression on paper merely because everybody else seems to be using it. If you learn to reflect on language and experience, notebook in hand, you can develop a talent for figurative language. It takes time. So does everything else about writing.

Ten

False Rules and What Is True about Them

*E*nglish has rules. Break them, and you make it hard for readers and yourself. Readers falter if you use a plural verb with a singular subject or if you use a double negative. They stumble if you do not use the possessive case when it is needed, and broken parallelism in your prose ruptures their concentration. Misspelled words make readers back up because they know something is wrong and have to pause to find out what it is. When you violate the rules, intelligent readers will suppose you are ignorant of the writing conventions and therefore not worth their time.

Many people complicate matters by making up false rules. These rules burden inexperienced writers and may make prose sound stilted and somehow wrong. Any examination of prose in good magazines and books shows that professional writers break these "rules" all the time. Yet these rules have a vigorous life. Writing is a complicated business, one of the most difficult acts of the human brain. False rules seem to grant security, to reduce writing to a formula that anybody can understand, to make it less threatening. The people who tout false rules are like astrologers; they can always find an audience even if experience proves them wrong. Unfortunately, some people in that audience teach English in high schools and colleges.

Writing is more than obeying rules; writing is observation and imagination, order and revelation, style and form. The multiplication of false rules is much like the welding armor onto a car; in the end the car may be perfectly safe, but it is also too heavy to move.

The false rules evolved out of genuine needs. They became false because some people made them absolute when in fact they are relative to our purposes when we write. Although the rules are wrongly expressed, they rest on substance, and we should take the substance into account even as we reject the silliness and the pedantry of the extremes.

Common False Rules ·

Here are some of the most common false rules, with a few notes about what may be true about them.

1. Don't use the first person.

Every college freshman knows this one because so many high school teachers order their students never to say *I* or *we*. So instead of the first person we get impersonal stiff constructions like these:

> It is the opinion of this writer that . . .
>
> This writer would be forced to agree . . .
>
> This writer has shown . . .
>
> The reader is made to feel . . .
>
> This writer was hit by a truck when she . . .

The best argument for the first person is that we see it in all kinds of professional prose. I find it especially valuable in reviews of books and movies to avoid the tedious repetition of phrases such as "the reader" or "the audience." Walter Jackson Bate, writing about Samuel Johnson, demonstrates the graceful use of the first person without recourse to the tiresome impersonality of *the reader*.

> Even if we knew nothing of the state of mind he was forced to battle during this psychological crisis, the edition of Shakespeare—viewed with historical understanding of what it involved in 1765—could seem a remarkable feat; and we are not speaking of just the great *Preface*. To see it in perspective, we have only to remind ourselves what Johnson brought to it—an assemblage of almost every qualification we should ideally like to have brought to this kind of work with the single exception of patience; and at least some control of his impatience, if not the quality of patience itself, might have been passable if this period of his life had not been so distressing.[1]

The first person appears in accounts of events the writer has observed, though he may not be a part of them. Neil Sheehan's *A Bright Shining Lie: John Paul Vann and America in Vietnam* tells the tragic story of a Marine Lieutenant Colonel whose self-delusion stands as a symbol of the entire American experience during the Vietnam war. Sheehan is a reporter for *The New York Times*. Because Sheehan covered the war and knew Vann, he sometimes interjects his own memories into the account and speaks in the first person.

> We picked up news of the dimensions of the Viet Cong buildup in the Delta—in retrospect, the first stage in the creation of the second Viet Minh—at the beginning of August. We would have learned about it sooner but we had all been unable to leave Saigon for a look at the war

since June because of the Buddhist street demonstrations and the constant threat of another suicide. Mert Perry of *Time* heard of a big fight in Kien Hoa Province in July in which eleven helicopters had been hit. I knew the captain who was the advisor of the 7th Division battalion involved in the battle from a march through the rice paddies long before. He came to Saigon at the beginning of August for a weekend leave, and I ran into him by chance on the street.[2]

One may read hundreds of pages in this large book without encountering Sheehan's use of the first person, but where his own experience intersects his subject, he uses the first person without hesitation.

Writers expressing their opinions about a controversial subject use the first person to avoid any ambiguity about where they stand. Here is a passage from Stephen Jay Gould's essay called "Racist Arguments and IQ":

> I do not claim that intelligence, however defined, has no genetic basis—I regard it as trivially true, uninteresting, and unimportant that it does. The expression of any trait represents a complex interaction of heredity and environment. Our job is simply to provide the best environmental situation for the realization of valued potential in all individuals. I merely point out that a specific claim purporting to demonstrate a mean genetic deficiency in the intelligence of American blacks rests upon no new facts whatever and can cite no valid data in its support. It is just as likely that blacks have a genetic advantage over whites. And either way, it doesn't matter a damn. An individual can't be judged by his group mean.[3]

Yet modern writers do not use the first person indiscriminately. It is fairly rare in serious journalism. In a recent issue of *The New York Times Magazine* picked up at random from the pile here by my desk, I found four feature articles that did not use the first person and one that did. Even in an informal journal such as *Sports Illustrated*, articles written in the first person are not numerous.

Ask yourself this: Am I writing about myself, or am I writing about something else? Don't get in the way of your subject. Professional writers do not say, "In my opinion, the Middle East is the most dangerous place in the world." They say simply, "The Middle East is the most dangerous place in the world." If a writer signs her name to an article, every reader with common sense will understand that the assertions in the article represent the writer's considered opinion and not some universal truth carved in stone by the almighty finger of God.

My inexperienced writers sometimes think they must write a personal and emotional commentary at the end their papers. They want to let me know their hearts are in the right place. Passionate writing may have a place now and then. But most of the time the facts standing alone—sometimes starkly alone—have such weight and power that the writer's emotions seem trivial and distracting. In the following paragraph, social historian Robert Proctor writes of Nazi Germany's medical policy of putting to death those children judged to be incurably ill or handicapped. The children were removed from their homes supposedly for special and improved treatment, but instead they were killed. Says Proctor:

> Methods of killing included injections of morphine, tablets, and gassing with cyanide or chemical warfare agents. Children at Idstein, Katenhof, Görden, and Eichberg were not gassed but were killed by injection; poisons were commonly administered slowly, over several days or even weeks, so that the cause of death could be disguised as pneumonia, bronchitis, or some other complication induced by the injections. Hermann Pfannmüller of the hospital at Eglfing-Haar slowly starved the children entrusted to his care until they died of "natural causes." This method, he boasted, was least likely to incur criticism from the foreign press or from "the gentlemen in Switzerland" (The Red Cross). Others simply left their institutions without heat, and patients died of exposure. Nazi medical men could thus argue that their actions were not technically murder, for they were simply withholding care and "letting nature take its course." Parents were informed with a standardized letter, used at all institutions, that their daughter or son had died suddenly and unexpectedly of brain edema, appendicitis, or other fabricated cause; parents were also informed that, owing to the danger of an epidemic, the body had to be cremated immediately.[4]

Proctor would have ruined the force of this stark paragraph had he interjected his opinion that killing infirm children represented savagery. Merely by providing these grim details he implies a moral commentary. He trusts us to know what side he stands on, and he does not insult us by assuming that we have to be coached about the correct emotions to have in response to these horrors. He keeps the focus on his true subject—Nazi medicine—and not on himself.

Wayne C. Booth's "implied author"—mentioned in Chapter Two—should come to mind here. Never write to make readers suppose that you are trying to be cute or domineering or hateful. Don't show off; avoid drawing unnecessary attention to yourself. Stick to the business of telling readers what you know. When we blatantly insert ourselves into our story, we are like thoughtless people who invite friends to a movie and then spend so much time talking that they are not allowed to enjoy the show.

Avoid giving the impression that when you say, "I think," you install yourself in an impregnable fortress, immune to any counterargument. Many people today suppose that all opinions are equal and that those who express themselves vehemently enough and sincerely enough deserve respect and even admiration. These people imagine that others are guilty of bad taste or at least discourtesy if they disagree with opinions strongly stated. Many an oral argument ends with the offhand and sometimes surly remark, "Well, you have your opinion, and I have mine." The speaker declares that he will not argue any more, telling his adversary that *she* should not argue any more because it will not help; she will not change his mind. He may also be saying that he does not have any other arguments to muster in his cause and that he does not want to be upset by the evidence. He has an opinion. His opinions are sacred. Trying to get him to change his opinion is like trying to get him to change his religion.

We live in a society in which people have the right to say just about anything they please. What they say may be dull, brilliant, foolish, bizarre, or simply ordinary. This freedom does not confer equality on all opinions. Educated people know that if they are to win respect among thoughtful readers, they must support opinion with evidence. They must give some good reason why they have their opinions and persuade others to accept them or at least to believe them worthy of respect.

Command of the evidence allows you to make statements without using the first person. Eugene D. Genovese, in his classic book about slavery in the South before the Civil War, writes about the music of the slaves:

> The slaves' talent for improvisation, as well as their deep religious conviction, drew expressions of wonder and admiration from almost everyone who heard them sing.[5]

Genovese is not compelled to place an "I think" before this opinion; he assembles evidence to show that it is so, and the evidence convinces us without a needless first-person pronouncement that would call more attention to the author than to what he is saying about slaves.

Barbara Tuchman, discussing the ineptitude of Patrick J. Hurley, the American ambassador to China in 1945, writes:

> It happens that Hurley was a man whose conceit, ambition, and very vulnerable ego were wrapped up in his mission to the point of frenzy.[6]

Tuchman makes her case by assembling piles of evidence; she does not have to preface her opinion with a feeble "I think."

When you deliver yourself of an "I think" before a judgment in writing, you may appear to be granting that other people can think anything they want. But if you present evidence for your assertions, you can convey an impression of confidence that your audience will take seriously.

So the false rule about the first person contains some truth. You should avoid using the first person except when it is clearly called for. In the following instances, the first person may be in order.

When you deliberately assume a conversational tone as in a regular newspaper column, a letter, or a book like this one, you may use the first person. The conversational tone may help you create a sense of intimacy with your readers. Most books about writing share the assumption that we all perform the same task and that the author has something to share with others who write. Most books like this one are chatty—perhaps too much so. E. B. White, John McPhee, George Orwell, Joan Didion, Ann Tyler, and many other modern essayists use (or used) the first person as a matter of course. Their writing tells about what happens to them, their reactions, their conclusions. They share their experiences to enlarge our own. Some subjects lend themselves to informality; some do not. You will not find a chatty book on brain surgery or leukemia. For such subjects informality would be in bad taste.

For serious subjects, use the first person only if your experiences are essential to your essay. If you report on research that you have done alone or with colleagues, you may use the first person or the passive voice, depending on your own taste. Most scientific journals use the passive voice:

> One thousand people were questioned about their preferences for automobiles. They were asked whether performance was more important than economy, whether they needed a large back seat, and whether color might influence their choice of a new car. They were asked whether they had more confidence in American cars or in Japanese makes.

Some writers prefer to use the first person in such reports, making their prose more informal and lively. That is the style of *Consumer Reports*, the nation's most popular and most respected consumer magazine. Here is a paragraph from an article about tests on strollers for young children:

> Parents and other adults do the most to keep the perils at bay, of course, but they should have an ally in the manufacturer. Unfortunately, the companies whose strollers we tested for this report don't always bear their fair share of the load. Although baby strollers have been significantly improved in recent years, more than 10,000 babies and children under five are injured seriously enough every year in carriages and strollers to require emergency hospital treatment.[7]

If you sign your name to a formal essay or report, you may venture an occasional comment in the first person. Like Stephen Jay Gould, you may wish to assert your own choice among conflicting opinions. You cannot use the first person singular if you have not signed the essay. If you write a memo to represent the views of your university on a controversial issue like investments in South Africa, you may use the editorial *we* to show that your thoughts represent the official policy of your institution. But you cannot say "I" since no one knows who you are if your name is not on the piece.

2. Never write a sentence fragment.

This false rule should be amended to read, "Never write a sentence fragment unless you know what you are doing." If you cannot tell the difference between a sentence and a sentence fragment, get yourself a good English handbook and work on the problem until you beat it. But good writers who know what they are doing use sentence fragments for special effects. From Ellen Goodman:

> I think that self-consciousness about health, the desire to take responsibility for the shape of our lungs and calf muscles, is positive, and I agree that we are our own best screening system. But there is a risk. A risk that as we focus on the aspects of self-health we begin to look at all illness as self-inflicted and even regard death as a kind of personal folly.[8]

From Lewis Thomas:

> Now all that has changed. I cannot think that way anymore. Not while those things are still in place, aimed everywhere, ready for launching.[9]

From Richard Selzer:

> What is it, then, this thing, the knife, whose shape is virtually the same as it was three thousand years ago, but now with its head grown detachable? Before steel, it was bronze. Before bronze, stone—then back into unremembered time.[10]

We can scarcely read any modern writer without running into sentence fragments. Fragments provide a rapid pace, especially effective in the context of a series of events or thoughts or described objects. If the context is clear, fragments are both readable and efficient. They get readers quickly from place to place.

Sometimes you can begin a paper with a series of fragments, but most of the time your fragments depend for meaning on the sentences that come immediately before them. They can usually be joined to the immediately preceding sentence by a comma, a dash, or a colon. Instead of telling you never to use them at all, teachers should tell you to use them with care. Care means seeing to it that fragments do not become tiresome as a result of your using them too often or that they do not become confusing because you use them out of a proper context.

3. Don't split infinitives.

Before we talk about split infinitives, we should be sure we know what they are. An infinitive can be split only by inserting a word or phrase between the infinitive marker *to* and the verb that makes the infinitive. The split infinitives below are in italics.

Many expected Bosworth *to really intercept* passes in his enormous mouth.

Spinks trained hard for months *to bravely fight* for 91 seconds.

Clemens granted the interview *to finally and completely tell* Red Sox fans how much he despised them.

These are not split infinitives:

To be truly understood, Paul wanted his life to be an open book.

Unfortunately, the pages were far too dull *to be carefully read* by anyone with taste.

Many people who know nothing else about grammar know about split infinitives and know they do not like them. For their dislike they reckon on a literalistic understanding of the infinitive form. In most languages, the infinitive is one word. *Hacer*, *faire*, and *facere* are infinitives meaning "to do" in Spanish, French, and Latin, respectively. Each is one word. Rigorists insist that infinitives in English should always be considered as one word and that to split an infinitive is barbaric. Their reasoning seems confirmed by our use of infinitives in English, especially by our habit of referring to an infinitive with the pronoun *it*: "To write was everything to her; it was a compulsion that sometimes alarmed her friends." Here the pronoun *it* refers to the infinitive *to write*, a singular entity used as a noun. The rigorists believe that to split an infinitive violates an integrity of the noun the infinitive may represent.

Nevertheless, common sense tells us that English infinitives are not one word but two, and even the most casual observation reveals that good writers occasionally split infinitives. Here is a paragraph from *Time* about the disappearance of a Japanese explorer Naomi Uemura, who vanished on a mountain-climbing expedition:

He became a national hero in 1970 when, as a member of the first Japanese team *to successfully climb* Mount Everest, he was the first to reach the 29,028-ft. peak.[11]

Writing is governed by flexible standards set by editors. Most editors nowadays publish split infinitives, and I think it is futile to rave against split infinitives as if they represented decadence and sloth.

Still, moderation is in order. Although professional writers occasionally split infinitives, they do so *only* occasionally, and they usually sense some good reason for doing so. Several split infinitives used in a short essay may cumulatively make the essay sound clumsy. They seem to break down the natural rhythms of speech that make for clear writing and easy reading. We rarely split infinitives when we speak. We should be moderate in splitting them when we write.

Beyond rhythm is efficiency. Most split infinitives are not bad because they violate a sacrosanct rule but because the adverb that does the splitting is unnecessary. Suppose you write, "He wanted to really work hard." You can drop the *really* and have a better sentence. *Really* is a pointless intensifier. The same is true of most split infinitives; the adverb that does the splitting is usually unnecessary, and dropping it makes the sentence stronger.

Remember, too, that many people detest split infinitives with an irrational passion. I once knew a university official who picked split infinitives out of letters addressed to him with fastidious disgust. He thought that anyone who split an infinitive was wholly ignorant. People like him are surprisingly numerous in the world, and you should at least know that they exist when you write.

I don't split infinitives. I don't know why, but I do not feel comfortable splitting. Split infinitives disturb some delicate sentence balance in my head. Perhaps the feeling is an illusion. Perhaps it is the lingering memory from my seventh-grade English teacher. Perhaps it is my recollection of people like the university official I just mentioned. Whatever it is, my aversion to the split infinitive is so strong and so habitual that I do not fight it. I revise sentences to eliminate split infinitives, and something old-fashioned in me makes me notice when others split them.

You are much more likely to find split infinitives in journalism—newspaper and magazine writing—than in trade books. The more time editors have with a manuscript, the more likely they are to eliminate split infinitives. But the split infinitive is so common nowadays in so many things we read that writing teachers become a little foolish when they try to indict splitters with high crimes and misdemeanors against the English language.

4. Don't end a sentence with a preposition.

Prepositions are small words—such as *in, at, by,* and *of*—that never change their form no matter how they are used; they connect nouns or pronouns in prepositional phrases that serve as adjectives or adverbs in a sentence. Prepositions allow the strength of nouns and pronouns to modify other elements in a sentence.

In the night he dreamed *of horses*.

The prepositional phrase *In the night* works as an adverb modifying the verb *dreamed*; so does the prepositional phrase *of horses*. Without prepositions, we could not easily express these ideas: *Nightly he dreamed horsely*. Some study might reveal the meaning of such a sentence, but the task would be difficult.

The dictionary *on my desk* is my favorite book.

The prepositional phrase *on my desk* serves as an adjective modifying *dictionary*, a noun.

To place a preposition before its object follows the general rule of English syntax that related elements in a sentence should be as close to each other as possible. To end a sentence with a preposition deprives that preposition of a natural object on which to rest, and this apparent disorder may be unsettling. "The committee voted *against*." Against what? "The hamburger came *with*." With what?

But often it seems unnatural to be strictly formal in putting prepositions before their objects. We can easily say this: "That was the argument I fought against." We can change the sentence to read, "That was the argument against which I fought." But only a robot would talk like that. You can revise the sentence to read, "I fought against that argument"; but if you have been talking about several arguments and want to identify the particular one you have fought against, you may wish to say, "*That* was the argument I fought against."

In developing a writing style we each make deliberate choices between alternatives that sometimes differ only slightly from each other. I can see an important difference in emphasis between the sentences, "That was the argument I fought against" and "I fought against that argument."

5. Don't begin a sentence with a conjunction.

Conjunctions join sentence elements—words, phrases, or clauses. The common coordinating conjunctions—*and, but, for*, and *or*—join equal elements. Other conjunctions, such as *if, although, whether*, and *even*, join dependent elements.

I do not know the origin of the rule that sentences should never begin with a conjunction, but it is quoted to me frequently, usually by men over 60. Yet any glance at a newspaper or magazine shows that professional writers frequently begin sentences with conjunctions. John F. Kennedy used conjunctions to begin fifteen sentences in his short inaugural address in 1961. E. B. White, one of the finest essayists of our time, used conjunctions to begin many of his sentences. Lewis Thomas, one of our best writers about science, does the same.

So the false rule would seem to have little validity among those who write English best.

Using a conjunction to begin a sentence emphasizes the connection between the thoughts of two consecutive sentences. With a conjunction at the start of a sentence, you say something like this: "Pay attention. This sentence is closely related to the thought in the sentence immediately before it. But it is important enough to stand by itself, to begin with a capital letter so you have to take careful note of it."

As I have pointed out earlier, most sentences develop some thought in the sentence immediately preceding them. Although you may wish to emphasize such connections now and then, your readers will become immune to the effect if you use the device too often. Use of too many conjunctions as sentence openers can look like a verbal tic, an eccentricity of style that can become as annoying as a restless child's steady kicking against the back of your seat at the movies. Used with circumspection, the device of beginning an occasional sentence with a conjunction can hold paragraphs together and make your prose a little more fluid. But remember the almost implacable habit of writers in English: Around 80 percent of all sentences begin with the subject.

6. Avoid the pronoun you.

If you have read this far, you know I have violated this false rule again and again—for a reason. I have written these pages in an informal, conversational style, and in conversations we address readers as *you*. We do the same in letters.

In more formal writing, to say *you* may seem wordy and out of place. No one would write this sentence in a formal essay on cancer: "If you study cancer long enough, you will discover that it is not one disease but a large group of diseases that share certain lethal qualities." It's much better to say this: "Cancer is not one disease but a group of related diseases." Nor should you use the pronoun *you* in an essay about history: "You have to sympathize with the Germans in World War I, facing as they did powerful enemies in both the east and the west." You should instead say something like this: "In World War I, Germany faced powerful enemies in both the east and the west."

Even in informal writing the second person should be used sparingly. No one can sensibly write a sentence like this one: "To serve in one of the first submarines, you had to be brave or foolish or both." Your readers did not serve in one of the first submarines; you cannot meaningfully include them in your sentence. Say this instead: "Crew members on the first submarines had to be brave or foolish or both."

Nor can you say this: "When you have been a famous athlete most of your life, you sometimes can't bear it when the cheering stops." Most of your readers have not been famous athletes all their lives. Write this instead: "Famous athletes sometimes can't bear it when the cheering stops."

It's all right to use *you* in various informal contexts. Articles that give advice or describe processes often use *you*:

> Most of the cameras give you no say in the exposure. A few, however, have a backlight switch, which lets you correct the exposure when strong light is coming from behind a subject.[12]

Personal essays often address the reader. Here is Alice Walker writing about the Reverend Martin Luther King, Jr.:

> You know, if you have read his books, that his is a complex and revolutionary philosophy that few people are capable of understanding fully or have the patience to embody in themselves.[13]

7. Avoid contractions.

Here much of the advice about the pronoun *you* can be repeated. Contractions do well in informal or semiformal prose—like the prose in this book. You may sometimes loosen stiff prose by using contractions. Most teachers accept contractions in college papers, and contractions serve well enough in letters or personal essays.

They serve less well in formal essays. I feel uncomfortable using them in scholarly books and articles because I find them a little too conversational, a little too informal for a serious subject that I want to be taken seriously by the audience who will read the article. I have not seen contractions in dissertations, in formal books about history or philosophy or literary criticism, in business reports, or in articles in medical journals. Less formal publications such as *Sports Illustrated* use them but not excessively. (Of course when you are quoting a source that uses contractions, you quote exactly as the words were written.)

8. Use that to introduce restrictive clauses, which to introduce nonrestrictive clauses.

Restrictive clauses add essential information to the core statement of a sentence; *nonrestrictive* clauses add information that may be parenthetical, interesting, and valuable, but not essential to the meaning the writing is trying to convey. You cannot leave a restrictive clause out and preserve the meaning of the core statement; you may omit a nonrestrictive clause without damaging the core statement. The restrictive clause in the following sentence is in italics:

> Of all my teachers, the one *who gave me the lowest grades* taught me the most.

Leave out the italicized clause, and you have nonsense. Grammarians call the clause *restrictive* because it restricts the noun it modifies. We are not talking about just any teacher; we are talking about the one teacher *who gave me the lowest grades*.

Here is a sentence that includes a nonrestrictive clause, one that does not restrict the meaning of the noun it modifies but merely adds some information.

> My English teacher, *who was also my next-door neighbor*, knew me from the time I was born.

Now we have a clause that can be deleted from the sentence without harm to the main statement. The clause is parenthetical; it adds interesting but not essential information. It does not restrict the noun *teacher*.

Many people, especially those over 60, believe that restrictive clauses should be introduced with *that* and that nonrestrictive clauses should be introduced with *which*. At times they become irate when anyone suggests that this rule is only a foolish and cumbersome false rule that few writers observe or even think about. We have just seen that in clauses that refer to people, *who* can introduce both restrictive and nonrestrictive types. Why all the fuss?

Back in 1906, the English grammarian H. W. Fowler hit on the idea of using *that* to introduce restrictive clauses and *which* to introduce nonrestrictive clauses. He rightly believed that writers should make a clear distinction between the two types. Fowler wanted people to write sentences like these:

> The song that Sam played in the movie *Casablanca* was called "As Time Goes By."
>
> The ocean, which we could see from our house, changed color according to the shifting light of the sun through the clouds.

Because the distinction between restrictive and nonrestrictive clauses is necessary, many people have taken Fowler's suggestion as a law of language. Fowler himself knew better. Calling restrictive clauses "defining" and nonrestrictive clauses "non-defining," he wrote the following:

> If writers would agree to regard *that* as the defining relative pronoun, and *which* as the non-defining, there would be much gain both in lucidity and in ease. Some there are who follow this principle now; but

it would be idle to pretend that it is the practice of either most or the best writers.

Fowler was much more charitable than his modern disciples who have turned the that/which "rule" into a fetish. After the first edition of this book appeared, some outraged readers called my office to express their fierce indignation that a writing teacher should be so decadent as to deny the "rule" any authority. The fact remains that few writers and editors care much about it. We use *that* or *which* according to some indefinable sense of which one sounds better in a particular sentence. The rule is impossible to observe in sentences such as the one immediately preceding this one or in common usage such as this: "That which makes the rule invalid is its impossibility." Neither can the "rule" hold in who/whom clauses, and it cannot help us in restrictive or nonrestrictive phrases.

But recall the motive of the "rule": You must make a distinction between the two kinds of clauses. The only sure way to do this is to use proper punctuation. Restrictive clauses are not set off by any kind of punctuation; nonrestrictive clauses are usually set off by commas, although you can also use parentheses and dashes.

On occasion the meaning of a sentence changes according to whether the writer uses commas to make a clause nonrestrictive or does not use them to make the clause restrictive. Here is an example:

> The novel, which Charles wrote in Virginia, sold more than 30,000 copies.

This sentence includes a nonrestrictive clause, one that gives some added information about the novel under discussion. Charles seems to have written only one novel. He happened to write it in Virginia. But here now is the sentence with the nonrestrictive clause turned into a restrictive clause by the omission of the commas.

> The novel which Charles wrote in Virginia sold more than 30,000 copies.

Now we are talking about one novel among many. Charles's other novels not written in Virginia may have sold more or less. The one written in Virginia sold more than 30,000 copies. The restrictive clause marks off this novel from others.

The that/which rule is false, and few writers observe it. But you must be conscious of whether your clauses are restrictive or nonrestrictive, and you must punctuate accordingly. Otherwise you may confuse your readers by obscuring your meaning.

Conclusion

Don't be seduced by false rules, but don't go to the other extreme and suppose that English has no rules at all. Consider the motives behind the false rules, and observe the cautions that I have mentioned here. Always be aware of your audience. If, for example, you don't know if your teacher will accept contractions, ask her. Also, try to be efficient in your writing. That is, use as few words as possible to express as clearly as you can the meaning you want to convey. That principle will help you cut needless intensifiers out of your prose—especially intensifiers that split infinitives. Read carefully to learn the practices of other writers. Use common sense.

Eleven

Grammar and Mechanics

Most Americans, given half a chance, will moan loudly about their ignorance of English grammar, sometimes in tones that smack suspiciously of pride, as if knowing grammar were almost as embarrassing as remembering the names of stars on the old Lawrence Welk Show. To some, grammar seems almost effete, a collection of perplexing rules that ought to be ignored by hearty men and women. Others take an opposite view. They believe that grammar is the soul of writing, and that schools ought to be marching students through grammar books in lockstep.

In both views of grammar there is a piece of the truth. Grammar drills don't accomplish much. The soul of writing is to have something to say. If you don't have anything to say, no one will read your prose merely for its flawless grammar. High school students would profit much more from developing the habit of writing than from doing unending drills in the parts of speech and from filling in the blanks of tedious grammatical exercises. Yet writers destroy the effectiveness of what they say when they make mistakes in grammar. Their readers lose respect for them, and the writing itself may be confusing.

Most of us know more grammar than we admit. We start learning grammar as we learn to talk. When grammar works, children communicate with their families. When they communicate, they get what they want. As they succeed, they remember the speech patterns that gave them success, and they use the patterns again to satisfy their next desire.

Most of us continue to use the grammar we picked up as children. We often cannot recall the technical terms. Not many educated people can name the parts of speech, but they use them well enough. Few can make a lightning distinction between a conjunctive adverb and a conjunction, but they use without difficulty conjunctive adverbs like *moreover* and conjunctions like *and* without difficulty.

Since about 1890 the grammar of literary English has been remarkably stable. It works in print and on radio and television and in our daily utterances. We can understand Australian movies and English newspapers. A few differences crop up. The English usually write this: "If one persists on betting on the horses, one will lose one's shirt." An American will usually write this: "If one persists on betting on the horses, he will lose his shirt." The English use plural verbs with many collective nouns. They say this: "The committee are undecided." Americans say, "The committee is undecided." Yet Americans may also say, "The majority are sure of themselves." These slight variations do not seriously impede communication between Americans and Australians or New Zealanders or the English or the Scots or the Irish.

Grammar cannot be a science; like the rest of language, it is a collection of proved conventions or patterns that allow communication to go on. Despite the best efforts of scholars on linguistics, we do not know just how those patterns developed. Why have we rejected *ain't* as a contraction for *am not* or *is not*? Why is "he don't" wrong and "he doesn't" right? Why can't we write this: "Thomas Jefferson and Karl Marx was both heirs to John Locke"? The only worthwhile answer is that the "erroneous" sentences are contrary to conventions developed over the centuries.

These conventions used to be much looser than they are now. The coming of mass literacy and the newspapers and magazines that feed literacy have created a much more inflexible grammar than that which Shakespeare or Chaucer used. Mass production of anything works best by standardization. Standard forms are easier to teach and easier to learn and also easier to recognize. When only a few people could read and when readers read aloud—as they did in the Middle Ages—grammar could be much more flexible. But when readers rapidly scan print in silence, irregularities trip them up and make them go back to read a line again before they can understand it. A standard grammar—like standard tools of all kinds—helps a mass society work.

A few writing experts contend today that to enforce the conventions of grammar smacks of elitism. They say that conventional English is only one dialect among many and that all dialects are equal. No humane person could suggest that we scorn those whose dialect learned at home is different from conventional English. But it is a serious misreading of both past and present to say that all dialects, including conventional English, are equal in a large and literate society. Those who do not learn to use conventional English are at a lifelong disadvantage.

Television and other mass media are homogenizing the conventions even more. In my native South, among the rural people where I grew up, the word *ain't* is disappearing. People my age still use it; their children use it much less. Why is it going? I suspect that it is passing away because people are not seeing it on television, and the thousands of hours the average American child spends before the tube affects language more than all the English teachers in America combined.

Students often have problems in grammar because writing is so different from speaking. Often they get lost in the physical process of writing, of moving a pen or a pencil laboriously across the page, so that the brain runs off and leaves the hand behind. Writing goes so slowly and painfully for them that they lose track of their sentences. If you think you have severe problems in grammar, try reading your own work aloud to yourself. You will pick up a lot of your errors. Writing with a computer liberates us from much of the physical toil of writing and allows us to see our errors better and revise them away. You can also buy yourself a good handbook. Handbooks usually contain a great deal of grammar presented in a readable way and provided with an index that lets you find items quickly. However you write, you can help yourself by more writing. Grammar, like everything else in writing, gets better as we practice it more.

Persistent Problems

In the following list, I have tried to compile descriptions of the problems in grammar and punctuation that most afflict my students. (Punctuation is part of grammar in that it is one of the forces that holds sentences together and helps us arrange them.) It is not an exhaustive study. But it will help you overcome most of the common errors.

I hope something else will happen as you study this section: I want you to gain confidence in your own knowledge so you can use the language more effectively. Each of the issues I list represents a means of making writing richer, more textured, more attractive. It's a shame, for example, that many people will avoid the subjunctive mood of verbs altogether because they fear to use the subjunctive incorrectly. The subjunctive is uncommon in English, but now and then it adds a certain elegance to language. You can get away with using the simple past tense for your verbs, but using the various perfect tenses can add subtlety to your thought that makes your work more interesting.

Punctuation seems unimportant to most of my students; punctuation is such a little thing, a matter of dots and squiggles on a page.

Why bother with it? But knowing something about punctuation helps us hold sentences together more adeptly. To know punctuation is also to give ourselves some confidence in handling some of the complex structures of the English sentence that make for variety and compression.

In most of my recommendations on punctuation I have followed the advice of *A Manual of Style* published by the University of Chicago Press and generally called "The Chicago Manual of Style." The looming authority of this celebrated work is so great it should be a reference book in every writer's library.

1. Make the subject and verb agree in number.

If the subject of a sentence is singular, it must join a singular verb; if the subject is plural, the verb must be in the plural form. In nearly all verbs, except the irregular "to be" verbs and "to have" (am, are, is; was, were; has, have), the only variation between singular and plural forms is in the third-person singular of the present tense. We say, "I dance, you dance, we dance, they dance," but "she *dances*." The simple past of most verbs uses the same form for both singular and plural: "I danced; he danced; they danced." Helping verbs will vary like the present tense, but since the most common helping verbs are "to be" and "to have," we don't have to learn a lot of special forms. In this regard English is simpler than languages that do not use helping verbs. So we can be grateful for some simplicity in our complicated tongue.

We are all most likely to make errors in subject-verb agreement when we insert a clause or phrase between a subject and a verb. The danger becomes acute when the phrase is a preposition with a plural object. That happens in incorrect sentences like this: "Each of the cars were fast." *Each*, the subject of the sentence, is singular. A prepositional phrase like *of the cars* can throw writers off and in a case like this influence them to use the plural verb *were*. The sentence *should* read like this: "Each of the cars *was* fast."

Anybody, everybody, anyone, each, every, neither, nobody and *someone* are all singular and require a singular verb.

> *Each* of the players *is* eligible until final exams.
>
> *Every one* of the coaches *chews* gum.
>
> *Nobody knows* what happened to the Johnsons.
>
> *Everybody* in the audience *is* applauding.
>
> *Each* of the choices *is* possible; *neither is* desirable.

Now and then a compound subject considered as a unit takes a singular verb:

Cops and robbers *is* an old American children's game.

But don't assume that readers will see the unity you may see in a compound subject. You may write, "The gathering and classifying of data goes on relentlessly in all the sciences." In your mind *gathering and classifying* may be a single act, and you may use the singular verb *goes*. But many readers will assume that they are two acts, and you will confuse them by using a singular verb. Except in a few idiomatic expressions, use the plural verb with a compound subject.

Some collective nouns occupy a shadowy borderland. Most Americans will accept these sentences: "A number of movies produced last year *were* filled with violence and sex"; "A majority of the team *were* unable to graduate."

2. When a singular noun subject of a sentence is joined by *or* or *nor*, the verb should be in the singular.

Neither economics *nor* history *is* an exact science.

A tub *or* a shower is in every room.

3. When a plural noun in a compound subject is joined by *or* or *nor* to a singular noun, the verb agrees with the nearest noun.

Neither the singer nor her *managers are* happy.

Neither her managers nor the *singer is* happy.

Try to revise sentences like these to eliminate the awkwardness of the constructions: "The singer and her manager are unhappy."

4. Use the correct verb form after the adverb *there*. In a sentence beginning with *there*, the verb must agree with the subject, which usually comes immediately after the verb.
Don't say, "There is singing and laughter upstairs tonight." Say instead, "There are singing and laughter upstairs tonight." Don't say, "There are the team." Say, "There is the team."

5. Use the nominative case for a pronoun when it is the subject of a dependent clause, even if the clause itself serves as an object.
Don't say, "He was prepared for whomever might ask a question." Say, "He was prepared for whoever might ask a question." *Whoever* is the subject of the verb *might ask* and so must be in the nominative case.

Don't be confused by parenthetical clauses within dependent clauses. A parenthetical clause has no *grammatical* effect on the subject of a dependent clause of which it is a part. Therefore don't say, "The woman *whom* he believed was drunk was in a coma." The *he be-*

lieved is a parenthetical clause. Say this: "The woman *who* he believed was drunk was in a coma." The pronoun *who* governs the verb *was*.

Now complications enter. When you write a pronoun that is the subject of an infinitive, the pronoun is in the objective case.

> She supposed *him* to be a friend.
> We imagined *her* to be wise and good.

The pronoun is in the objective case even if the infinitive is understood rather than written:

> She supposed *him* a friend.
> She thought *her* beautiful.

The subject of an infinitive acts as the agent of action the infinitive describes. Any subject of an infinitive always follows a transitive verb, one that takes a direct object. Infinitives themselves are nonfinite verbs; we sometimes call them *verbals*. A nonfinite verb cannot express past or present time by itself. To express time, a verbal must be joined to a finite verb: "He wanted to be famous." The past tense of the finite verb *wanted* adds time to the infinitive (verbal) *to be*, which has no time of its own. We could as easily say, "He wants to be famous," or "He will want to be famous."

If the infinitive has a subject, the subject becomes part of an infinitive phrase and serves as the direct object of the preceding transitive verb.

> They told *us* to be careful.

6. Use the objective case for a pronoun that serves as a direct object, an indirect object, or the object of a preposition. Do not use the objective case for a pronoun that serves as a subject.

Don't say, "Just between you and I, his poetry is terrible." Say this instead: "Just between you and me, his poetry is terrible." Don't say, "He laughed at Clara and I." Say, "He laughed at Clara and me." Don't say, "Me and Wilma spoke to them last night." Say, "Wilma and I spoke to them last night." Don't say, "Her and me decided to bicycle in France." Say, "She and I decided to bicycle in France." Don't say, "Myself and Richard invite you to the staff party." Say, "Richard and I invite you to the party."

7. Form the possessive case correctly.

My students have more trouble with the apostrophe marking the possessive case than with any other mark of punctuation. About half of them cannot form the possessive in accordance with the conventions of English. To form the possessive, you must use the apostrophe according to the guidelines outlined below.

To form the possessive of singular nouns, add *'s* ("apostrophe *s*") at the end:

> Ann's job; Gertrude's voice; Doc's friendship; the hotel's buffet; Israel's troubles; the superintendent's office

Use *'s* even when the singular noun ends in *s*:

> Burriss's house; Erasmus's first book; Charles's pen

The rule is not observed in some traditional phrases:

> For goodness sake!
> In Jesus' name

Be sure to add the *'s* to words that end with z or x:

> Groucho Marx's films; Berlioz's music

To form the plural possessive use the simple apostrophe after words whose plurals end in *s*:

> the Joneses' street; the dogs' door

If the noun has an irregular plural that does not end in *s*, form the possessive by adding *'s* just as you would if the noun were singular:

> children's literature; men's clothing; women's rights

8. Use the correct verb tense.

Tense is the time of a verb. English has six tenses:

> *Present*:   I play.
> *Simple past*:   I played.
> *Simple future*:   I will play.
> *Present perfect*: I have played.
> *Past perfect*:   I had played.
> *Future perfect*:   I will have played.

Each tense has a *progressive* form that expresses continuing, or progressive, action within the time noted in the tense:

> *Present progressive*:   I am playing.
> *Past progressive (imperfect)*:   I was playing.
> *Future progressive*:   I will be playing.
> *Present perfect progressive*:   I have been playing.
> *Past perfect progressive*:   I had been playing.
> *Future perfect progressive*:   I will have been playing.

The present tense may do several things, one of which is reporting habitual action:

Birds *migrate* every year.

The sun *rises* every morning.

Wars *are caused* by stupidity.

Habitual action extends to verbs that describe the action in literature, because the written word is assumed to be always speaking:

David Copperfield *is* not as interesting as other characters in the book.

Socrates *teaches* that the way to wisdom begins with the command, "Know thyself."

The United States Constitution *links* the right to keep and bear arms to serving in the militia—what we call today the National Guard.

The present progressive tense is the most idiomatic way we have of speaking of something happening right now:

She *is coming* down the street.

They *are repaving* the highway between Boston and Lynn.

The present progressive can become a future tense by the addition of an adverb of future time:

She is coming *tomorrow.*

They are playing softball *next Sunday.*

Adding *do* or *does* to the present tense of a verb shows emphasis. The present emphatic is used in negations:

I *do not* like snakes.

She *does not* like people who *do not* like snakes.

The present emphatic is also used to affirm something that someone else has denied. For example, someone may accuse you of disliking rock music, and, if you have any hearing left, you may say, "I *do* like rock music."

The present tense creates confusion for writers who get carried away with the sense of action conveyed by the present. Such writers often use the present tense to describe past action, especially when they write about history or an exciting story. For example:

Franklin Roosevelt is elected because he promises to do something about the Depression, and Hoover keeps saying that the Depression is almost over. Roosevelt takes over in March 1933, and at his inaugural address he promises bold action and tells the American people that the only thing they have to fear is fear itself, and Hoover tells them that

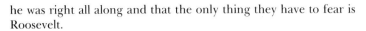

he was right all along and that the only thing they have to fear is
Roosevelt.

Narration in the present tense may be successfully used sometimes.
Thomas Carlyle used it to great effect in *The French Revolution*. But in
general you should avoid the present tense when writing about the
past. That is the common style of British and American historians.
The present sounds strained in telling English-speaking readers
about the past, and it may be confusing.

The simple past is usually formed by adding *-ed* as a suffix to the
present stem of the verb. *I play* becomes *I played*. The past participle is
made in the same way. *I have played*. But English is complicated by
having about three hundred irregular verbs. They are irregular because they form the past tense or the past participle in some way
other than by adding *-ed*. We say, "I draw," but not "I drawed." We
say, "I drew," and "I have drawn." We say, "I see," but not, "I seed."
We say, "I see," "I saw," and "I have seen."

We usually learn irregular verbs as we learn to talk and hear others use them. In some regions of the country common speech di-
verges from standard English. In the farming community where I
grew up, people said, "I seen him when he done it," and, "He drawed
me a plan for the house, and I taken a lot of time to study it over."
These were intelligent, sensible people. Similar people in other regions today may use verbs in nonstandard forms. When you are in
doubt, consult a dictionary—the most valuable tool a writer has.
Any good dictionary lists the various standard forms of irregular
verbs.

The simple future tense is formed with *shall* and *will*. Strict grammarians used to insist that *shall* be used with the first person and *will*
with the second and third persons. American writers generally ignore
this distinction. We nearly always say, "He will be 50 on his next
birthday," and, "We will be happy to see you at the party." Today in
American English *shall* seems to indicate an emphatic statement.
"They shall not pass." "I shall be there." It is almost as if *shall* were
always in italics in our minds.

We should give a few more words to the progressive form, which
shows action that continues. The past progressive, or imperfect, is the
most common form. Use it to show action going on while something
else is happening: "I *was traveling* west during June." The sentence
means that while June was going by, I was traveling West. Here are
other examples:

He *was sleeping* when the robbery occurred.

The team *was holding* its post-game prayer meeting when the
gamblers came in to pay off the players.

We call the past progressive the *imperfect* because the end of the action is not described. That is, the action of sleeping continued as long as the robbery occurred, and the action of holding the prayer meeting went on an indefinite length of time. We are not told how long in either sentence.

Think of the progressive as duration. The action continues for a time—or continued or will continue. Don't use the progressive when the past will do.

9. Avoid illogical mixing of verb tenses.

The simple verb tenses are seldom difficult. We combine them logically. We would never think of saying, "I was there when you will come." We can say, "I am arriving when you will be there" because we understand that the present progressive verb phrase *am arriving* becomes a future tense because of the adverbial clause that follows it. Sometimes we stumble a moment when we consider how to join the past tense with the present, but a little thought usually leads us aright. We can mix past and present, as in the following sentences, when someone in the past made a statement that continues to be "true" for all time.

> Plato believed that the soul is immortal.
>
> Thomas More thought that death is not the worst fate.
>
> John Maynard Keynes taught that governments should use deficit financing during depressions.

Normally the past tense in a first clause will demand a past tense in a second clause, and we usually join such clauses without difficulty:

> He played baseball because he loved the game, not because he was paid a high salary.
>
> Players for the Boston Red Sox thought he was crazy.

Problems with mixing tenses usually arise when the perfect tenses are used. The present perfect always conveys a sense of action that started in the past and continues to the present, where either the action itself or its effects continue. The present perfect tense is formed by using the present tense of the verb *to have* with the past participle of the main verb in the construction.

> We *have worked* since yesterday afternoon.

The work started in the past and is still going on at the time the sentence describes.

The present perfect tense can easily be used in combination with the present tense:

He *has been* a great baseball player, but his greatest days are behind him, and he is retiring at the end of this season.

She *has been grinding* rust off the car all afternoon with the electric sander, and now she *is* tired.

The present perfect tense can be used with the future, since both tenses join at the time when the statement about future action is made.

They *have been traveling* all night, and they *will travel* all day today and tomorrow.

The past perfect tense uses the past tense of the verb *to have* with the past participle of the main verb in the construction. It always implies that an action ended before or just as another action began:

They *had been waiting* an hour when the train *arrived*.

The waiting ended at the moment the train arrived; both actions took place in the past.

The past perfect cannot be used before the present perfect. We cannot say, "Country music had been popular and has remained so." A reader wants to know this: "It had been popular before what?" The past perfect sets up the expectation of an end point, and if you do not have an end point, you must provide one or change the sentence:

Country music *had been* popular before 1950, but in that year it *attracted* national attention.

Here the prepositional phrase *before 1950* provides the end point that the past perfect leads us to expect, and the later clauses go on from that point to make another statement.

Sometimes we imply the end point, especially in oral English. Speaking of a classmate who came to an early-morning history class in a tuxedo, a friend may ask, "Did you know that John came to class this morning in a tuxedo?" You ask why, and your friend says, "He *had been* at a party all night long." From the last sentence spoken by your friend, you infer an end point already mentioned in an earlier sentence. The implied thought is this: "John had been at a party all night long and came to class in the morning in his tuxedo." The end point of the action *had been* is his arrival in class.

You also cannot properly use the past perfect with the present tense. You should not say, "He had to learn to walk before he learns to run." You should not use the past perfect as a substitute for the simple past. That is, don't say, "Henry VIII had been born in 1491" unless you intend to follow that sentence with another related to it by the simple past. It is better to say, "Henry VIII was born in 1491."

You may use the past perfect in a paragraph whose sentences lack a dependent clause only if the end point of the past perfect is clearly stated in another sentence:

> Henry VIII came to the throne in 1509. He *had not been meant* to be king. He *had been born* the second son of Henry VII. His older brother Arthur *had been heir* to the throne, but Arthur died. A persistent legend holds that young Henry *had been destined* to become a priest, but Arthur's death changed that destiny and the destiny of England as well.

Here we have several sentences in the past perfect, all moving toward the end point stated in the first sentence.

The past perfect tense is used too much, especially in the writing of history. Use the simple past unless the past perfect is clearly needed.

The future perfect tense describes a future act that must be concluded before or just as another future act begins.

> We *will have been* here a week before you arrive.

> The apples *will have been picked* before then.

As in all perfect tenses, the future perfect makes you think of the time when one action ends and another begins. The action in the future perfect tense must end before some future moment or just as some future action begins.

Always recall that perfect tenses imply a time considered as the end point of an action, a time when the action of the sentence is complete from the point of view of the sentence. You may say, "I have been waiting for an hour," using the present tense. You may go on waiting for another hour, or you may now be ending your wait, but neither possibility is the concern of this sentence. This sentence is concerned with the action that has gone on for an hour, and that hour is complete by the time the sentence is written or spoken.

10. Use the subjunctive form of the verb in dependent clauses that make a statement contrary to fact.

> I wish I *were* in the Caribbean.

I am not in the Caribbean; hence the use of the subjunctive *were* is appropriate.

> If he *were* more tactful, he would have more friends.

He is not more tactful; so he does not have more friends.

The subjunctive form of the verb is much more common in French or German or Greek than in English. Verbs can either be in the *subjunctive* or the *indicative* mood. The indicative is used to represent simple statements of fact. The subjunctive always carries with it a mood of doubt or yearning or fear or command that in English lingers only in a few uses. Indeed it is used so seldom that the chief problem of the subjunctive is that insecure people afraid of being incorrect may use it inappropriately.

The subjunctive is not used, for example, after every *if* in a sentence. Use the subjunctive only to make a statement that is clearly contrary to fact, as in the examples above. Don't use it for factual statements that may involve some uncertainty about the past. You should say this, "If what she said *was* true, he was guilty." This is a simple indicative statement. You do not know whether she spoke the truth or not. You merely make the statement that if she did speak the truth, he was guilty. That is a fact. The indicative is used in factual statements. If you knew beyond any doubt that she was lying, you would say this: "If what she said *were* true, he was guilty."

Had and *should* may express the subjunctive. "Should you win the Nobel Prize, I will help you spend the money." It is entirely uncertain that you will win the Nobel Prize. But if you do, I will help you spend the prize money. "Had the Germans not feared Russia so much in 1914, they might have beaten France quickly." The Germans did fear the Russians; they did not concentrate all their army in France; and they not only did not win the war quickly, but they did not win it at all. The subjunctive use of *had* introduces a condition clearly contrary to fact.

11. Use commas according to standard practice.

The comma appears more than any other punctuation mark in English. It is important for you to use it according to standard practice to avoid confusing readers.

A. Use the comma with a coordinating conjunction to separate independent clauses in a sentence.

Independent clauses can usually stand alone as sentences. The coordinating conjunctions are *and, but, nor,* and *for,* and sometimes *yet* and *so.* The comma and the conjunction bind separate independent clauses together.

Dolphins have brains bigger than those of humans, *but* they spend all their time in the water, *and* they can't even play checkers.

The star tailback of Sourmash State University could not read simple English after four years of college, *nor* could he find a pro team willing to hire him.

It is incorrect to use a comma alone to hold independent clauses together. Do not use a comma like this:

> Intercollegiate football games used to be for the participants, now the fans—often overweight and unable to climb a flight of stairs without puffing—demand that teams win at any cost, even if they must cheat.

The absence of the coordinating conjunction *but* after the comma confuses us. For a moment we think the participants are now the fans. We have to get to the end of the sentence to sort out its meaning. The fault here is called a *comma splice*; that is, the writer tries to splice the clauses together with a comma, but the comma cannot do the job. The sentence is fine when we add the appropriate conjunction:

> Intercollegiate football games used to be for the participants, but now the fans—often overweight and unable to climb a flight of stairs without puffing—demand that teams win at any cost, even if they must cheat.

You can use a semicolon instead of a conjunction to separate independent clauses:

> He cheated on the test; it did not help his grade.

B. Use a comma after a long introductory clause or phrase that precedes the subject of an independent clause.

> Because the temperature on the highway was 115 degrees in the California desert, the air conditioning in the diner nearly knocked me flat.

> Backed up against Antwerp, the Belgian army furiously counter-attacked the Germans in September 1914.

> Having failed to win peace in Massachusetts by negotiation and compromise, the British decided to use force.

C. Use commas to set off parenthetical clauses and phrases that add descriptive material not essential to the principal assertion of the sentence.

Here is a sentence that contains a parenthetical phrase set off with commas:

> Jim kept the fountain pen, *a gift from his father*, for the rest of his long life.

The phrase *a gift from his father* adds information to the sentence but is not essential to the main assertion of the sentence. The writer might choose to develop something from the detail that the fountain pen was a gift from a father to a son. But the main assertion of this sentence is that Jim kept the pen for the rest of his long life. The assertion would remain the same without the phrase, so the phrase is set off by commas.

This sentence contains a parenthetical (or nonrestrictive) clause set off by commas:

> The personal computer, *which was unknown only a decade ago*, now is an indispensable tool for thousands of writers.

The parenthetical clause adds an interesting detail, that a device as common as the personal computer was unknown only ten years ago. But it is not essential to the core assertion of the sentence, that the personal computer is now an indispensable tool for thousands of writers.

Do not set off clauses and phrases that are necessary to the main assertion. Here is an example of an essential clause not set off by commas:

> The churchmen *who opposed Galileo* feared that his teachings would undermine the faith.

The clause here is essential to the main assertion. The writer is not speaking of all churchmen but only of those who opposed Galileo. Without the clause, the main assertion of the sentence would not make sense. At least it would not make the sense that the writer intended.

Be careful here. You can change the meaning of a sentence by setting off a clause or phrase with commas. Suppose you say this:

> Faculty members *who are slipshod and lazy* rob their students.

This sentence means that only faculty members who are slipshod and lazy rob their students. By not setting off the dependent clause with commas, you indicate that it is essential to the meaning of your sentence. You are writing about one kind of faculty member. But suppose you say this:

> Faculty members, who are slipshod and lazy, rob their students.

The commas tell us that you mean that all faculty members rob their students. You happen to add the information that faculty members are also slipshod and lazy, and so you deliver a double insult. You condemn the teaching profession for robbing students, and you announce that all members of that profession are slipshod and lazy.

Some writers set off all appositives with commas, but this habit may lead to confusion. Suppose you write this sentence:

> In his novel, *For Whom the Bell Tolls*, Ernest Hemingway made the Spanish Civil War a modern tragedy.

The commas make the book title parenthetical, something that could be left out without damaging the meaning of the sentence. They tell readers that the main assertion is this: "In his novel Ernest Hemingway made the Spanish Civil War a modern tragedy." The original sentence implies that Hemingway wrote only one novel and that it was called *For Whom the Bell Tolls*. But in fact Hemingway produced many novels, and the writer should not set off the title of the book with commas.

D. Use the comma to set off adjectives that modify the same noun.

Johnson was the strong, silent type.

E. Use a comma to set off interjections or transitive adverbs at the beginning of a sentence.

Consequently, we thought Johnson was boring.

Indeed, his wife thought Johnson was boring.

F. Use a comma to set off words or phrases in a series of three or more elements.

She wrote books, articles, and poems.

Lincoln's mighty words in the Gettysburg Address made the Civil War a struggle for government "of the people, by the people, and for the people."

G. Use a comma to set off direct quotations.

John Lyly said, "If one write never so well, he cannot please all, and write he never so ill, he shall please some."

H. Use a comma correctly with other punctuation.

A comma at the end of quoted material goes inside the quotation marks:

"Hating people is like burning down your own house to get rid of a rat," said Harry Emerson Fosdick, one of the greatest of Protestant preachers.

But a comma goes outside parentheses or brackets at the end of the material so set off.

In hard times (the thought is from Euripides), friends show whether they are to be trusted or not.

She wrote me that she hated my "mispellings" [sic], but she said that my content was fairly good.

12. Use the dash circumspectly.

Many writers love the dash. It helps us add some of the seemingly spontaneous thoughts that break into our mind while we are writing a sentence. It provides a sense of a telegraphic style. It allows us to digress slightly or to signal readers that we want to them to pay special attention to what follows.

The first thing to do with a dash is make it correctly. On a typewriter or a computer, the dash is composed of two hyphens without a space between them, typed with no spaces between the last word before the dash and the first hyphen or between the last hyphen and the first word after the dash—like this. If you use one hyphen - like this, you will confuse readers and upset the people who set your work into type.

Use the dash to set off an emphatic phrase:

Baseball players now charge for their autographs—up to $25.00 a signature!

You can also use the dash to set off an emphatic clause:

Longstreet surveyed the field at Gettysburg and wanted to withdraw, and events proved him right. But he could not get his way for one reason—Robert E. Lee wanted to attack, and Lee was in command.

Dashes, like parentheses, sometimes set off slight digressions or definitions within a sentence. Dashes seem to be a little more emphatic than parentheses, though that depends on the writer.

Renaissance painting—assuming there was such a thing as the Renaissance—emphasized the human figure and a somewhat idealized human expression.

Sometimes for emphasis you may want to write a compound subject, follow it with a dash, and make a statement about that subject with a clause.

Beethoven, Chopin, and Liszt—these are perhaps the greatest of the romantic composers.

It's not good to use dashes to set off more than one element in a sentence. Writer's occasionally do so, but the effect can be confusing.

Be circumspect. You can often use a colon, parentheses, or a simple comma to set off elements that you might also set off with a dash. Too many dashes in a piece of prose always give me the uncomfortable feeling that the writer is extremely nervous and wants to emphasize everything. The effect is a little like being yelled at.

13. Use standard American forms for quotations.

Use double quotation marks to set off direct quotations. If material you are quoting includes material in quotation marks, use single quotation marks (the apostrophe key) to set off those words within quotation marks in the original.

> Speaking of Sioux chief Sitting Bull, Evan S. Connell says, "A feminine element very often radiates from sexually powerful males and in the case of Sitting Bull this was so unmistakable that one journalist, fascinated by the oval face between long braids, spoke of his 'manhood and womanliness.' "[1]

English practice is the opposite of American practice; English publishers use apostrophes or single quotation marks where we use the double marks and the double marks where we use the single marks. Follow American practice.

Commas go within closing quotation marks; semicolons and colons go outside.

> "You write in water," said Erasmus of work that had no result.
>
> "Hell will never be full until you be in it"; such was a Scottish proverbial insult.
>
> "Whom the gods love dies young": John F. Kennedy died when he was 46 years old.

Do not put quotation marks around block quotations. Use indented blocks for quotations more than four or five lines long. In typed or computer-generated manuscripts, the blocks should be indented five spaces from the left margin. The indention of a block of text is indication enough that you are quoting. If you add quotation marks, readers will assume you are beginning the quotation with a quotation from someone else.

The lines in the block quotation should be double-spaced. Within the block quotation you use quotation marks exactly as they appear in the quoted material. I have elsewhere in this book recommended that you not use block quotations whenever you can avoid them. It is better to paraphrase and to quote smaller sections of a text than one usually quotes in a block. However, in books such as this one, block quotations are necessary, and everyone has to use them now and then. When you do use them, study the examples in this book if you have questions about the right form.

Do not use quotation marks to set off slang terms, clichés, or other words that you wish to apologize for. Only inexperienced writers use these apologetic quotation marks. They seem to say, "I know this is a cliché or some other lazy language, but at least I have put it in quotation marks to let you know that I know I'm being lazy." When

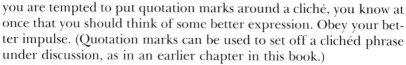
you are tempted to put quotation marks around a cliché, you know at once that you should think of some better expression. Obey your better impulse. (Quotation marks can be used to set off a clichéd phrase under discussion, as in an earlier chapter in this book.)

But do use quotation marks to indicate a usage by others that you do not share yourself.

> In a communist "people's democracy," the people had very little voice in anything their government did.

14. Use ellipsis marks correctly.

My students seem to have excessive trouble using ellipses properly. Ellipsis marks indicate that some words have been left out, usually out of a quotation.

Make ellipsis marks by using the period key on your typewriter or computer. Put a space between the last word before the ellipsis and the first ellipsis dot; make the dot, space again, make the second dot, space again, make the third dot, space again, and then resume the quotation. You should not make ellipsis marks without spaces between the marks like this (...). Ellipsis marks should always be spaced . . . like this. Otherwise the rapid reader will stumble and will have to back up and reconsider what you have written.

Here are a few sentences from Paul Fussell's book *The Great War and Modern Memory*:

> Recourse to the pastoral is an English mode of both fully gauging the calamities of the Great War and imaginatively protecting oneself against them. Pastoral reference, whether to literature or to actual rural localities and objects, is a way of invoking a code to hint by antithesis at the indescribable; at the same time, it is a comfort in itself, like rum, a deep dug-out, or a woolly vest.[2]

Here is part of a paper that quotes from this text, using ellipses to indicate some omitted words:

> Fussell argues that English troops in World War I used the pastoral tradition as an anodyne against the horrors they met in the trenches. He says, "Pastoral reference . . . is a way of invoking a code to hint by antithesis at the indescribable; at the same time, it is a comfort in itself."

The ellipsis marks show that words have been omitted between "reference" and "is," and by checking the original, you can see what those words were. Notice that there is a space between "reference" and the first dot and a space after each of the dots, including the space between the last one and the word "is."

Notice, too, that there are no ellipsis marks after "itself," although it is not the last word in Fussell's sentence. The quotation marks are sufficient to show readers that the writer has stopped quoting. Any reader assumes that Fussell's text goes on; no reader needs ellipsis marks to understand that the paper is not quoting everything Fussell says.

Neither do you need ellipsis marks at the beginning of a quotation, even if you are quoting only part of a sentence. The quotation marks tell readers that you are quoting, and readers assume that you cannot quote all of your source. You don't need to create typographical monstrosities like this:

> Lincoln said that the Civil War was fought so that " . . . government of the people, by the people, and for the people . . . " might endure.

Remember always that the function of ellipsis marks is to show that you are leaving something out between your first quotation marks and your last. They are a kind of certification of your honesty, showing readers that you are not quoting something exactly as the author wrote it. The quotation marks themselves set off your quotation from what you choose not to quote from your source.

Sometimes you may leave out a whole sentence, several whole sentences, or an entire paragraph from a long quotation. Then you must punctuate the last sentence before the ellipsis marks. You put the period at the end of that sentence, make a space, and write the ellipsis marks according to standard practice.

> David Donald speaks of the difficulties a man as large as Thomas Wolfe had when he wrote. "He tried to keep to a fixed schedule. He began working on his book about midnight and, because no chairs or tables were ever quite comfortable for a man of his height, he usually stood while he wrote, using the top of the refrigerator as his desk. . . . Often in the early afternoon Abe Smith, his former student at New York University, now a young, married businessman, came by to type his interminable manuscript."[3]

The writer quotes David Donald, Wolfe's biographer, and the ellipsis marks show that words have been omitted after the sentence ending with "desk." That sentence is punctuated with a period. Then there is a space, an ellipsis dot, another space, a second dot, another space, a third dot, and another space before the quotation takes up again.

15. Use colons to set off lists and some quotations.

> She wanted three things: a good job, respect, and loyal friends.

Note that the colon comes at the end of an independent clause. A colon should not break into an indepedent clause. You should not say this: "She wanted: a good job, respect, and loyal friends."

You can see from the many examples in this book that colons frequently come at the end of text just before a block quotation.

Colons can also join independent clauses when the second clause is meant to be a consequence or a clarification of the first:

> Jackson was furious: someone had given him a monkey for Christmas, and he hated pets.

16. Observe the rules for parallelism.

Parallel grammatical forms can add power to your writing. The most simple parallelism is the series—"Churchill said, 'I have nothing to offer but *blood, toil, tears, and sweat*' "—but phrases and clauses can also make parallel forms.

Parallel forms are joined by the coordinating conjunctions *and, but, or, for,* and *nor.* The words, phrases, and clauses joined by these conjunctions must be equal in form. In the example from Churchill above, the conjunction *and* helps join four nouns—*blood, toil, tears,* and *sweat.*

> I have heard the chimes at midnight and seen the sun at dawn.
>
> He liked neither beer nor wine.
>
> I shall sing a song, for I am happy.

The most common errors in parallelism are in a series. Here is a faulty parallelism:

> We came home, ate dinner, and we watched the All-Star game.

The correct form is this:

> We came home, at dinner, and watched the All-Star game.

Appendix One

Sexist Language

❖ ❖ ❖

For centuries ordinary English seemed to imply that only men were important. We have now progressed to a different perception. Women have demanded fair and equal treatment not only in jobs and education and social life but also in language. The consequences for writing have been confusing. The discussion in this section will not, alas, clear up all the confusions, but some of its advice may be helpful. At the very least it will show where the confusion is most troublesome and will help clarify some problems just a little. How do we keep language from being sexist and at the same time keep it natural and fluent? That is the question.

The most troublesome problem in sexist language is this: What do we do with the English custom of using *he, his,* or *him* when we use the pronoun to refer to an indefinite singular noun or pronoun that may indicate either male or female? In common English we have for years written this: "What do we want our reader to think about our writing? We want him to believe that we know what we are talking about, that we respect his point of view, and that we hope he will seriously consider ours." We know that "our reader" may include male or female. What do we do now, with the different consciousness of this age?

With the preceding example the solution is easy. We turn the singular into the plural, and we say this: "What do we want our readers to think about us? We want them to believe that we know what we are talking about, that we respect their points of view, and that we hope they will seriously consider ours."

At times we must use the singular, as in a sentence like this: "The thief entered the house by breaking a pane of glass in the back door, cutting himself in the process, and left a trail of blood through the kitchen. The wound must not have been serious since he not only stole my computer but came back to take two large boxes of computer paper as well."

Now what are we to do? In some sentences we might write both the feminine and the masculine pronoun, but in this sentence the effect, to me at least, seems clumsy. "The thief entered the house by breaking a pane of glass in the back door, cutting himself or herself in the process, and left a trail of blood through the kitchen. The wound must not have been serious since he or she not only stole my computer but came back to take two large boxes of computer paper as well."

We can use the masculine and feminine pronouns when repetition is unnecessary. We can write easily enough, "The company promised to give the first prize winner a week's stay in any hotel in the country that he or she may choose." But we get into trouble when we write this: "The company promised to give the first-prize winner a week's stay in any hotel in Hawaii that he or she may choose and promised also that he or she might take along a companion and that he or she would also be given free use of a rental car for the week and free meals in the restaurant of his or her choice." Here again we can revise to eliminate the difficulty: "First prize was a week's stay in any hotel in Hawaii for the winner and a companion, a free rental car for a week, and free meals in any restaurant in the islands."

Occasionally we can use the pronoun *one* as a substitute for *he* or *she*: "Anyone who works the night shift for twenty years will discover that one's view of life changes in ways incomprehensible to one's neighbors." To many such usage is uncomfortable.

I often hear well-educated people say things like this: "Anybody who works the night shift for twenty years will discover that their view of life changes in ways incomprehensible to their neighbors." The plural pronoun *their* (or *them*) offers a nonsexist solution to the problem of *he* or *she, her* or *his.* That solution is not grammatically correct, and it makes me wince, perhaps because it runs so counter to my early teaching about English; it may not offend younger readers. I do not expect it to be adopted soon by most editors and professional writers, but who can tell? I see it now and then in advertising and even in slick-paper magazines. Anyone who says English cannot change to accept uncomfortable usage does not know what they are talking about.

To me, even the ungrammatical use of *their* to refer to a single person is much better than the "he/she" or, worse, "s/he" that I see occasionally in memos. We should always be able to read writing aloud, and I do not see how we could read "he/she" or "s/he" aloud in any sensible way. It also looks wretched on the page.

My own solution, used in this book, is first to do my best to revise away the problem. Most editors of books and magazines seem to have adopted this procedure. You think and rewrite and use a plural instead of a singular, or you change your text even more. When I have to use a singular form, I vary the pronoun, using *he* sometimes and *she* sometimes. A few people I know—including some feminists—argue that male writers should use the pronoun *he* and that female writers should use *she*. Many writers in my observation have now adopted this usage. Yet to many it seems awkward, and woman writers as diverse as Barbara Tuchman and Mina Shaughnessy have used the traditional *he* without feeling that they betray other women. I must admit that *he* comes to me much more naturally, and I confess that I do not believe this particular pronoun has much of an effect on the fate of women's rights. In France and Hungary, where the languages allow a neuter singular pronoun, women are traditionally discriminated against and oppressed in both law and custom. But we should not take the bad example set by others as an example for ourselves. Maybe we can do better than the French and the Hungarians. In our society the very attention that we give to the matter is a positive sign.

I find myself torn. I don't want to offend an audience unnecessarily. An offended audience for whatever reason is one that will not take your work seriously. Just now hardly any subject related to writing offends people more than the issue of sexist language. The problem for writers is that some men and women will be offended no matter what we do. If we sound clumsy in our efforts to avoid sexist language, we are going to offend traditionalists, of whom there are many. If we refuse to take note of social change and go on using *he* and *him* as if everyone on earth worthy of consideration were born male, we will offend the large and rapidly growing number of people who believe that clumsiness of language is a small price to pay for sexual equality.

Aside from the difficulties with pronouns, we can easily avoid some of the traditional offenses of sexist language. You don't have to say *policeman*; you can say *police officer*. I have no special problem writing *chairperson* rather than the traditional *chairman*. Some journals now use the word *chair*, a word that seems to be taking hold. *Freshperson* seems unbearably clumsy as a substitute for *freshman*, but we can always say *first-year student* instead.

Where once we spoke of *mankind*, we can now say *humankind*; where once we wrote *man*, we can usually find a substitute. Instead of saying, "The average man," we can say, "The average person." Instead of saying, "Man is the highest form of life," we can say, "The human species is the highest form of life." Whenever you are tempted to use a word that seems to show superiority of men over women, pause to think of another, sex-neutral word. You can nearly always find one.

Some words should be abandoned. *Poetess* for a woman now seems degrading—though *actress* does not. Women should never be

referred to as "the fair sex" or "the distaff side," as if the only interesting quality of a woman were appearance and her only job to stay in
the home. A wife should never be called her husband's "better half,"
a term patronizing at best. The word *lady* often has a negative connotation these days, for many feel that it sets women apart and implies that they are worthwhile only if they act like characters in a
nineteenth-century etiquette book. The word *woman* is better.

Above all, readers should not be addressed as though the only
important people among them were men. Never identify women by
telling who their husbands are unless that information has some special importance. I recently received a notice about a conference on
Thomas More where Mary Ellen Bork, president of the St. Thomas
More Society of Washington, D.C., was to be one of the speakers. The
circular identified her as "Wife of Judge Robert Bork." The conference was sponsored by a conservative religious group—perhaps one
reason for a labeling of Mrs. Bork so offensive to feminists and others
who are often taken to be radical. Mrs. Bork has a long and distinguished career of activity related to interests in Thomas More, and
having met her, I find her gracious and very bright. It seems gratu-
itous indeed to identify her by reference to her husband, no matter
how celebrated—or notorious—he may be or have been. In a news
story, that information might have been placed far down the text, for
it would interest some people naturally curious to know if Mrs. Bork
was related to the judge. But it is demeaning as a primary identi-
fication.

Take care also with the proper titles of women. The term *Ms.* is
now common, and I use it regularly to address correspondence to
women. A few women object to the title and prefer the more traditional *Mrs.* if they are married and *Miss* if they are not. Courtesy requires that you call people what they want to be called, and an occasional editor may prevent you from calling women by titles that both
you and they may prefer. But that conservatism seems to be breaking
down. Between the first and second editions of this book, *The New
York Times*, which had long held out against *Ms.*, has started using the
title regularly.

All these matters are difficult. They require a willingness to
change and a broad-mindedness about language. We are a long
way from resolving all the questions about sexist language that
arise. But we must do what we can to make ourselves more sensitive to an issue that is both real and important. Women are equal
to men. They ought to be treated that way, for to treat them any
other way is to demean men as well as women. The English-
speaking world is democratic, and our language should reflect our
profession.

Appendix Two

Clichés

*S*tudy the following list and avoid the expressions you find there. They have been worked to death. They may have had some power once, but it has long since been dust. On occasion you may find some special reason to use one of the phrases, and when we are pressed, we are all likely to tumble into using some of them because they come so easily to mind. That is just what is wrong with them. Although no one will hang you or beat you for letting a cliché creep into your prose, it's a good idea to change a cliché into simple English whenever you can. Instead of saying that a marathon is an "acid test," you can say that it is a test of stamina and character. That says more specifically what you might try to say using the cliché "acid test."

abreast of the times

absolute truth

acid test

across a wide [broad] spectrum

across the spectrum

add insult to injury

after all is said and done

against the current

agony of defeat

agree to disagree

all walks of life

a man [or woman] for all seasons

at this point in time

avoid like the plague

[the] ball's in his court

basic needs

basic truth

beat a hasty retreat

be that as it may

better half

better late than never

better part of valor

beyond a shadow of doubt

[the] birds and the bees

bite the dust

bitter end

bloody but unbowed

blue as the sky

bolt from the blue

❖

bottom line
bottom of my [her] heart
bottom of the barrel
bottom of the deck
brave as a lion
bright as a new penny
bring down the house
bring home the bacon
broad array
broad daylight
brown as a nut
brutally frank
brutal murder
burn the midnight oil
bustling cities
by the same token

calm, cool, and collected
cat on a hot tin roof
chip off the old block
cloud nine
cold as ice
cold, hard facts
cold light of day
come to grips with
communicate effectively
consensus of opinion
conspicuous by his absence
cool as a cucumber
could have knocked me over
with a feather
crack of dawn
crisis of confidence
critical juncture
crowning glory
crying on the inside
cut and dried

dead as a doornail
deaf as a post
deep, dark secret
deep as the ocean
diabolical skill
distaff side
doomed to disappointment
do or die
down and out
down but not out
down for the count
down the primrose path
dyed in the wool

each and every
[to] each his own
every dog has its day
every tub on its own bottom

face the music
factor
facts of life
fatal flaw
few and far between
filthy lucre
first and foremost
fit as a fiddle
fleecy clouds
fond memories
fond recollections
fresh as a daisy
frozen north

get the lead out
gone but not forgotten
go over like a lead balloon
go over with a fine-tooth comb

grave danger
green with envy
gutless wonder

hail fellow well met
hale and hearty
hands-on
happy as a lark
happy as a clam
happy medium
hard row to hoe
head up [the committee]
heady mixture
hearts and minds
heave a sigh of relief
higher than a kite
highest priority
high spirits
hit the nail on the head
hotter than hell [Hades]
hush fell over the crowd
hustle and bustle

imminent danger
in a nutshell
in a very real sense
innocent as a new-born babe
in some cases
integral part
in terms of
in the final analysis
in this day and age
it goes without saying
it is incumbent upon
it is interesting to note
it stands to reason

ladder of success
larger than life
last but not least
last straw
learning experience
lick and a promise
light as a feather
like father, like son
little lady
live and learn
live from hand to mouth
live like a king
lying through her teeth

mad as a hatter
make a shambles of
man about town
meaningful experience
meaningful relationship
method in her madness
mind like a steel trap
miss is as good as a mile
mitigate against
more sinned against than sinning
more than meets the eye
murmur of approval

neat as a pin
needle in a haystack
never, ever
nip and tuck
nip in the bud
nose to the grindstone
no sooner said than done
nothing ventured, nothing gained

not too distant future
nuclear holocaust
off his rocker
off the beaten track
off the track
off the wall
once and for all
one hundred and ten percent
one rotten apple spoils the barrel
ongoing
on the fast track
on this planet
other side of the coin
out of the blue

painfully obvious
paint the town red
paramount importance
pass the buck
pave the way
pebble on the beach
pencil thin
pertinent facts
pick and choose
pivotal figure
plain as the nose on your face
plain Jane
pleased as punch
poor but happy
poor but honest
precondition
preplanning
pride and joy
primrose path
prioritize
proof is in the pudding
proud owner

proud possessor
put your best foot forward
put your foot in it

quick as a flash
quick as a wink
quick as lightning

raise its ugly head
rank and file
rather unique
raving lunatic
rear its ugly head
rude awakening

sadder but wiser
scarce as hens' teeth
sell like hot cakes
sharp as a razor
sharp as a tack
short and sweet
short end of the stick
shot in the arm
shoulder to the wheel
sigh of relief
silver platter
simple as salt
sink or swim
skeleton in the closet
skin of your teeth
slow but sure
smart as a whip
smelling like a rose
sneaking suspicion
sober as a judge
soft place in my heart
sound as a dollar
spread like wildfire

stick out like a sore thumb
stock in trade
straight and narrow
strike while the iron is hot
sunny south
supreme moment
sure winner

tangled skein
tangled web
tempest in a teapot
tender mercies
tested in the fire
thin as a rail
tired but happy
to all intents and purposes
tried and true
truth is stranger than fiction
twinkling of an eye

undercurrent of excitement

unstinted praise
up in arms

viable alternative
vicious circle [cycle]
vital role

walk a chalk line
walking on air
walk the line
walk the straight and narrow
wet blanket
when the going gets tough, the tough get going
white as snow
work like a dog
work like a horse
wreak havoc

Appendix Three

Glossary of Terms

❖❖❖

Throughout this book I have used many terms that should be familiar to you from the early study in grammar that most of us endure. This glossary will help you brush up on some definitions that you may have forgotten.

absolute   A phrase beginning with a noun followed by a present or past participle and modifying the entire clause rather than any single element within the clause.

> The guys hung out on the corner, *their motorcycles parked in a row on the street*.
> The Philistines inhabited the valleys, *their iron weapons keeping Israel confined to the hills*.

Sometimes the participle in an absolute is understood. In the following example, the participle *being* is understood after the noun *mind*.

> She sat staring into space, *her mind in another world*.

accusative   The standard grammatical term for what Americans call the objective case. The accusative is the case for pronouns that are direct objects, indirect objects, or objects of prepositions.

> He loved *her*.
> She bought *him* the bicycle.
> He worried about *them* on their trek to Mars.

Pronouns in the accusative case include *me, us, him, her, them,* and *whom*.

adjective   A part of speech that adds some description or *modifies* nouns or pronouns.

The streets were *glossy* with rain.

Rotting ice floated in the lake.

Heavy people run a *larger* risk of heart disease than *thin* people.

Adjectives answer questions like, What kind? Which one? How large? How many? What color?

adverb   A part of speech that adds description or modifies verbs, adjectives, and other adverbs. In common usage, adverbs may modify an entire clause.

The plane rose *swiftly*.

In a moment it was *nearly* invisible.

Unfortunately, she will be away for a year.

case   The form of a noun or pronoun that indicates its use in a sentence. Nouns change form only to make the possessive case, which shows ownership or some special relation. Pronouns change form to show that they are actors, recipients of action, or possessors.

The possessive case of single nouns is formed by adding an apostrophe and an *s*, even to words that end in *s*.

Dickens's novels; Melville's works

The possessive case of plural nouns is formed by adding an apostrophe to nouns whose plurals end in *s* and an apostrophe and an *s* to those whose plurals end otherwise.

The Raiders' passing game; the children's books

The case of definite pronouns is usually indicated by their forms. The subjective case includes the following: *I, you, he, she, it, we, they*. The possessive case includes the following: *my, mine, your, yours, his, hers, its, our, ours, their, theirs*. The objective case includes the following: *me, him, her, us, them*.

Indefinite pronouns do not change form except in the possessive case. The possessive of pronouns follows the same rules that govern the possessive of nouns:

anybody's; everybody's

clause   A sentence element with a subject and a verb. Clauses can be *dependent* or *independent*. See these definitions in the glossary.

conjunction   *Coordinating conjunctions* include *and, but, or, nor*, and *for*, and sometimes *yet* and *so*. *Subordinating conjunctions* include such words as *although, because, if, though, unless, whether*, and *when*.

The parts of a sentence joined by a *coordinating* conjunction should have equal grammatical importance. Coordinating conjunctions may join independent clauses:

She loved cars, *but* he preferred bicycles.

They may also join words in a series:

McDonald said she would take bread, crackers, *or* biscuits.

Subordinating conjunctions most often join dependent clauses to other clauses:

He got angry *when* he could not find a parking place.

dependent clause   A clause that serves as a noun, an adjective, or an adverb for another clause.

Noun clause: He said *that he loved the University of Vermont.*
Adjective clause: The house *that he painted* was the wrong one.
Adverb clause: *When the sun rose* she was already hard at work.

finite verb   A verb that has tense (a synonym for *time*). Finite verbs can be *present*, *past*, *future*, *present perfect*, and *future perfect*. They differ from *infinitives* in that infinitives, strictly speaking, cannot have time.

free modifier   A participial or participial phrase that occurs at the end of a clause, set off by a comma and modifying the *subject* of the clause.

Rain fell through the night before Waterloo, *soaking both French and English troops.*

In the following sentence the participial phrase is *not* a free modifier because it modifies not the subject but the last noun in the clause before the participle.

He looked out to the sun *rising over the blue wall of mountains to the east.*

Note that there is no comma after *sun*.

gerund   A verbal used as a noun in a sentence. Gerunds almost always take the form of the present participle.

Walking delighted her.

independent clause   Sometimes called a *main clause*. An independent clause can usually stand by itself as a complete sentence. A more technical definition is that an independent clause does not serve as a noun, adjective, or adverb for another clause.

> *Charles Darwin arrived at the idea of biological evolution* after he had thought for years about the differences he observed in species.

infinitive   A nonfinite form of a verb made by placing the infinitive marker *to* before the present stem; a nonfinite form of the verb has no tense. The infinitive of *make* is *to make*; the infinitive of *sit* is *to sit*. Occasionally you may see a past infinitive, made of the verb *have* and the past participle of the infinitive verb: "*To have sat* during his commencement speech was a great tribulation." Strictly speaking the infinitive here is *to have*, timeless until the participle *sat* is added to it.

Infinitives often work as nouns in a sentence:

> He struggled *to write*.

Infinitives that act as nouns can become the antecedents of pronouns:

> He struggled *to write*; it was his only ambition.

Infinitives can also serve as adjectives or adverbs:

> Her desire *to succeed* ruled her life. [adjective]
> She stood up *to read*. [adverb]

A *split infinitive* occurs when a word, usually an adverb, is placed between the infinitive marker *to* and the verb, as in the phrase "to *really* win."

interjection   A part of speech that denotes sudden emotion. Interjections include words like *ouch* and *wow*, as well as common obscenities and blasphemies.

intransitive verb   An intransitive verb describes a condition or an act that does not carry to an object.

> She *thought*.
> We *waited*.

linking verb   A linking verb joins a subject and an adjective or a subject and another noun or noun substitute. The most common linking verbs are forms of *to be*.

> Burriss *was* always friendly.
> Lanier *is* an architect.

Linking verbs are intransitive.

nominative case   The nominative case is used for pronouns that serve as subjects or subjective complements in clauses.

> *He* thought often of home.
> She was the one *who* he thought could best do the job.
> Could *she* be guilty?
> "It was *I*," I confessed.

The nominative forms of pronouns are *I, we, who, he, she*, and *they*. The form *you* is the same in both the nominative and the objective (or accusative) case.

nonrestrictive clause   A clause that adds information to a sentence without being essential to the main statement the sentence makes. Nonrestrictive clauses are set off with commas:

> Jesse Owens, *who ran brilliantly at the Olympic games in Berlin in 1936*, died of lung cancer from smoking one pack of cigarettes a day.

noun   The part of speech denoting substantives capable of being described. Nouns may be persons, places, things, actions, thoughts, or anything else capable of having an adjective used to describe it. The articles *a, an*, and *the* always signal a noun to follow, though the noun may be separated from the article by adjectives.

object   All objects in a sentence must be nouns or pronouns, or they must be clauses or phrases that serve as nouns or pronouns.
Direct objects receive the action of transitive verbs:

> Kant taught *philosophy*.
> He said *that time and space were essential to existence*.
> Frank Bernstein loved *to help people*.

Indirect objects do not receive action, but they show the purpose of action. You can often identify an indirect object by mentally placing a *to* or a *for* before it and seeing if it makes sense.

> My parents bought *me* a computer.
> Lincoln told *Americans* the truth about slavery.

The *object of a preposition* completes a prepositional phrase.

> High cholesterol in the *blood* may cause heart attacks.
> Between you and *me*, I would say that he bullies people.

objective case   The same as the *accusative case* (see definition in this glossary).

participle   The form of a verb that may be used either in a verb phrase or in an adjective. Present participles end in -*ing*. Past participles usually end in -*ed*, but English has about 300 irregular verbs that form the past participle in unpredictable ways.

preposition   A part of speech that never changes its form. Prepositions serve to introduce phrases that include a noun or a pronoun. The prepositional phrase allows the noun or pronoun to be used in an adverbial or adjectival sense in the sentence.

> The alumni slush fund *at Sourmash State University* [adjective] caused the athletic program to receive the death penalty *from the NCAA* [adverb].

pronoun   A part of speech used as a substitute for nouns and noun phrases.

> *Definite pronouns* are such words as *I, she, it, we, they, him, her, them, our.*
> *Indefinite pronouns* are such words as *anybody, everybody*, and *everyone.*
> *Reflexive pronouns* are such words as *itself, themselves*, and *myself.*
> The *relative pronouns* are *which* and *that.*
> The *demonstrative pronouns* are *this, that, these*, and *those.*

restrictive clause   A clause essential to the basic statement made in a sentence. Restrictive clauses are not set off by commas.

> We loved the snow *that fell on Christmas Eve*, but the snow *that fell on the day of the wedding* kept the bride from showing up.
> That *which is impossible to do* is immoral to command.

transitive verb   A transitive verb conveys action from a subject to an object. The object can be a noun, a pronoun, or a noun phrase or clause.

> She *designed* the plans for the house.
> He *said* that he loved the Pyrenees.

verbal   A nonfinite form of a verb—that is, a verb form that has in itself no sense of time. Verbals include *participles, infinitives*, and *gerunds* (see definitions in this glossary). They may be used as nouns or adjectives and sometimes as adverbs.

Notes

INTRODUCTION

[1]John Simon, *Paradigms Lost*, New York, Penguin Books, 1981, p. 18.
[2]Simon, p. 45.
[3]Dennis E. Baron, *Grammar and Good Taste*, New Haven, Conn., Yale University Press, 1982, p. 141.
[4]David B. Kaminsky, *Aspiration Biopsy For the Community Hospital*, New York, Mason Publishing, 1981, p. 1.
[5]Quoted in E. D. Hirsch, Jr., *The Philosophy of Composition*, Chicago, University of Chicago Press, 1977, pp. 60–61.
[6]Hirsch, p. 61.
[7]Giovanni Boccaccio, *The Decameron*, trans. Frances Winwar, New York, Modern Library, 1955, p. 16.
[8]Richard Selzer, "The Knife," *Mortal Lessons*, New York, Simon & Schuster, 1976;

CHAPTER 2

[1]Montaigne, Essays, 3:1, *Oeuvres complètes*, Paris, Editions Gallimard, 1962, p. 767.
[2]Montaigne, 2:10, p. 389.
[3]Lewis Thomas, "The Ilks," *The Lives of a Cell*, New York, Viking Press, 1975, p. 107; *Modern American Prose*, p. 373.
[4]Annie Dillard, "Jest and Earnest," *Pilgrim at Tinker Creek*, New York, Harper & Row, 1974, p. 5; *Modern American Prose*, p. 138.
[5]Joan Didion, "Bureaucrats," *The White Album*, New York, Simon & Schuster, 1979; *Modern American Prose*, p. 91.
[6]Jill Smolowe, "No Winners, Only Losers," *Time*, November 21, 1988, p. 91.
[7]Stephen Jay Gould, "Women's Brains," *The Panda's Thumb, More Reflections in Natural History*, New York, W. W. Norton & Company, 1983, p. 152; *Modern American Prose*, pp. 242–43.

[8]Lewis Thomas, "To Err Is Human," *The Medusa and the Snail*, New York, Viking Press, 1979, p. 36; *Modern American Prose*, pp. 384–85.

[9]Ron Fimrite, "Bring Back Day Games," *Sports Illustrated*, October 31, 1988, p. 88.

[10]Joan Didion, "Bureaucrats," *The White Album*, New York, Simon & Schuster, 1979; *Modern American Prose*, p. 95.

[11]Lewis Thomas, "To Err Is Human," *The Medusa and the Snail*, New York, Viking Press, 1979, p. 36; *Modern American Prose*, pp. 384–85.

[12]Thomas, "To Err Is Human," p. 40; *Modern American Prose*, p. 387.

[13]Gould, "Women's Brains,"; *Modern American Prose*, pp. 247–48.

CHAPTER 3

[1]Thomas More, *The Confutation of Tyndale's Answers* (eds. Louis A. Schuster, Richard C. Marius, James P. Lusardi, and Richard J. Schoeck), New Haven, Yale University Press, 1973, pp. 20–21.

CHAPTER 4

[1]Gilbert Allardyce, "What Fascism Is Not: Thoughts on the Deflation of a Concept," *American Historical Review*, April 1979, p. 367.

[2]Barbara Tuchman, *Practicing History*, New York, Knopf, 1981, p. 23.

CHAPTER 5

[1]Loren Eisley, "Charles Darwin," *Scientific American*, February 1956, pp. 62–72; *Modern American Prose*, p. 167.

[2]James Baldwin, "Notes of a Native Son," Boston, Beacon Press, 1955; *Modern American Prose*, p. 52.

[3]Alice Walker, "Beauty: When the Other Dancer Is the Self," *In Search of Our Mothers' Gardens*, New York, Harcourt Brace Jovanovich, 1975; *Modern American Prose*, p. 443.

[4]Barbara Tuchman, *The Proud Tower*, New York, Macmillan, 1966, p. 68; *Modern American Prose*, p. 408.

[5]Loren Eiseley, "Charles Darwin," *Scientific American*, February 1956, pp. 62–72; *Modern American Prose*, p. 166.

[6]Loren Eiseley, "The Judgment of the Birds," *The Immense Journey*, New York, Random House, 1956; *Modern American Prose*, pp. 179–180.

[7]William Manchester, *The Glory and the Dream*, Boston, Little, Brown, 1974, p. 93.

[8]John McPhee, "The Swiss at War," *La Place de la Concorde Swiss*, New York, Farrar, Straus & Giroux, 1984; *Modern American Prose*, p. 331.

[9]Annie Dillard, "Seeing," *Pilgrim at Tinker Creek*, New York, Harper & Row, 1974; *Modern American Prose*, p. 131.

[10]Lewis Thomas, "Late Night Thoughts on Listening to Mahler's Ninth Symphony," *Late Night Thoughts on Listening to Mahler's Ninth Symphony*, New York, Viking Penguin, 1982; *Modern American Prose*, p. 389.

CHAPTER 6

[1]Robert A. Caro, *The Years of Lyndon Johnson: The Path to Power*, New York, Alfred A. Knopf, 1982, p. 413.

[2]Stefan Kanfer, "The Protean Penman," *Time*, December 19, 1988, p. 80.

[3]Stephan Jay Gould, "The Criminal as Nature's Mistake," *Ever Since Darwin, Reflections in Natural History*, New York, W. W. Norton, 1977; *Modern American Prose*, p. 236.

[4]Barbara Tuchman, "In Search of History," *Practicing History*, New York, Alfred A. Knopf, 1981, p. 18; *Modern American Prose*, p. 398.

[5]Annie Dillard, "Transfiguration," *Holy the Firm*, New York, Harper & Row, 1977; *Modern American Prose*, p. 149.

[6]Norman Mailer, "Into Orbit," *Of a Fire on the Moon*, Boston, Little, Brown, 1970; *Modern American Prose*, p. 299.

[7]Tuchman, *Practicing History*, p. 20; *Modern American Prose*, p. 400.

[8]Annie Dillard, "Seeing," *Pilgrim at Tinker Creek*, New York, Harper & Row, 1974; *Modern American Prose*, p. 131.

[9]Robert W. Creamer, "First Inning: 1876–1901," in *The Ultimate Baseball Book*, ed. Daniel Okrent and Harris Lewine, Boston, Houghton Mifflin, 1981, pp. 14–15.

[10]John McPhee, "Oranges," *Oranges*, New York, Farrar, Straus & Giroux, 1967; *Modern American Prose*, p. 322.

[11]Phillip Caputo, *A Rumor of War*, New York, Holt, Rinehart & Winston, 1977, p. 163.

[12]Richard Selzer, "The Knife," *Mortal Lessons*, New York, Simon & Schuster, 1976; Modern American Prose, p. 344.

[13]Bruce Catton, *The Coming Fury*, Garden City, N.Y., Doubleday, 1961, p. 247.

[14]William Faulkner, *Light in August*, New York, Random House, 1932, p. 147.

[15]Kirkpatrick Sale, *Human Scale*, New York, Coward, McCann & Geoghegan, 1980, p. 129.

[16]Barbara Tuchman, *A Distant Mirror*, New York, Alfred A. Knopf, 1978, p. 139.

[17]George Orwell, *Homage to Catalonia*, Boston, Beacon, 1955, p. 86.

[18]Ellen Goodman, "Blame the Victim," *At Large*, New York, Summit Books, division of Simon & Schuster, 1981; *Modern American Prose*, p. 219.

[19]Norman Mailer, "The Siege of Chicago," *Miami and the Siege of Chicago*, New York, 1969; Modern American Prose, p. 290.

[20]Tom Wolfe, "Las Vegas," *The Kandy-Kolored Tangerine-Flake Streamline Baby*, New York, Farrar, Straus & Giroux, 1963; *Modern American Prose*, p. 517.

[21]Malcolm Cowley, *And I Worked at the Writer's Trade*, New York, Viking, 1978, p. 100.

[22]Richard Selzer, "Imelda," *Letter to a Young Doctor*, New York, Simon & Schuster, 1982; *Modern American Prose*, p. 356.

[23]John McPhee, "The Swiss at War," *La Place de la Concorde Swiss*, New York, Farrar, Straus & Giroux, 1984; *Modern American Prose*, p. 331.

CHAPTER 7

[1]"The Collective Behavior of Fads: The Characteristics, Effects, and Career of Streaking," *American Sociological Review*, August 1988, p. 572.

CHAPTER 8

[1]John Simon, *Paradigms Lost*, New York, Penguin Books, 1980, pp. 17–18.

[2]Quoted in Dennis E. Baron, *Grammar and Good Taste*, New Haven, Yale University Press, 1982, p. 218.

[3]Baron, p. 206.

[4]*Harper Dictionary of Contemporary Usage*, eds. William Morris and Mary Morris, New York, Harper & Row, 1975, p. 312.

[5]Charles Darwin, *Life and Letters*, vol. VIII, p. 58 (cited in O.E.D.).

[6]N. R. Kleinfield, *The New York Times*, November 23, 1983, p. C-1.

CHAPTER 9

[1]Loren Eiseley, "The Judgment of the Birds," *The Immense Journey*, New York, Random House, 1956; Modern American Prose, p. 180.

[2]Tom Wolfe, "Las Vegas," *The Kandy-Kolored Tangerine-Flake Streamline Baby*, New York, Farrar, Straus & Giroux, 1963; *Modern American Prose*, p. 513.

[3]John McPhee, "The Swiss at War," *La Place de la Concorde Swiss*, New York, Farrar, Straus & Giroux, 1984; Modern American Prose, p. 333.

[4]Phillip Caputo, *A Rumor of War*, New York, Holt, Rinehart and Winston, 1977, p. 129.

[5]Bertrand Russell, quoted in Ronald W. Clark, *Einstein: The Life and Times*, New York, World, 1971, p. 87.

[6]Richard Selzer, "The Knife," *Mortal Lessons*, New York, Simon & Schuster, 1976; *Modern American Prose*, p. 343.

[7]Norman Mailer, "The Siege at Chicago," *Miami and the Siege of Chicago*, New York, 1969; *Modern American Prose*, p. 292.

[8]Joseph Conrad, *Lord Jim*, New York, New American Library, 1965, p. 80, first published in 1899.

[9]Donald Davidson, "What Metaphors Mean," *On Metaphor*, ed. Sheldon Sacks, Chicago, University of Chicago Press, 1979, p. 40.

[10]*The New Yorker*, December 5, 1988, p. 132.

[11]Alexander L. Taylor III, "The Wizard Inside the Machines," *Time*, April 16, 1984, p. 56.

[12]"Block That Metaphor," *The New Yorker*, December 26, 1988, p. 90.

[13]Irving Howe, *World of Our Fathers*, New York, Simon and Schuster, Touchstone Books, 1976, p. 174.

[14]Norman Mailer, "The Siege of Chicago," *Miami and the Siege of Chicago*, New York, 1969; Modern American Prose, pp. 294–95.

[15]John Kenneth Galbraith, *A View from the Stands*, Boston, Houghton Mifflin, 1986, p. 217.

[16]John Kenneth Galbraith, *Economics in Perspective*, Boston, Houghton Mifflin, 1987, p. 60.

[17]*Elements of Literature*, eds. Robert Scholes, Carl H. Klaus, Michael Silverman, New York, Oxford University Press, 1978, p. 41.

[18]Alan Lupo, "File . . . and Forget," *The Boston Globe*, July 12, 1989, p. 15.

[19]Michael Kinsley, "The New Politics of Abortion," *Time*, July 17, 1989, p. 96.

CHAPTER 10

[1]Walter Jackson Bate, *Samuel Johnson*, New York and London, Harcourt Brace Jovanovich, 1977, p. 395.

[2]Neil Sheehan, *A Bright Shining Lie: John Paul Vann and America in Vietnam*, New York, Random House, 1988, p. 343.

[3]Stephan Jay Gould, "Racist Arguments and IQ," *Ever Since Darwin, Reflections in Natural History*, New York, W. W. Norton, 1977; Modern American Prose, p. 233.

[4]Robert N. Proctor, *Racial Hygiene: Medicine under the Nazis*, Cambridge (Massachusetts), Harvard University Press, 1988, p. 187.

[5]Eugene D. Genovese, *Roll Jordan Roll*, New York, Random House, Vintage Books, 1976, p. 249.

[6]Barbara Tuchman, *Practicing History*, New York, Alfred A. Knopf, p. 196.

[7]"Strollers," *Consumer Reports*, November 1988, p. 723.

[8]Ellen Goodman, "Blame the Victim," *At Large*, New York, Summit Books, division of Simon & Schuster, 1981; *Modern American Prose*, p. 219.

[9]Lewis Thomas, "*Late Night Thoughts on Listening to Mahler's Ninth Symphony*, New York, Viking Penguin, 1982; Modern American Prose, p. 390.

[10]Richard Selzer, "The Knife," *Mortal Lessons*, New York, Simon & Schuster, 1976; Modern American Prose, p. 346.

[11]*Time*, March 4, 1984, p. 47.

[12]"Compact 35 mm Cameras," *Consumer Reports*, November 1988, p. 706.

[13]Alice Walker, "Choice: A Tribute to Dr. Martin Luther King, Jr.," *In Search of Our Mothers' Gardens*, New York, Harcourt Brace Jovanovich, 1983; *Modern American Prose*, p. 441.

CHAPTER 11

[1]Evan S. Connell, *Son of the Morning Star: Custer and the Little Bighorn*, San Francisco, North Point Press, 1984, p. 231.

[2]Paul Fussell, *The Great War and Modern Memory*, New York, Oxford University Press, 1975, p. 235.

[3]David Donald, *Look Homeward: A Life of Thomas Wolfe*, Boston, Little Brown, 1987, p. 254.

Acknowledgments

JOHN CLIFFORD and ROBERT DIYANNI   Excerpts from *Modern American Prose*, second edition, 1987, McGraw-Hill, Inc.

JOAN DIDION   Excerpts from "Bureaucrats" from *The White Album* by Joan Didion. Copyright © 1976, 1979, 1989 by Joan Didion. Reprinted by permission of Farrar, Straus & Giroux, Inc.

ANNIE DILLARD   Excerpts from "Seeing" and "Jest and Ernest" from *Pilgrim at Tinker Creek* by Annie Dillard. Copyright © 1974 by Annie Dillard. Reprinted by permission of Harper & Row, Publishers, Inc.

LOREN EISELEY   Excerpts from "Charles Darwin" by Loren Eiseley. Copyright © 1956 by Scientific American, Inc. All rights reserved. And, excerpts from "The Judgment of the Birds," copyright © 1956 by Loren Eiseley. Reprinted from *The Immense Journey* by Loren Eiseley, by permission of Random House, Inc.

STEPHEN JAY GOULD   Excerpts reprinted from *The Panda's Thumb, More Reflections in Natural History*, by Stephen Jay Gould, by permission of W. W. Norton & Company, Inc. Copyright © 1980 by Stephen Jay Gould.

NORMAN MAILER   Excerpts from "The Siege of Chicago" from *Miami and the Siege of Chicago* by Norman Mailer. Reprinted by permission of Donald I. Fine, Inc.

WALLACE STEVENS   Excerpt from "Sunday Morning," copyright 1923 and renewed 1951 by Wallace Stevens. Reprinted from *The Collected Poems of Wallace Stevens* by permission of Alfred A. Knopf, Inc.

LEWIS THOMAS   Excerpts from "To Err Is Human" from *Medusa and the Snail* by Lewis Thomas. Copyright © 1976 by Lewis Thomas. Originally published in *The New England Journal of Medicine*. Reprinted by permission of Viking Penguin, a division of Penguin Books USA, Inc.

BARBARA TUCHMAN   Excerpts from *Practicing History* by Barbara Tuchman, © 1981 by Alma Tuchman, Lucy T. Eisenberg, and Jessica Tuchman Matthews. Reprinted by permission of Alfred, A. Knopf, Inc.

Index